Welcome to the hard world!

Climbing is hard. Hard rock, hard routes, hard moves, hard tr
is just hard. Climbing is a lifestyle and most of us dedicate
the years climbing I visited countries all
over the world and that is definitely one
of the real great aspects about climbing
– you can find rock in almost every country.
And for me climbing is the best way to travel!
The countries described in this edition of the
Rock Climbing Atlas have their own, unique
character – life, culture, traditions – and that
gives these countries its fascination. Plus…
there is tons of first class rock! Go there and
check it out. There is no way that you would
come back disappointed!

Great days out there and enjoy climbing!

Alexander Huber

Even though we have some great crags in the UK, I'd rather climb overseas, especially at those
places where the sun is always shining and the chances of rainy days are small. I think this
Rock Climbing Atlas is a great source of information when deciding where to go climbing next,

there are so many great places
described here that I'm certain
it would be a tough decision.
No matter what you decide, I'm
sure you'll have a great time.
Climb on!

Richard Simpson

Published by: Rocks Unlimited Publications
Printed by: Roto Smeets GrafiServices, Utrecht

Graphical design: Irene Pieper from NIHIL Climbing
Authors: Wynand Groenewegen & Marloes van den Berg
Editor: Daniel Jaeggi

This Rock Climbing Atlas does not contain any topos or detailed route information because we would like to encourage our readers to purchase local climbing guidebooks. The proceeds of guidebook sales tend to support local climbers and underpins route development, and we hope that our actions, and those of our readers, may contribute to the preservation and enhancement of the climbing areas we describe.

Although we have put every effort and taken reasonable care in preparing this guide, we cannot guarantee and we do not accept any liability for the accuracy or completeness of the content. Prices can go up, campsites shut down, climbing areas close, new routes appear, airline schedules change, etc. Please visit our website www.rockclimbingatlas.com for updates and please let us know if you find anything to be inaccurate or missing. Our email address is info@rockclimbingatlas.com. Feedback, comments, and suggestions are highly appreciated.

The publisher, authors and the editor accept no responsibility for any consequences arising from the use of this guide, and do not accept any liability for any damages or injuries incurred. The Rock Climbing Atlas is not a climbing safety book and has no instructions or directions with regards to any aspect of climbing safety. You are strongly advised to seek professional instruction before participating in any climbing related activity. Climbing is an activity with a danger of personal injury or death. Participants should be aware of and accept these risks and be responsible for their own involvement.

The inclusion of a crag in this guide confers neither the right of access to the crag or the surrounding land, nor the right to climb on the crag.

First edition November 2006

ISBN-10: 90-78587-01-6
ISBN-13: 978-90-78587-01-9

South Eastern Europe
Rock Climbing Atlas

Rovinj, Croatia

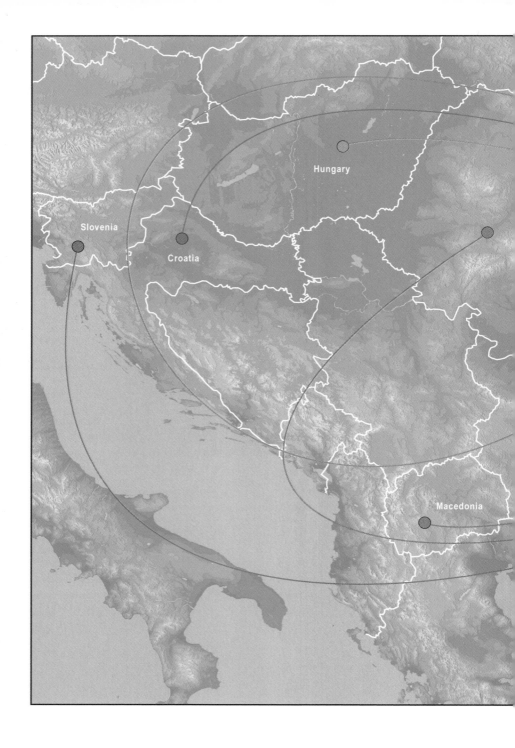

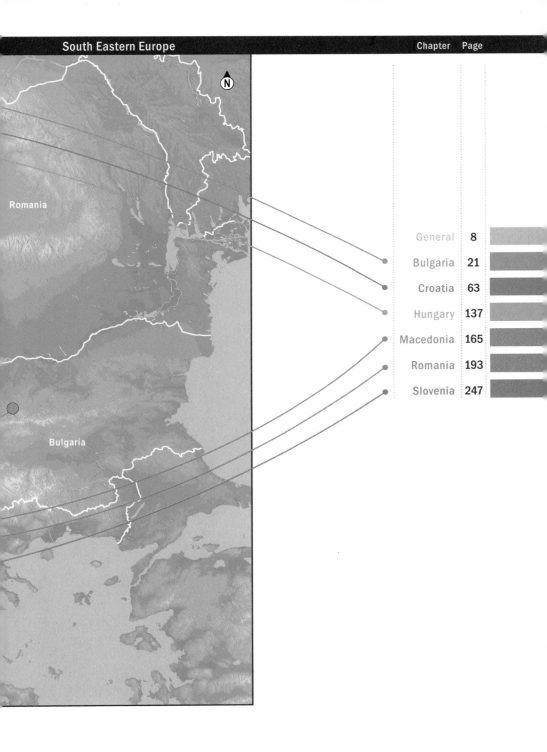

Romania

Bulgaria

Vika Kollerova on Evanjelijum (5c), Cliffbase, Croatia

Contents

Climbing has truly become an international sport. Roll up at any major crag in Western Europe and you'll find climbers of more nationalities than you have fingers on your hand! It's remarkable, actually, and it's probably due to a combination of cheap air fares, the internet and an increasingly global cultural outlook. What's more remarkable, though, is that if you travel just a little bit further outside the confines of the popular and much visited climbing destination in Western Europe - for example to the countries in South Eastern Europe - you'll find virtually no foreign climbers at the crags. What's going on? Is it the poor quality of the rock or the climbing? No way! If anything the rock is better because it hasn't seen the massive traffic some western crags get. Is there a lack of developed climbing areas? Definitely not! You'll find more routes here than you could complete in a lifetime and, although it is true that there is lots of undeveloped rock, this offers massive potential for new-routing. What about the ease of getting there? Come on! There are many cheap flights crossing Europe, with many more routes being opened by low-cost operators, and what's an extra hour on a plane when you're on a trip, anyway? The cost? Hah! The further you travel, the cheaper things -usually- get!

No, people don't travel further afield because they don't know where to go and so they stick to tried and trusted climbing venues. Want to do something different and escape the crowds? Want to experience some truly fantastic climbing? Then you've got to go southeast, and we're going to tell you exactly how to get there!

This Rock Climbing Atlas will equip you with all the essential facts and knowledge to go climbing in South Eastern Europe. The quality and quantity of the climbing is phenomenal - there's everything from bouldering to trad big-walls, steep sport routes to relaxed multi-pitch classics. You'll experience beautiful landscapes, charming towns and villages, friendly local people and we can guarantee you'll broaden your cultural perspective. And you'll escape the crowds and the polish so common in the West!

For each country we cover, we'll tell you all you need to know to get there and travel around. We tell you about the most interesting climbing areas there, and give you the essential run-down – how to get there, what the climbing is like, where to eat and sleep, what to do on rest days and which crags are family friendly. We don't provide you with topos or detailed route descriptions – we strongly believe in sustainable tourism and encourage you to buy the local topo, supporting the local climbers and economy – but we give you more than enough to get you to the crags and ready to go.

We selected the climbing areas included based on the beauty of the area, the number and quality of the routes (the area should be big and challenging enough to keep you busy for around a week), the quality of the climbing (in terms of protection and solid rock), and accessibility, including ease of accommodation. In compiling the Rock Climbing Atlas, we not only relied on information and opinions from local climbers, but we also checked all the areas ourselves. We aim to tell it like it is and don't hesitate from mentioning both the good and the bad!

There are countries that are not included in this guide but that belong geographically to South Eastern Europe - Albania, Bosnia-Hercegovina, Moldova, Serbia and Montenegro. The reason for their omission is the lack of climbing there. However, this is not to say that there is a lack of rock and, given the growth in popularity of climbing in these countries, it could well be that they find inclusion in future editions of the Rock Climbing Atlas!

Have a nice journey into the unknown and climb safely!

The layout of The Rock Climbing Atlas has been designed to be extremely easy to use. Each country has its own extensive introduction after which the climbing areas are described in more detail. The crags within each climbing area are then described. We use only symbols where necessary and the written descriptions are supplemented by many photos. In this way, we hope to give you the best, and most accurate, description of the climbing possibilities.

Country introduction

We will always start with some general comments about each country, to give you a feel for the place and to present some general information. This is followed up by some more specific **Climbing information**. We also give a brief overview of all the **Climbing areas** in the country by showing these on the country map. Herewith we quote the number of routes and whether it is a sport, trad or bouldering area.

① Climbing area not included in this Rock Climbing Atlas

② Climbing area included in this Rock Climbing Atlas

Sport climbing

Traditional climbing

Bouldering

Total number of routes

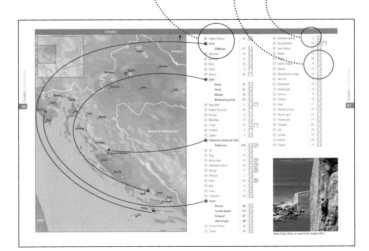

We then present a lot of practical information. In the **Climate** section there is information about the average climate in the country, including average temperature and rainfall figures. We pick the figures to be most representative of the conditions in the climbing areas in the country, but be aware that these are averages and that variations can be extreme! Later, in the individual 'Climbing area / When to go' sections the specific weather conditions for the climbing area are given plus a recommendation for **When to go**.

Getting there gives you the most important information about the best and cheapest travel options to get to the country from abroad. Where applicable, we give you options for travel by plane, train, bus, car and boat. In many cases we give you details of websites containing up to date travel and ticket information.

Moving around provides you with similar information for travel within the country. We try to provide you with travel information for both public transport and car, except when it's impossible to get to the climbing areas by public transport. Car rental can be very useful if flying into a country and we give details of the best places to hire a car. We also provide information about how to get from the airport to the centre of town.

Next we describe the **Accommodation** options with average prices, including campsites, guest-houses and hotels. The local **Food & Drinks** is also described and here we give average costs for eating out in restaurants, having a cappuccino or a beer in a bar and the costs of supermarket food. Moving onto climbing related things, we tell you where you can pick up **Local climbing guidebooks** and topos/route information for the crags we describe. The information provided here is general and will tend to include locations of climbing shops in large towns and cities – local outlets are described in the climbing area sections. Finally we give **Facts about the country**, including important information such as visa requirements, emergency numbers, currency and exchange rates, safety, language, mobile phone usage, internet access and if the water from the tap is safe to drink.

Month	Average temperature (°C)	Average rainfall (mm)
Jan	6	79
Feb	6	64
March	8	65
April	13	65
May	17	58
June	21	50
July	23	38
Aug	23	58
Sept	20	73
Oct	16	75
Nov	11	111
Dec	7	99

Climate table Istria.
Average temperatures at the Dalmatian coast
are approximately 2 degrees higher.

Climbing area information

Here you'll find a general description of the climbing area along with information about the best time of year to go. A map shows the whole area with the various crags and, along with further sketches and GPS waypoints, should be enough to allow you to get to each crag painlessly. However, it goes without saying that a general map of the area or the country is always useful!

► Recommendable

Spring

Spring   Summer   Autumn   Winter

► Not recommendable

Winter

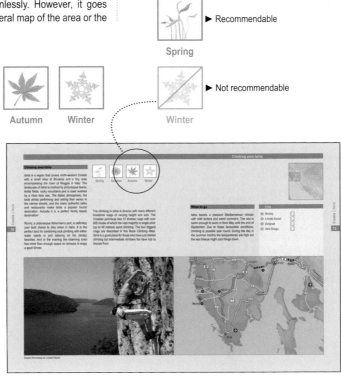

The next section tells you **How to get to the area** and **how to move around** and provides precise details of how to reach the climbing area. We will always tell you if the crags are accessible with public transport or if you'll need your own car. If public transport is an option, we'll give you as much information as possible but we don't publish exact timetables, since this information is very liable to change. Still, we'll give you frequencies and journey times, which should allow you to make good plans. We try to give you fare information where possible and we quote prices for 2nd class travel. Of course, we also give links to websites with local travel information.

Where to stay tells you about the accommodation possibilities. Where camping is an option, we'll always include one or two campsites as well as possible other types of accommodation.

Campsite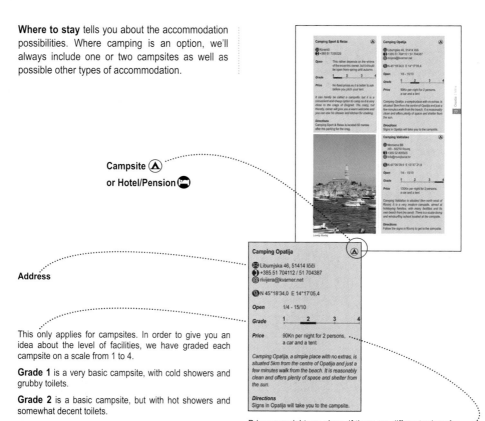

or Hotel/Pension

Address

This only applies for campsites. In order to give you an idea about the level of facilities, we have graded each campsite on a scale from 1 to 4.

Grade 1 is a very basic campsite, with cold showers and grubby toilets.

Grade 2 is a basic campsite, but with hot showers and somewhat decent toilets.

A grade 3 campsite will have warm showers, clean toilets and a few other facilities such as a bar and a playground for children.

A grade 4 campsite is luxurious with all kind of facilities.

Prices per night are given. If there are different prices for the low and the high season this is stated as well. High season normally is July and August. Prices for hotels are for a double room with an en-suite bathroom, unless otherwise stated.

Where to buy groceries tells you about the local shops and the best and cheapest places to buy supplies.

In the Country Introduction section there is information given about the relevant climbing guidebooks. In the **Where to find the local climbing guidebook** section, detailed information about the local guidebooks is given, as well as addresses of the shops where you can buy them. If there is no local guidebook, we tell you where you can find information and/or topos on the internet.

Of course, websites come and go so check *www. rockclimbingatlas.com* for the latest information.

Finally, we tell you **What else is there to see & do** in the area besides climbing. We wrote this section particularly for those on longer trips or those climbing as part of a general (family) holiday, but everyone appreciate good rest days too! We don't intend to give a complete overview of all possible activities but we highlight those we think are the most interesting.

Crag details

In this section we present the most important information about the crags. Besides some general comments about the crag and the climbing, there is a comprehensive **Crag details** page where all the required information can be found at a glance.

One star means the climbing is fantastic in terms of quality of the routes and the setting.
Two stars means a visit is absolutely mandatory.

The **GPS waypoints** of the parking and/or the exact location of the crag are provided. We use the grid latitude / longitude hddd°mm'ss.s.

This gives the **time** required to get to the crag **on foot** from either the campsite Ⓐ or car-park P .

Sport climbing

Traditional climbing

Bouldering

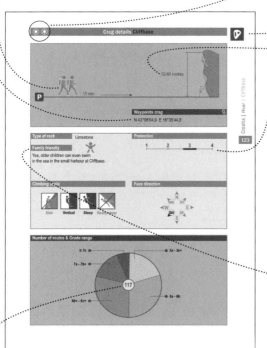

Route length, minimum and maximum. Maximum length is given for the longest multi pitch or trad routes where applicable.

We give a grade for the **quality of protection**. This always only applies to the sport routes at each crag and not to trad routes.

Grade 1: shouldn't try this one unless you prefer to go solo....

Grade 2: distances between bolts exceed 4 metres. You have to have good nerves or shouldn't climb above your level.

Grade 3: approximately every 3 metres a bolt

Grade 4: approximately every 2 metres a bolt

Family friendly means there is sufficient flat ground at the crag to take little children along and the approach from the parking or campsite is not too taxing. If applicable we give this information per sector.

The number in the middle of the pie chart indicates the **total number of routes**. This applies to the sport routes and multi pitch routes count as one route, unless otherwise stated. With regard to the **grade range** the most difficult pitch in a multi pitch route is included. We used the French sport grade system.

Sport route: a route that is protected with drilled bolts.
Multi pitch routes: sport routes of at least two rope lengths.
Trad routes: routes on which the leader has to place all protection. On these routes you will always need to take friends, nuts and slings although there might be some fixed protection.

Symbols

Roads

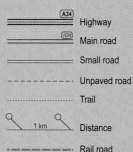

(A34)	Highway
(N34)	Main road
	Small road
- - - - - - - - -	Unpaved road
....	Trail
1 km	Distance
▬ ▬ ▬ ▬ ▬	Rail road

Landscape marks

～～～	River
————	Stream
◆	City or Village
⁄ ⁄ ⁄ ⁄ ⁄	Sea or Lake
🌳🌳🌳	Forest
/\\	Crag
◯ ◯	Boulders

Symbols

P	Car-park	✈	Airport
Signpost		Bus station / Stop	
Bridge		Train station	
Ⓝ North		House	
Supermarket		Church	
Restaurant		Mountain hut	
Hotel / Pension		Monastery	
Campsite		Water source	

The next page shows a **Detailed drawing** with the exact location of the crag, unless it is very obvious where it is. We must note that the map scale used is only approximate and features should not be interpreted literally. Where useful, we also include some point to point distances.

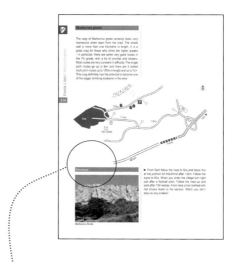

Finally, **Directions** to the crags by car and/or by public transport are given.

Climbing and swimming in Croatia (2-3 weeks)

This guide is packed with places that are close to the sea. Croatia's very attractive peninsula, Istria, is high up on the list of top climbing & beach spots! You can camp next to the sea and the crags are never too far away. Head for Rovinj, which is a charming little town and perfect base.

After one week take the boat to Cliffbase on the island of Hvar. The crag on this easy going island is often called 'Little Thailand' and has some routes directly above the water. A deep water solo of 300 metres (!) could be child play here. Then if you have another week left, the Paklenica National Park is a great place to end your trip. The park has, besides sport routes, a few big walls with routes of several hundred metres, many of which are even completely bolted! As with almost all climbing areas in Croatia you can camp near or on the beach and dive straight into the sea after having sweated it out in the National Park. You can't go wrong with Croatia!

Climbing in Slovenia (1 week)

If you don't have much time and you are looking for some very good single and multi pitch routes in the 6th, 7th and 8th grade, go to Osp and Mišja Peč in the south of Slovenia. The quality of the rock is high, the variety of routes is simply huge and the approach to the crags is very short – the campsite in Osp is only a few minutes on foot away from the first route. Osp itself lies very close to the border of Italy, which is perfect if you fancy a night out in Trieste.

Discover the secrets of Bulgaria (2-3 weeks)

As the distances between the different climbing areas and the most interesting places in Bulgaria are short, two weeks can easily be enough to soak up the best of the country. A trip of three weeks allows you more time to fit in, maybe, some hiking

Klemen Vodlan on the beautiful Dr. Ivan Merz (6b+), Omiš, Croatia

in one of Bulgaria's great National Parks. Renting a car is a good option but it's perfectly possible to travel around by public transport.

If trad climbing is your thing, make sure you don't miss the big-walls of Vratza, only two hours from the capital Sofia. The pure sport climbers are better off in Lakatnik, one hour from Sofia, with a wide variety of routes and where wild camping is most pleasant. A great rest day activity is to visit to the magnificent Rila Monastery. This is also the starting point for beautiful hiking trails.

Another great climbing destination is Veliko Tărnovo. One could easily spend a week here, discovering the different crags and the wonderful town itself. A nice trip could start in Varna, where there are cheap charter flights in summer, and spend some days at the Black Sea. Your trip would have it all!

Bucegi Mountains after having relaxed in Braşov, one of Romania's most appealing cities. Go for the trad climbing in Coştila or try the sport routes at Sinai. This latter is definitely not the place for an easy holiday as the majority of the routes are tough! While in this beautiful area, get your walking boots on and explore the trails.

After the Bucegi Mountains head north to the Bicaz Gorge, where the routes get even more difficult. You could easily spend a week here before you cross the country diagonally to Băile Herculane. On the way, make a stop over in Sighişoara and see where Dracula lived! Spend the rest of your time in Băile Herculane and, again, enjoy the beautiful surroundings. Don't forget to take a thermal bath while you're there. If you enter Romania from Hungary by car in the north, a detour around the beautiful Maramureş province is worth considering, even though there is little climbing there.

Climbing and sightseeing in Romania (3-4 weeks)

Climbing in Romania is of an unexpectedly high standard. Either by car or by public transport, Romania makes for a very interesting destination for climbing and a bit of exploration. Start in the

Get the best out of South Eastern Europe (6-8 weeks)

If you have the time and you are eager to experience the best climbing South Eastern Europe has to offer, then take your car, pack it with gear and hit the

Maramureş, Romania

road. Eight weeks would be perfect to really enjoy the climbing in this part of Europe without rushing. Six weeks is tight but you can always skip one or two countries.

Get started and warm up in Slovenia, in Osp and the surrounding crags. After a few days of climbing there you'll need a rest day, which you can use to drive to picturesque Rovinj in Croatia. Relax at the seaside and have dinner in the old part of town. There is enough climbing in the area to last you a good few days – when you get sore, the time has come to continue. Follow the road along the Adriatic all the way down to Split, which is a nice place to spend a few days and nights. You can also head directly to the Paklenica National Park and spend some more days there. From this point it takes 2 days to drive to Macedonia but you can take a break in beautiful Dubrovnik, in the south of Croatia. The trip via Serbia and Albania to Macedonia makes a great journey on its own. As your fancy takes you, head for Matka near Skopje or Demir Kapija not far from the border of Greece. From here you could also head to Greece instead of Bulgaria. Check out the Rock Climbing Atlas, Greece & the Middle East, for great climbing destinations there.

The first stop in Bulgaria after Macedonia could be Lakatnik, a great place to enjoy fantastic sport routes. You can also skip this area and spend this time in the Rila Mountains, where there is some wonderful hiking. Either way, make sure you don't miss Bulgaria's highly attractive medieval capital, Veliko Tărnovo, where there's good climbing and enough culture to keep you happy.

After four or five days continue to Romania - Dracula country! Prepare yourself for a long, but interesting drive, to Bucharest. Spend a day in this lively capital before setting off to the wonderful Bucegi Mountains. This is a great area for both climbing and hiking. Make the Bicaz Gorge your next destination in Romania but beware, the majority of the sport routes here are very difficult. Fortunately, there are many trad routes in all grades. Whatever you do, a stay in the Bicaz Gorge is unforgettable.

Băile Herculane makes a good alternative to the Bicaz Gorge. The good atmosphere in the town and the wide choice of mid-grade routes on good solid limestone makes this an attractive climbing destination. When you have seen it all, prepare for the journey back home. If there is time, cross Romania's Maramureş province - you won't regret this.

The roads in Hungary are of a good quality and this country can be crossed easily in two days. Try to have a night out in Budapest, which is one of Europe's most attractive capitals. Climbing in Hungary is also possible but it's not quite as good as what you've been used to. Still, it might be worth it for the novelty factor! From Hungary head home and reflect on a super trip!

Great destinations for families with children

Rovinj, in Croatia, is one of the best destinations for families with children. Camping next to the sea is possible at very nice, child-friendly, campsites. The crags offer lots of easy short routes for children too - when they get tired of climbing there is enough space for them to play and a calm sea to keep them busy. The crags around Rovinj offer plenty of challenges for (adult!) climbers.

Many families visit the Paklenica National Park too. Most campsites, which are only about 2km away from the park, are situated along the sea making it perfect for children. The entrance to the park, which is easy accessible, offers routes for beginners as well. Of course if you are into multi-pitch climbing you'll need someone to look after your children during the day, there's lots of that here!

Another great family-friendly climbing destination is Bled, in Slovenia. Bled also has very good campsites with excellent facilities for families with children. Besides excellent crags with a wide variety of routes that are suitable to take children along, there are lots of other things to do in and around Bled. These include hiking in The Triglav National Park, sightseeing and (easy) river activities such as rafting and canoeing.

Climbing area	Crag							Easy routes	Moderate routes	Difficult routes
Bulgaria										
Vrachanska Mountains	Vratza	P		•	•	•		•	•	•
Iskar Gorge	Lakatnik	P		•	•	•		•	•	•
Veliko Tărnovo	St. Trinity	P		•	•	•			•	•
	Usteto	P		•	•	•			•	•
Croatia										
Istria	Rovinj	P		•	•	•	•	•	•	
	Limski Kanal	P		•	•	•	•	•	•	
	Dvigrad	P		•	•	•	•	•	•	
	Vela Draga	P		•	•	•	•	•	•	•
Split	Brela	P		•	•	•	•	•	•	•
	Omiš	P		•	•	•	•	•	•	•
	Marjan	P		•	•	•		•	•	•
	Markezina greda	P		•	•	•		•	•	•
Hvar	Cliffbase	P		•	•	•	•	•	•	•
Paklenica N.P.	Paklenica	P		•	•	•		•	•	•
Hungary										
Geresce Hills	Tardos	P		•	•	•			•	•
Mátra Hills	Mátra	P			•				•	•
Macedonia										
Matka	Matka Hut	P		•	•	•		•	•	•
Demir Kapija	Demir Kapija G.	P		•	•	•		•	•	•
Romania										
Bucegi Mountains	Sinaia	P		•	•	•		•	•	•
	Coştila			•	•	•		•	•	
Bicaz	Bicaz Gorge	P		•	•	•		•	•	•
Turda	Turda Gorge	P		•	•	•		•	•	•
Cerna Valley	Băile Herculane	P		•	•	•		•	•	•
Slovenia										
Bled-Bohinj	Bodešče	P		•	•	•			•	•
	Bohinjska Bela	P		•	•	•			•	•
	Bitenj Potok	P		•	•	•			•	•
	Bitnje	P		•	•	•			•	•
	Bohinj	P		•	•	•		•	•	•
Osp-Trieste	Osp	P		•	•	•			•	•
	Mišja Peč	P		•	•	•				•
	Črni Kal	P		•	•	•		•	•	
	Val Rosandra	P		•	•	•		•	•	
	Napoleonica	P		•	•	•	•		•	•
Celje	Kotečnik	P		•	•	•			•	•
	Kamnik	P		•	•	•			•	•

N 48°29'18,2 W 114°14'94,3

What if you knew you could always find your directions to unfamiliar crags? What if you had an eXplorist™ GPS?

The Magellan® eXplorist family offers real value in a lightweight, rugged, water-resistant handheld GPS. Easy to operate with just one hand, it features TrueFix GPS technology, an advanced, intuitive file management system and plenty of memory for all your tracks and route history.
The eXplorist 210 has 22mb of memory whereas the eXplorist 400, 500 & 600 use Secure SD cards for memory storage.
Which eXplorist is the right one for you?

For more information, please go to www.magellanGPS.com
or call 00800 MAGELLAN (00800 62435526)

BE THERE.™

MAGELLAN®

Magellan® eXplorist™ GPS

...Europe's best kept secret...

Bulgaria

Ida Gandeva is at home on Nezen Kravopietc (7c),
Sector Vrajite Dupki at Lakatnik

Want an active holiday? Bulgaria has it all – climbing, hiking, skiing, horse riding, alpinism, swimming and caving... Want to relax? Amazing landscapes, sunny beaches, healing spas, monasteries and churches, hospitable towns and villages... Bulgaria has it all! This wonderful country has something to offer for everyone and, for climbers, it is a rock-filled dreamland.

Bulgaria always has had a lot to offer to active outdoor people. Around the whole country, there are many unique places and fabulous landscapes, peppered with fantastic monasteries, and the warm hospitality of the people makes a visit complete. Since the fall of the communism in 1989, the Bulgarian people have had a hard time as the standard of living has decreased significantly. Nowadays wages are still low and unemployment high, but the country is changing rapidly and a lot of effort is being made to join the European Union in 2007.

The country is rich with hundreds of monasteries reflecting the soul of Bulgaria. Some of them date back to Byzantine times, others were built in the 20th century to replace destroyed ones. Bulgaria's monasteries have always played an important role in retaining the nation's values during difficult times. The most popular monastery is the Rila Monastery. This UNESCO World Heritage site lies 117km south of Sofia and is popular because of its size, natural surroundings, architecture, wall paintings and ancient history, and is well worth a visit.

Trekking and hiking in the Rila, Pirin or Rodopi mountains is a great way to enjoy Bulgaria's natural environment and cultural traditions, and is a great escape from urban life. All of Bulgaria's mountains are accessible and suitable for a wide range of activities both in summer and winter. The highest peak is Mount Mussala (2,925m.) in the Rila Mountains.>>

It would make a great trip to combine climbing in Bulgaria with trekking in one of its mountainous regions or sightseeing around the country.

Rock climbing in Bulgaria is growing fast - more and more climbing areas are being developed and many new routes are being put up in existing areas. These days there are over 21 climbing areas with a total of around 1500 climbing routes and endless amounts of traditional climbing. Plus, bouldering and deep water soloing are getting ever more popular. Bulgaria really is Europe's best kept secret!

Climbing information

Bulgaria offers many opportunities for alpine and traditional climbing, as well as for sport climbing. The best trad climbing areas are found at Vratza, in the Malyovitsa region of the Rila Mountains, and there are a variety of spots in the Pirin Mountains. There is a distinct lack of route information for the Rila and Pirin areas so we'll only describe the Vratza region into detail. The Malyovitsa region, by the way, is also great for ice climbing in winter.

The Iskar Gorge and Veliko Tărnovo are Bulgaria's best two sport climbing areas and are described into detail in this Rock Climbing Atlas. Two other areas

that are worth mentioning, but are not described, because there are not so many routes, are the Vitosha climbing area close to Sofia (and therefore very popular with locals) and Kamen Briag on the Black Sea (a good deep water soloing area).

Climbing area Vrachanska Mountains

The town of Vratza, situated in the Vrachanska Mountains, offers unlimited possibilities for trad climbing together with some good sport climbing. This beautiful area is perfect both for the intermediate and the experienced climber, and especially for those after climbing big walls.

Climbing area Iskar Gorge

For many Bulgarian climbers, Lakatnik located in the stunning Iskar Gorge is the most popular sport climbing area with many excellent bolted routes of all grades in a beautiful setting.

Climbing area Veliko Tărnovo

The splendid rock climbing conditions combined with the relaxing city of Veliko Tărnovo and the charming villages and monasteries in the surrounding area makes this a top European climbing destination!

Yavor Panov swings through on Koza Nostra (6c) at Kamen Briag

polartec.com

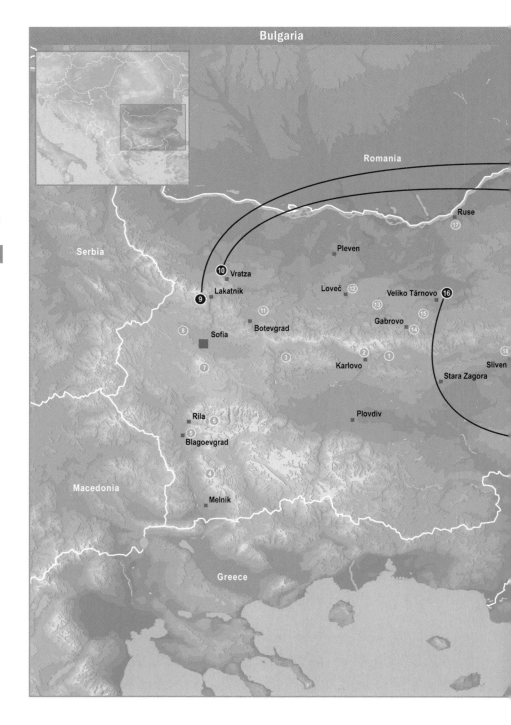

 By public transport

Bulgaria has an extensive network of bus and train services and most tourist sights are easily accessible by public transport. There are both private and public buses connecting all cities and major towns. Private buses are more comfortable and only a bit more expensive than the public buses – if you're covering larger distances they're the better option. Trains are also a good alternative to the buses and are generally cheaper too. The Bulgarian State Railways website *www.bdz.bg* provides comprehensive domestic train information in English.

Both international and domestic buses arrive at the well organised central bus station (Kniaginia Maria Luiza blv) in Sofia. It's located next to the central railway station, north of the city centre.

Taxi fares are very low in Bulgaria and are a good alternative if you're travelling shorter distances.

 By car

There is a road tax for all Bulgarian roads, payable by buying a vignette, which you stick on your windscreen. This costs €3 and is valid for a

Monument of the Asens in Veliko Tărnovo

week - it can be bought at larger petrol stations. Unfortunately, corruption can still be encountered when dealing with customs and the traffic police. Stay polite, but also stand your ground if you feel you are being unfairly treated.

Petrol stations are widespread in Bulgaria but you should always fill up if you are planning to stay in a mountain region for a longer period of time. Prices are slightly less expensive compared to Western Europe. In case your car brakes down call 146 for road assistance.

Car rental in Bulgaria can be a real bargain, as long as you don't care what the car looks like! Bargains start at €15 per day. Check out *www.visitbulgaria. net/rentacar* and *www.bulgariacarrent.com*. Newer cars can be rented with the usual international car rental companies for almost double the price. There are car rental offices at the airports in Sofia and Varna, as well as at other central locations.

Accommodation

Campsites in Bulgaria are not very common at all - those that do exist tend to be located next to noisy roads. Luckily, wild camping is permitted and this is the accommodation option of choice for Bulgarian climbers, allowing them to camp close to the crags.

Budget accommodation is widely available and relatively cheap. The choice varies between private accommodation, guesthouses, hostels, hotels and even some monasteries! Prices vary between €10 to €20 for 2 people. If you're looking for a bit of luxury, 3 to 4 star hotels are usually also not expensive and you can get an excellent double room for around €25 in many towns.

Food & Drinks

Bulgaria has without a doubt the best cuisine of South Eastern Europe, with its many salads and traditional clay pot meals and the Turkish and Greek influences are easily recognisable. Going out for dinner is fun and cheap. Fun, because outside the touristy areas, and even in many restaurants in Sofia, you'll get a menu written in Cyrillic only.

If your Cyrillic is not too good and the waiters don't speak English, you never know what you are about to get! We can guarantee that it will be delicious though. For a very good and large meal the bill rarely exceeds €5 per person. A salad (often large enough for a main course) costs €1 to €2. The shepherd's and shopska salads are always good.

A cappuccino costs €0.75 (but don't expect "real" cappuccino) and a local beer in a bar is €1.

Supermarket prices for basic things as yogurt, cheese and bread are also pretty low and the same goes for fruit and vegetables bought at the markets. Don't forget to try the Bulgarian yogurt and the red wine from Melnik!

Climbing guidebook

The excellent internet site *www.climbingguidebg.com* is your bible for climbing in Bulgaria. It shows not only all the climbing areas but often detailed information about routes as well. The route information can be downloaded for free after you have registered, which does not cost anything either. While important sections of some climbing areas are translated into English, unfortunately the majority is in Cyrillic.

For the Vrachanska Mountains area the website does provide good and sufficient information in English. It is advisable to download all the topo's prior to departure to Bulgaria.

Lakatnik has a guidebook written completely in English, with clear photographs of the routes. You can buy this at climbing shops in Sofia. Veliko Tărnovo also has its own basic guidebook with English text that can be bought in Veliko Tărnovo. You can find shop addresses in the 'Climbing area sections'.

Rila Monastery

Facts & figures

Population:	8 million
Religion:	Orthodox Christian (83%)
Capital:	Sofia
Time zone:	GMT +2
Telephone code:	+359

Money

Currency:	Leva (BGN)
Exchange rate:	€1 = 1.95 Leva
ATM machines:	widespread

Language

Good day	*Zdraveyte*
Thank you	*Blagodarya / Merci*
Goodbye	*Dovizhdane*
Yes / No	*Da / Ne*
Right / Left / Straight	*Nadyasno / Nalyavo / Naprvo*
Rock climbing	*Skalno katerene*

Visas & formalities

EU	*Other European nationalities*	*USA / Canada*	*All other nationalities*
No visa required for a period of up to 90 days.	Most other European nationalities do not require a visa for a period of up to 90 days. UK and Irish nationalities do not require a visa for a period up to 30 days.	No visa for a period of up to 30 days.	Most other nationalities do not require a visa for a period of up to 90 days. Check *www.mfa.government.bg* for more information.

Safety

Although the economy of Bulgaria has declined significantly over the last few years and statistics show a slight increase in crime levels, tourists are, in general, no more a target than in any other major citiy. However do pay extra attention where you park your car and be careful not to leave valuables inside.

Emergency numbers

Police:	166
Fire Brigade:	160
Ambulance:	150

Use of mobile phone

Reasonable coverage in the whole country.

Internet access

Almost every small town is connected to the rest of the world via internet and prices are remarkably cheap, as little as €1 for an hour.

Water

Water in Bulgaria can be found everywhere and it comes out of the ground at every possible opportunity. Ironically, water from natural sources is safe but it is better not to drink the tap water! Even small shops sell bottles of water, with sizes up to 5 and 10 litre bottles. A 5 litre bottle costs €0.90.

Climbing area Vrachanska Mountains

Spring

Summer

Autumn

Winter

The fantastic limestone crags of Vratza are situated in the Vrachanska Mountains in the north of Bulgaria, part of the "Vratza Balkan National Park" covering 1409 hectares. This park offers wonderful hiking opportunities and contains some of the most beautiful caves in the entire country and has unique cave fauna. There are, amongst others, rare and endangered species of Egyptian vulture, short-toed eagle, peregrine falcon, long-legged buzzards and eight different species of bats found in the more than 500 caves and karst precipices.

The town of Vratza, nestled in the foothills with the Leva river flowing calmly through it, is also a nice place to spend some time. The surrounding villages and monasteries offer plenty of sightseeing options for rest days.

In the area there are many opportunities for trad climbing. There are around 247 traditional climbing routes up to 400 metres in length, and most of them are well documented. Additionally, there are 85 well bolted sport climbing routes in a range of styles. Some full-on climbing awaits you!

Mountain rescue service
There is an organized group of the Mountain Rescue Service in Vratza. During holiday days they are based in the Alpine house. The phone number for emergencies is + 359 88 323510.

When to go

You can enjoy climbing in Vratza in spring, summer and autumn. However the best time to go is in spring and autumn. During mid summer it can get very hot and the longer trad routes aren't really viable, as the big walls mainly face south. On the other hand, there is enough shade at the sport climbing sectors to hide from the sun during warm days.

Passage Vrattzata

Crag

Ⓐ Vratza

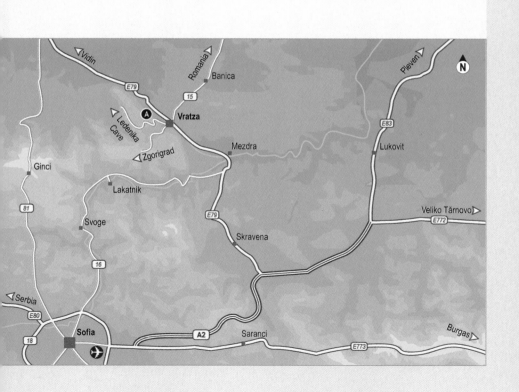

How to get to the area & how to move around

Once in Vratza you won't need a car to move around and there are enough accommodation options close to the crags. However, having a vehicle does make it easier to combine the climbing here with that at Lakatnik, only an hour's drive away.

 By public transport

The best way to get to Vratza from Sofia is by bus which leaves every hour [2h, 8 Leva]. Buses for Vratza depart from the central bus station in Sofia. In Vratza take one of the taxis from the bus station to get to your accommodation - this will cost about 7 Leva.

 By car

The 116km trip from Sofia to Vratza takes a little less than two hours. Road number 16 is very scenic and well maintained.

Where to stay

There is no campsite in Vratza, but wild camping is permitted next to the stream on the grass field close to the Vrattzata Passage. This is where local climbers usually camp. Water is available from fresh water sources along the road. Vratza also has several hotels for a more comfortable stay. The two hotels described are perfectly located close to the Vrattzata Passage. More information about Vratza and hotels can be found at *www.visit.vratza.com*.

Hotel Tourist (Турист)

 Vratza
 +359 92 661528
@ hotel@vratza.com

N 43°11'53,4 E 23°32'44,3

Price A double room is 30 Leva per night

The Hotel Tourist is basic and without much charm, but it's also without any major disadvantages except that the hotel charges half price for Bulgarians. This double pricing is really frustrating but bargaining does not help. The hotel is a few minutes walk from the centre of town.

Directions
Follow the signs for Ledenika. The hotel is situated at the beginning of the road from Vratza towards Ledenika and the Vrattzata Passage.

Hotel Chaika (Чайка)

 Vratza
+359 92 622367
@ chaika_hotel@abv.bg

Price double rooms start at 40 Leva per night

Hotel Chaika is probably far too luxurious for the average climber, but it does offer excellent value for money.

Directions
This hotel is situated along the road from Vratza towards Ledenika, just before the Vrattzata Passage. Follow the signs for Ledenika and you will pass the hotel on your left.

Where to buy groceries

Close to the Hotel Tourist there is a small supermarket and there are more to be found in the centre. On the west side of the main shopping street local women sell fresh fruits and vegetables from their own garden.

If you are camping out you might not even have to cook for yourself - as there are only few tourists in Vratza restaurant prices are genuinely low Bulgarian prices. Hotel Chaika serves delicious meals (only stay away from the fish!) in a classy setting for definitely non-classy prices. There are a few more restaurants in the centre.

Where to find the local climbing guidebook

The website *www.climbingguidebg.com* provides up to date and excellent route information and most important text is available in English. Be sure to print the information before leaving home.

What else is there to see & do

Visit other villages
Around Vratza there are some very nice small Bulgarian villages, such as Pavolche and Zgorigrad, where the villagers still value their local traditions. Walking around and talking to the locals is a great way to experience Bulgarian culture.

Monasteries
Close to Vratza, 29km to the south east, lies the beautifully situated Cherepish monastery, named "The Assumption of Virgin Mary". For more information about monasteries in this region have a look at *www.bulgarianmonastery.com*.

Hiking
The Vratza Balkan National Park offers good opportunities for hiking and has magnificent views all around. In the park lies one of the most beautiful Bulgarian caves named Ledenika. The cave is mostly covered in ice during winter. The entrance to this cave is clearly signposted.

There are lot's of imposing statues in Bulgaria, this is one in Vratza

Sofia National Theatre

Vratza

The Vratza crags (or also referred to as Vrattzata) are dominated by big walls with many isolated towers. The climbing area is divided into 31 massifs and there are approximately 332 routes in total. The majority of those routes involve trad climbing but there are also 85 very well equipped sport climbing routes that are worth the visit.

Vratza boosts the longest wall in Bulgaria, the Central wall. If you love long and hard traditional climbing, this is the place to be! The mount of fixed protection on the traditional routes varies from nothing to pegs and good drilled pitons and bolts. The information on *www.climbingguidebg.com* provides sufficient and reasonably reliable information about the routes, fixed protection and necessary gear. Most of the text is translated into English.

For sport climbing the place to be is either at the caves or at the Vrattzata Passage. The Big Cave and The Small Cave is the only place where you can climb when it is raining. The Small Cave has 34 very overhanging routes, mostly in the 7th and 8th grade. The Vrattzata Passage is very popular due to its easy accessible location and the well equipped sport routes. Here the routes at Malkata Vratza (Little Vratza) and the Bezengi massif are popular and technical climbers will love them. Slabs are the name of the game at Bezengi - if you can't find a tiny pocket here for the fingers, you have to balance on your feet until you do encounter one.

Relaxed climbing

Pure slab climbing at Sector Bezengi, The Slab (6b)

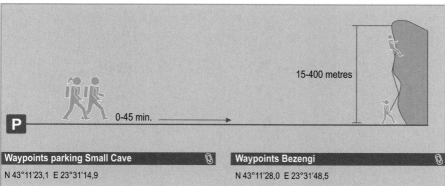

Waypoints parking Small Cave

N 43°11'23,1 E 23°31'14,9

Waypoints Bezengi

N 43°11'28,0 E 23°31'48,5

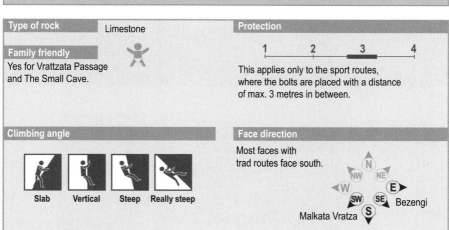

Type of rock

Limestone

Family friendly

Yes for Vrattzata Passage
and The Small Cave.

Protection

1   2   3   4

This applies only to the sport routes,
where the bolts are placed with a distance
of max. 3 metres in between.

Climbing angle

Slab   Vertical   Steep   Really steep

Face direction

Most faces with
trad routes face south.

N
NW   NE
W   E
SW   SE   Bezengi
Malkata Vratza   S

15-400 metres

0-45 min.

P

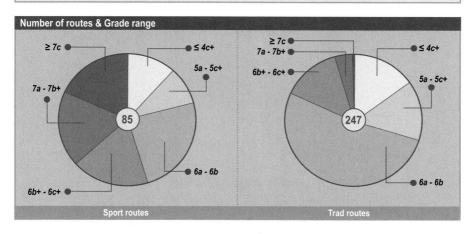

Number of routes & Grade range

≥ 7c
7a - 7b+
6b+ - 6c+
≤ 4c+
5a - 5c+
6a - 6b

85

≥ 7c
7a - 7b+
6b+ - 6c+
≤ 4c+
5a - 5c+
6a - 6b

247

Sport routes   Trad routes

Vratza

Tourist hotel in front of Kemera and East Massif

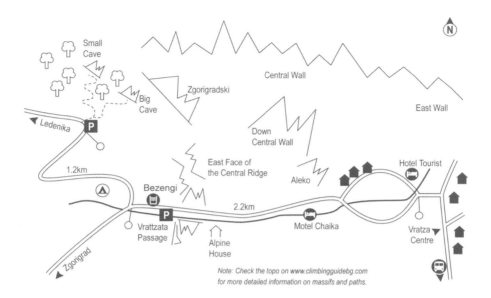

Small Cave

Central Wall

Big Cave

Zgorigradski

East Wall

Ledenika

P

Down Central Wall

1.2km

East Face of the Central Ridge

Aleko

Hotel Tourist

Bezengi

2.2km

Vratza Centre

Vrattzata Passage

Alpine House

Motel Chaika

Zgorigrad

Note: Check the topo on www.climbingguidebg.com
for more detailed information on massifs and paths.

Directions

The small cave

► The Vrattzata passage running at the feet of the rocks is situated 2km south west from Vratza town. Once you are in Vratza, follow the signs for Ledenika cave which will take you to the Vrattzata passage.

Climbing area Iskar Gorge

The marvellous Iskar Gorge, which is over 150km long, starts from the valley of Sofia. The river Iskar and the high rising walls of the gorge form an exceptional décor for a very attractive climbing area which has been developed close to the town of Lakatnik.

Lakatnik lies in the central part of the Iskar Gorge and is very popular with Bulgarian climbers because of its many fantastic sport climbing routes and wonderful location. As Lakatnik is only 63km from Sofia, it is easy and quick to reach. The town of Lakatnik itself has little to offer and that's even an understatement - a trip here will be for climbing reasons only! If you happen to be here during the week it is not uncommon to have the crags all to yourself.

Spring   Summer   Autumn   Winter

When to go

The climbing is good from April through to late November and, for die-hards, it can also be good on sunny winter days. In July and August it is normally too hot to climb as the crags mainly face south.

Where next? - Paolina Miteva on Kolkoto-tolkova (6a), Sector Vrajite Dupki

Crag

Ⓐ Lakatnik

Yavor Panov in action on Trite Kelesha (7c), Sector Vrajite Dupki

How to get to the area & how to move around

As Lakatnik is easy to reach by train and as camping close to the crags is the best option, it is not necessary to have your own wheels.

 By public transport

The most convenient way to get to Lakatnik from Sofia is by train. There are multiple trains daily between the central railway station of Sofia and Lakatnik [1½h, 3 Leva]. See the detailed drawing for the route from the railway station to the crags.

View over Lakatnik from camping spot

By car

Lakatnik lies north of Sofia and can be reached in a bit more than an hour via road number 16.

Where to stay

There is no official campsite and there are no hotels in or around the small village of Lakatnik. The good news is that there are a few great spots close to Sector Alpine Meadow to pitch your tent. There is even a small shelter with a table and some chairs. The best spots, with views over Lakatnik, are found a bit further from this shelter. To get there take the path up from the right side of the shelter and continue east for five minutes.

You can also stay with the locals at one of the houses along the road to Sector Vrajite Dupka. You won't find a sign indicating that rooms are offered, but the done thing is just to knock on the door and ask. A donation of 10 Leva will be asked for.

Svoge offers a wider range of accommodation in case you are interested in staying in a hotel or hostel. The town is located south of Lakatnik along the road to Sofia.

Sector Alpine Meadow

Lakatnik

It is hard to beat Lakatniks' scenery

Where to buy groceries

It is best to buy most groceries in Sofia since there is only a very small store in Lakatnik selling basic things as yogurt, canned food, rice, but no bread. To get to this store turn left after you have crossed the railway and then take the first street on the right. The store is located on a corner on your right after a few hundred metres. Another, even smaller, store is located at the corner of the road leading to Sector Vrajite Dupka.

Fresh drinkable water can be collected at the waterfall next to the restaurant at the start of the track leading to Sector Alpine Meadow. This restaurant serves cheap meals, a great place to counteract the healthy life!

Where to find the local climbing guidebook

The guide, which covers the routes of Lakatnik, is only sold at the Alpi climbing shop in Sofia, to the south of the centre. The guide is named "Lakatnik", costs 10 Leva and is written by Borislav Dimitrov.

Alpi climbing shop
✉ Gotze Delchev 9
Sofia
📞 +359 888 227736

What else is there to see & do

Sofia
Although Sofia is not as grandiose as other Eastern European capital cities, it still has a lot to offer and is a lively place. There are some great sights, such as the Aleksander Nevski Church, and some very good bars and restaurants for a swinging night out.

Hiking
Most of the other people you encounter in Lakatnik will be there for the hiking or for a visit to the cave. The cave is signposted from the restaurant. Several hiking trails start from here too.

Lakatnik

The area consists of three main sectors and in total there are over 280 routes. The majority of the routes are very well bolted and the quality of the rock is mostly excellent. The variety in climbing styles is huge - there are slabs, vertical walls and overhangs.

Sector Alpine Meadow (Alpiiska) is the oldest sector with 59 sport climbing routes ranging in length from 15 to 40 metres. There are also some longer trad routes that require nuts and friends, but we don't recommend these due to the poor state of the fixed protection and the amount of loose rock around.

Sector Vrajite Dupki has more than 200 routes across the grades and new routes are being put up every year. These routes are on excellent solid limestone and range between 15 and 20 metres in length. The protection is also excellent. This is the most popular and well liked sector at Lakatnik at least for the moment since the third sector, Sector Watermill, is now being developed with great enthusiasm. The first few routes at this sector have only been made in 2005 but the potential is also huge here.

Checking out the routes at Sector Vrajite Dupki

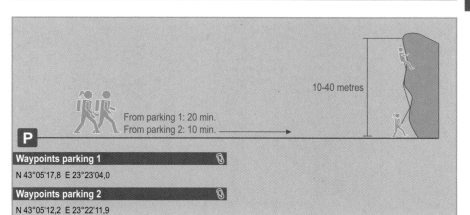

10-40 metres

From parking 1: 20 min.
From parking 2: 10 min.

Waypoints parking 1

N 43°05'17,8 E 23°23'04,0

Waypoints parking 2

N 43°05'12,2 E 23°22'11,9

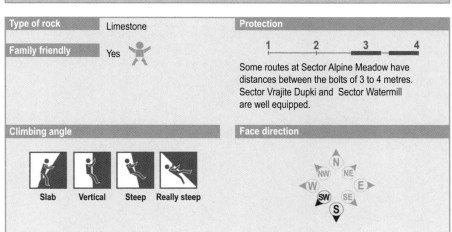

Type of rock   Limestone

Family friendly   Yes

Protection

1   2   3   4

Some routes at Sector Alpine Meadow have distances between the bolts of 3 to 4 metres. Sector Vrajite Dupki and Sector Watermill are well equipped.

Climbing angle

Slab   Vertical   Steep   Really steep

Face direction

N
NW   NE
W   E
SW   SE
S

Number of routes & Grade range

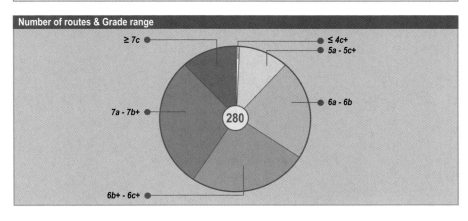

≥ 7c

≤ 4c+
5a - 5c+

6a - 6b

7a - 7b+

280

6b+ - 6c+

Ivajlo Radkov reaching for a tiny crimp on Thriller (8b+), Sector Vrajite Dupki

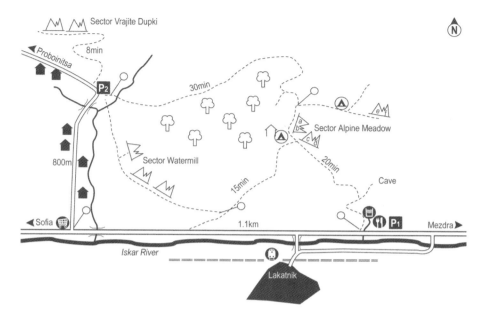

Directions

▶ Sector Alpine Meadow can be reached by a well maintained trail that starts from the waterfall next to the restaurant that lies along the main road Mezdra-Sofia. It takes about 20 minutes to get to the start of the routes. Sector Vrajite Dupki can be reached on foot from Sector Alpine Meadow, see the 'detailed drawing'. Another option is to drive here by car. From the restaurant go in the direction of Sofia and turn right after the bridge. After 800m there is a small parking place and a small river that offers some post-climbing refreshment. From here a path leads to the crag.

Climbing area Veliko Tărnovo

Spring   Summer   Autumn   Winter

Along the banks of the river Yantra the medieval capital of Bulgaria, Veliko Tărnovo, is spectacularly situated on a hillside. This wonderful town contains many medieval remnants from forgone times and offers lots of interesting museums. The old town is preserved with renaissance houses often functioning as handicraft shops or cafes. In summer there are lots of backpackers strolling around in its narrow streets, enjoying one of Europe's best kept secrets. There are also several very pleasant and fantastically situated monasteries around Veliko Tărnovo built during the time of the Second Bulgarian Kingdom. These former centres of cultural and spiritual life are absolutely worth a visit on rest days. The very charming traditional villages near Veliko Tărnovo offer yet another reason to take some rest days.

The climbing area of Veliko Tărnovo consists of the well developed crags of St. Trinity and Usteto, with in total almost 200 sport climbing routes. Almost every year these crags host one of the world cup climbing competitions. A third, smaller crag, Dryanovo, was still being developed at the time of writing. This crag has a great potential for a lot of fine routes.

The splendid rock climbing conditions combined with the very relaxing city of Veliko Tărnovo and the charming villages and monasteries in the surrounding area makes this a top European climbing destination!

Veliko Tărnovo

When to go

The best period for climbing is spring and autumn although the locals often climb during winter on sunny days as well. It can be very hot in mid summer, but climbing is still possible as there are plenty of routes that lie in the shade. However, bring anti mosquito repellent in summer times!

Crag

A St. Trinity

B Usteto

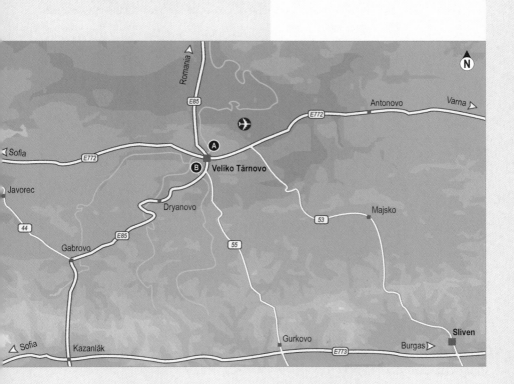

Saint Dimitrius church

Tsarevets during a light and sound show

How to get to the area & how to move around

It is convenient to have a car to get to the sectors of Veliko Tărnovo but it's not a necessity.

 By public transport from Sofia

Depending on your preference, both buses or trains will get you to Veliko Tărnovo from Sofia.

In summer, there are buses from Sofia to Veliko Tărnovo [4h, 12 Leva] leaving every hour from the central bus station. Buses are less frequent outside the summer period. The Pâtnicheski Prevozi Bus Station in Veliko Tărnovo is 4km from the town centre. From here a number of local buses head into the centre.

Another option is to take the train to Gorna Oryakhovitsa [3h, 11 Leva] which is 8½km from Veliko Tărnovo. Watch out - there are both "fast" trains and "express" trains, the express being faster. From Gorna Oryakhovitsa there are minibuses, taxis (8 Leva) and the bus No 10 that goes to the centre of Veliko Tărnovo.

 By public transport from Varna

From Varna there are plenty of daily buses to Veliko Tărnovo [4h, 10 Leva] leaving from the old bus station 2km north west of the city centre. Additionally there are 5 daily trains to Sofia stopping in Gorna Oryakhovitsa. See 'By public transport from Sofia' how to get to Veliko Tărnovo from here.

Great new route potential at Dryanovo

There is also a daily train between Budapest and Thessaloniki that stops at Gorna Oryahovitsa.

 By car

Veliko Tărnovo is 220km from Sofia and the journey takes about 3½ hours. From Varna it is about 225km to Veliko Tărnovo and it also takes around 3½ hours.

Where to stay

Veliko Tărnovo has several good hotels and lots of private accommodation. There are always local people around offering rooms to tourists. In the unlikely event that they don't manage to find you, the Tourist Information Centre (Ul Hristo Botev 5) also provides addresses for private accommodation. Try to get a room along the Stefan Stambolov street. Most private rooms here offer superb panoramic views away from the street noise.

There is no campsite in Veliko Tărnovo. However it is possible to wild camp behind the St. Trinity monastery. Cold and fresh drinking water is available at the parking lot of the monastery.

Hotel Trapezitsa

✉ Stefan Stambolov 79
☎ +359 62 622061
@ trapezitca_1902@abv.bg
🌐 www.trapezitca1902.com

Price   50 Leva per double room

This hotel is basic and, compared with the rest of Bulgaria, rather expensive but it offers reasonable value for money. The location, right in the centre of town, is in any case excellent.

Directions
The hotel is situated along the main road that goes through the centre and cannot be missed.

Endurance is needed for many routes at St. Trinity

Where to buy groceries

The place to buy the freshest and tastiest fruit and vegetables is the city market located at the corner of the streets "Nikola Gabrovski" and "Bulgaria". At the back of the market there is the CBA supermarket which will satisfy anyone's needs. Other smaller groceries shops are spread throughout the town.

Where to find the local climbing guidebook

The climbing guide of Veliko Tărnovo is for sale for 6 Leva at Hotel Trapezitsa. See the 'Where to stay' section for the address.

What else is there to see & do

Sightseeing in Veliko Tărnovo
This pretty town has a lot to offer. There are several museums, of which the archaeological museum exhibits the findings of medieval Bulgaria. If you like art, have a look inside the State Art Museum. Besides a tour around the various churches, a visit to the Tsarevets fortress on the east side of town is very worthwhile. There is a fabulous sound & light show that takes place on most evenings, which illuminates Tsarevets Hill. The show usually starts around 9pm. It's best to watch the 20 minute show from the side walk for free, which is what the locals do.

Visit the monasteries
At the very least, it's worth having a look inside the Holy St. Trinity monastery, also known as the Patriarch's monastery at the foot of the crags of St. Trinity. Another monastery worth a visit is the historical Dryanovo monastery situated about 4km away from Dryanovo town. It is situated in the picturesque gorge of the Dryanovo river where high rising limestone rocks dominate the whole landscape. This is also where there are a lot of new routes being put up. The monasteries of Kapinovo and Kilifarevo are also worthwhile. The tourist information centre in Veliko Tărnovo provides excellent maps showing all the cultural highlights of the region. More information on the monasteries can be found on *www.bulgarianmonastery.com*.

Visit the surrounding villages
If you have your own wheels (or hire a taxi) drive to one of the smaller villages around Veliko Tărnovo to experience Bulgarian life outside the cities. For example, Arbanasi makes a very enjoyable day trip. There are several historical monuments worth a visit, including the Arbanasi monastery. For a completely different kind of activity, horse back riding is another option in this pretty town.

Wall decoration in Veliko Tărnovo

St. Trinity

This crag is named after the 14th century monastery "St. Trinity" that is situated at the foot of the central part of the massif. This charming monastery gives an extra dimension to the great feeling one already has while climbing here. The crag is over 1 kilometre in length and has more than one hundred routes and this number continues to grow. The routes are very well equipped and there are some multi pitch routes of up to 80 metres as well.

The only downside of the climbing is that some harder routes contain artificial holds and in some places cement is even used. This was done on some routes that were used for world cup competitions. Nevertheless the climbing remains very enjoyable. The routes at sector 'The Cave' are wildly overhanging and a good dose of stamina is definitely needed. At other sectors the climbing requires more technical moves. In fact, St. Trinity offers something for every climber.

Monastery of St. Trinity

Lots of small overlaps at St. Trinity

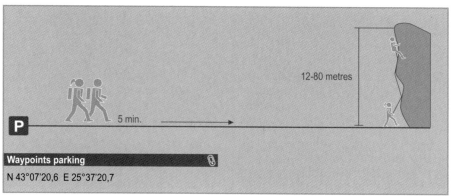

12-80 metres

5 min.

P

Waypoints parking

N 43°07'20,6 E 25°37'20,7

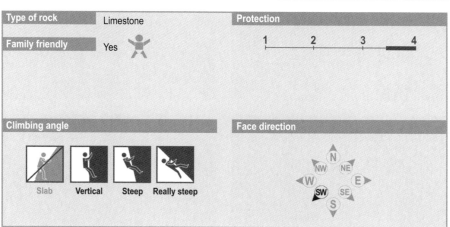

Type of rock	Limestone	Protection
Family friendly	Yes	

Protection: 1   2   3   4

Climbing angle

Slab   Vertical   Steep   Really steep

Face direction

N NW NE W E SW SE S

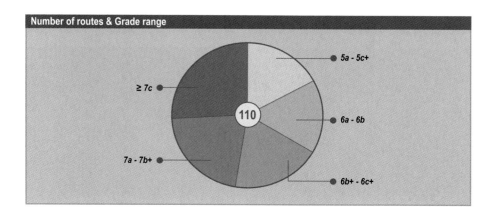

Number of routes & Grade range

110

- 5a - 5c+
- ≥ 7c
- 6a - 6b
- 7a - 7b+
- 6b+ - 6c+

Bulgarian champion Kalin Garbov on his beloved The Three Lions (8a) at St. Trinity

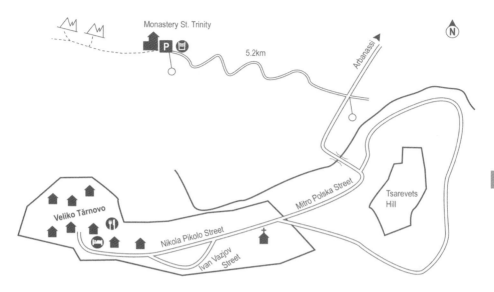

Directions

▶ From the centre of Veliko Tărnovo follow the road that goes around Tsarevets Hill. Cross the bridge on your right and take the second turning on the left. Follow this road for about 5km until you get to the parking lot of the monastery of St. Trinity. There is a footpath to the left of the monastery that clearly leads to the start of the routes.

If you don't have a car, a taxi can get you to St. Trinity and pick you up at the end of the day. The price of a taxi is around 5 Leva, one way.

Another very interesting crag for stronger climbers is to be found near the monastery of Dryanovo, 23km from Veliko Tărnovo. This crag is now being developed and had at the time of writing 14 routes between 7a and 8a. It has a great potential for a lot more hard routes. As soon as there is more information available it will be published on www.rockclimbingatlas.com.

Usteto

Usteto, 2km situated to the south of the city, consists of two crags, East and West, that are divided by a river. As the crags are near the city and the routes are not as hard as at St. Trinity, Usteto makes an ideal place for beginners and intermediate climbers. The East facing crag has most routes and offers many fifth grade routes. The best time for climbing here is in the afternoon when the crag is in the shadow. The West facing crag is further away from the road and therefore a bit quieter. Climbing is best in the morning before the sun appears.

Nice finger cracks!

Directions

▶ The crags of Usteto can be reached on foot from the centre, however, the smartest and easiest thing to do is to take a taxi as the way to get there is a bit tricky because you have to cross the highway. The ride should cost 3 Leva and all taxi drivers know the place. At the end of the day you could either walk the 25 minutes back or take another taxi.

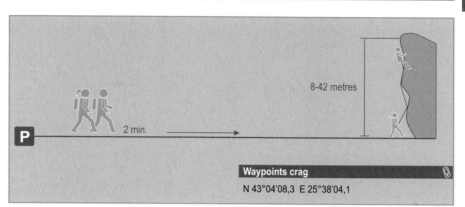

8-42 metres

P 2 min.

Waypoints crag

N 43°04'08,3 E 25°38'04,1

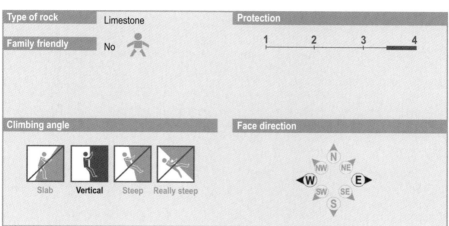

Type of rock	Limestone
Family friendly	No

Protection

1   2   3   4

Climbing angle

Slab **Vertical** Steep Really steep

Face direction

N
NW NE
W · E
SW SE
S

Number of routes & Grade range

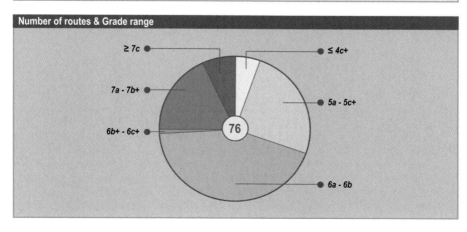

≥ 7c

7a - 7b+

6b+ - 6c+

≤ 4c+

5a - 5c+

76

6a - 6b

...where the rocks
touch the sea...

Croatia

Climbing at Cliffbase on Hvar Island,
photo by Hermann Erber

Croatia has some of the best climbing in Europe. Actually it seems as if the country is made of rock! With its beautiful coastline, old fishing villages and the sea always nearby, Croatia is undeniably a great climbing destination.

Since the bloody conflicts in the 90's, Croatia has been working very hard to rebuild itself and to join the EU as soon as possible. Tourists and climbers have already found their way to the beautiful towns, beaches and climbing areas of Croatia again. This is not without reason: the country includes 1,185 islands in the Adriatic Sea and has an amazing 5,835km of coastline full of cliffs and reefs. The coastal towns contain many traces of Roman settlements and Italian influences. Many of these towns, from Dubrovnik in the south to Rovinj in the north, are absolute jewels of Mediterranean architecture. Just outside the urban areas there are the most picturesque coves, bays, cliffs and beaches. No wonder the coastline of Croatia is considered to be one of the most beautiful in the Mediterranean.

But it is not just the coast that makes Croatia a popular tourist destination – inland there are a number of fantastic national parks. And if you're looking to combine climbing with other activities, such as scuba diving, windsurfing, hiking or biking, Croatia is the place to be. Simply exploring the towns of Dubrovnik, Split or Pula is also a great way to spend the day.

The wonderful Paklenica National Park has become a very well known rock climbing destination in Europe. But, besides this great area, Croatia has lots more excellent climbing, most of it being close to the sea. In short, it's a perfect climbing destination!

Last route of the day at Rovinj

Climbing information

Croatia has over 50 different crags - with endless potential for more - and all routes tend to be very well bolted, making it attractive for the pleasure seeking climber. There is even an excellent guidebook covering all crags in Croatia. In this Rock Climbing Atlas we describe the most interesting areas into detail - that is those areas where you could easily spend at least a week. The places not further described here are either very small or too hard to reach but, nevertheless, the climbing is often very good.

Climbing area Istria

Istria is Croatia's peninsula in the northwest and has 15 developed crags. Of these, the largest and most beautiful are: Rovinj, Limski Kanal, Dvigrad and Vela Draga. Climbing in Istria gives you the perfect combination of crags, beaches and picturesque small Mediterranean towns. This is an ideal destination to visit with children as well.

Climbing area Split

The crags in this area are all close to the city of Split, with the crag of Marjan actually situated in Split itself. Markezina Greda is just outside Split and the fine crags of Omiš and Brela are a bit further to the south. There is more than enough to choose from!

Climbing area Hvar

How does the prospect of a 300 metre deep-water solo sound? Good, you've come to the right place! This area includes the beautiful climbing at Cliffbase, which is in part directly above the sea, on the sparkling island of Hvar.

Climbing area Paklenica National Park

The Paklenica National Park offers some of the best climbing in Europe, especially for those interested in long multi pitch routes. Only 2km away from the beach, Paklenica makes a perfect destination for both hard climbing and relaxing in the sea.

Colourful Dubrovnik

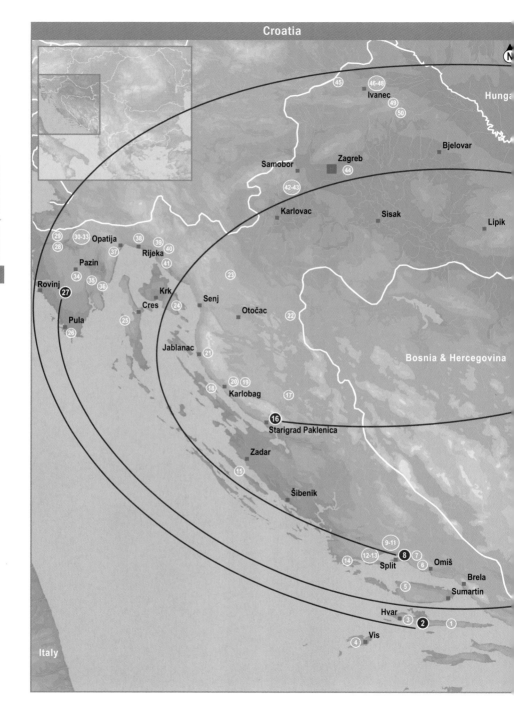

N

45
46-48
Ivanec
49
50

Bjelovar

Samobor
Zagreb
44

42-43

Karlovac
Sisak
Lipik

Hunga

29
30-33 Opatija
38
39
40
28
37
Rijeka
41
Pazin
34
35
36
Rovinj
27
Krk
Cres
24
Senj
Otočac
22
23
Pula
25
26
Jablanac
21
20 19
18
Karlobag
17
16
Starigrad Paklenica
Zadar
15
Šibenik
9-11
12-13
8 7
6
Omiš
14
Split
Brela
5
Sumartin
Hvar
3
2
1
Vis
4

Bosnia & Hercegovina

Italy

Climbing area	#		Climbing area	#	
1 Velika Stiniva	43		30 Istarske toplice	12	
2 Hvar			31 Raspadalica	34	
Cliffbase	117		32 Izvor Mirne	11	
3 Straćine	16		33 Nugla	14	
4 Komiza	13		34 Pazin	36	
5 Brač	59		35 Dolina Raše	9	
6 Ducé	9		36 Rabac	14	
7 Mosor	96		37 Mošćenićka draga	18	
8 Split			38 Veli vrh	19	
Brela	87		39 Kamenjak	23	
Omiš	81		40 Golubinjak	10	
Marjan	75		41 Antovo	8	
Markezina greda	57		42 Terihaj	15	
9 Rupotine	11		43 Okić	31	
10 Kaštel Sućurac	50		44 Gorsko Zrcalo	10	
11 Kozjak	6		45 Ravna gora	41	
12 Malačka	13		46 Vranja peč	11	
13 Trogir	27		47 Pokojec	60	
14 Vinišće	9		48 Zia	20	
15 Ugljan	5		49 Ljubelj	10	
16 Paklenica National Park			50 Kalnik	125	
Paklenica	376		51 Papuk	10	
17 Zir	7				
18 Pag	19				
19 Božin kuk	16				
20 Dabarski kukovi	49				
21 Strogir	17				
22 Plitvice	7				
23 Klek	20				
24 Krk	13				
25 Cres	11				
26 Vinkuran	28				
27 Istria					
Rovinj	96				
Limski kanal	118				
Dvigrad	87				
Vela Draga	68				
28 Ponte Porton	30				
29 Ćepić	46				

Boris Čujić on H.P.D. Imotski (7b+), Omiš

Climate

There are two climate zones: a mountainous climate prevails, very locally, in the interior with hot summers and cold snowy winters; a pleasant Mediterranean climate prevails along the Adriatic coast with an overwhelming number of sunny days (with 2,600 hours of sunlight per year, on average). The summers are dry and hot and the winters are mild and humid.

In general, the best time for climbing in Croatia is in spring and autumn. During summer you will have to climb either in the morning or late afternoon to avoid the heat. On the island of Hvar you can climb year round.

Month	Average temperature (°C)	Average rainfall (mm)
Jan	6	79
Feb	6	64
March	8	65
April	13	65
May	17	58
June	21	50
July	23	38
Aug	23	58
Sept	20	73
Oct	16	75
Nov	11	111
Dec	7	99

Climate table Istria.
Average temperatures at the Dalmatian coast are approximately 2 degrees higher.

Split

Getting there

 By plane

Croatia has eight major airports: Zagreb, Split, Dubrovnik, Pula, Rijeka (on the island of Krk), Zadar, Brac and Osijek. When flying to Croatia from elsewhere in Europe, you'll almost certainly be flying to one of the first five. Pula and Rijeka are near the climbing area of Istria. Try to book a flight to Split if you are planning to climb at the other three areas. Of these, the Paklenica National Park is close to Zadar, which is also worth checking out as a flight destination. Zagreb, the capital, is a few hours away from all the areas.

From Germany there are a few low cost airlines flying directly to Rijeka and Split, amongst others German Wings (*www.germanwings.com*). The volume of flights from the UK to Croatia is also considerable and they're inexpensive too. Try Easyjet (*www.easyjet.com*) or Thomsonfly (*www.thomsonfly.com*). From other European towns it is best to search for a charter flight or for connecting flights with low cost airlines. Flights from other continents will head for Zagreb.

Another interesting option is to fly to Italy (especially to Venice and Treviso) and catch a ferry. There are many low-cost airlines offering flights to several Italian cities, amongst them Ryanair (*www.ryanair. com*), and together with cheap prices, there is a lot of availability. Try to head for Ancona or Rimini (100km from Ancona). From Ancona there are several ferries to Split. See the 'By boat' text for more information about the websites of the ferry companies. Check *www.trenitalia.it* for train schedules between Ancona and other cities in Italy.

 By train

The main train stations in Croatia with connections to the rest of Europe are Zagreb, Pula, Rijeka and Split (via Zagreb). If you're travelling from north east Italy - Venice and Trieste – to Split, the detour via Zagreb can add quite a few hours to your journey, in which case it is better to travel by bus. A good website to check international train schedules is: *www.reiseauskunft.bahn.de*.

The famous bridge of Mostar (Bosnia)

Moving around

All the climbing areas in Croatia are easy to reach by public transport. It's more convenient to have your own wheels in Istria and Split, though this is not absolutely essential.

 Pula airport information

At the time of writing there were no shuttle buses operating between the airport and the centre or the bus station (located in the centre). A taxi should cost no more than €10.

By bus

There are frequent buses from major European cities to Croatia, especially in summer. The best place to start the search is via *www.eurolines.com*.

Rijeka airport information

There are regular buses between Rijeka airport and the central bus station in the centre of town [45min, €4].

By boat

There are currently only ferry services between Italy and Croatia. No services exist from any other European country. The following connections are possible:
- From Ancona to Zadar, Split, Vis and Hvar
- From Pescara to Split
- From Bari to Dubrovnik

For up to date travel information check:
- *www.jadrolinija.hr*
- *www.miatours.hr*
- *www.sem-marina.hr*
- *www.snav.com*

Split airport information

The airport is located near Trogir and is connected with the port, close to the main bus station, by the buses operated by Pleso Prijevoz or by local bus number 37. Both run frequently [30min, €4].

Dalmatian coast

By car

The easiest way to get to Croatia from Northern Europe is to drive to Munich, cross Austria via Graz and follow the directions to Maribor in Slovenia. Croatia is signposted as soon as you leave Maribor. The drive from Munich to the border of Croatia will take about 5 hours. If you head for Istria it is probably faster to drive via Ljubljana in Slovenia or via Italy.

Zagreb airport information

There is a direct bus connection between the airport and the main bus station (Aotubusni kolodvor) [25min, €3.75].

 By public transport

The train network is not as extensive as the bus network and trains are much slower than buses. Still, the train is a good way to see the country, if you have the time. Check *www.hznet.hr* for time schedules.

Judith van de Geijn enjoys Ribe 6a+ at Limski Kanal

Croatia has an extensive bus network and fares are relatively inexpensive. All cities are connected and even smaller towns can usually be reached by bus. There are express buses to cover larger distances in a short period of time. Autotrans (*www.autotrans.hr*) and Croatiabus (*www.croatiabus.hr*) are both well known companies. The fare for example from Zagreb to Split is about €18.

 By car

Roads are well maintained in Croatia and tolls are charged on some, but this is not too expensive. Make sure to drive during daytime with your headlights on - this is obligatory and the police are frequently on patrol.

The average price for car rental in Croatia is €37 per day for the cheapest category cars, if rented for 7 days or more. All international car agencies have offices at every airport and reservations can be made via their websites. Other sites worth checking include: *www.argusrentals.com*, *www. croatia.affordablecarrental-europe.com* and *www. weltrentacar.hr*.

Car rental in Italy is about €10 per day cheaper than in Croatia. Every Italian airport has car rental agency offices, however some of them will not allow you to take the car into Croatia, so check carefully. Hertz allows Ryanair customers to drive the rental car into Slovenia and Croatia (only when booked via Ryanair's website). In any case the trans-border permission should be marked on the hire documents or the car may be refused entry at the border. If you succeed in getting across without the appropriate authorisation, your insurance may well be invalid! The price of a litre of petrol or diesel in Croatia is comparable to most Western European countries.

Accommodation

Croatia has an excellent tourist infrastructure - almost every Croatian town worth visiting has a campsite and there is no shortage of hotels, apartments or private rooms for rent. Accommodation is well signposted from the roads. In general you won't need to book ahead, except maybe in the high season (mid-July to mid-August).

Campsites charge €12 to €16 for 2 persons, a tent and a car. There's a tourist tax of about €1 per person per day, but the actual price depends on the season and the region. Electricity may be included in the price or otherwise costs around €2 per day extra. Be aware that wild camping is prohibited in Croatia because, as a consequence of the recent war, mines are still spread throughout the country.

The cost of a hotel room or apartment really depends on the popularity of the location and the season. For a mid range hotel the price could easily add up from €50 to €80 for a double room. Expect to pay half that for a budget hotel. Prices in the low season for a decent apartment vary from €20 to €35 per day (with a minimum stay of three nights). Add 20-40% to these prices in July and August.

Private rooms in local homes can be booked through tourist offices in every town, but it is better to deal with proprietors directly. Not only is this type of accommodation the cheapest with excellent service, it is also the best way of getting to know the locals. Private rooms are marked with the sign 'Sobe' (meaning rooms available). You'll also find proprietors standing along the main road or at the bus station with a sign in their hands. Prices range between €9 to €20 per person per night depending on the duration of stay, location and season.

Treat yourself after climbing

Food & Drinks

Croatia doesn't have a particularly unique cuisine but, along the coast, excellent fish dishes are abundant.

Marko Miscevic on one of the best difficult routes at Omiš, Leon (7c)

Supermarkets and local markets are dotted all over the country and there is nothing you cannot buy in them. Supermarket prices are just slightly lower than in Western Europe.

A good meal of pasta or pizza (which most restaurants offer) costs around €5 in a standard restaurant. Along the coast grilled fish (for example mackerel) goes for €10. The prices for a drink in bars vary depending on how touristy the location is. Expect to pay between €1 and €1.50 for a cappuccino and between €1.75 and €2.50 for a beer. A scoop of (often excellent) ice cream only costs €0.60!

Climbing guidebook

The guidebook that covers all the rock climbing areas in Croatia, except Paklenica, is called "Climbing guide Croatia" by Boris Čujić (€21). The routes in Paklenica are contained in a separate book called "Climbing guide Paklenica", also written by Boris Čujić (€17).

There is another guidebook called "Climbing without frontiers" published by Sidarta (€20). This covers all the rock climbing areas in Istria including the crags in Italy around Trieste and those of Osp, Mišja Pec and Črni Kal in Slovenia.

Watch out for sea urchins

Facts & figures

Population:	4,5 million
Religion:	Roman catholic (88%)
Capital:	Zagreb
Time zone:	GMT+1
Telephone Code:	+385

Money

Currency:	Kuna (Kn)
Exchange rate:	€1 = 7,3Kn
ATM machines:	widespread

(A kuna is a weasel-like animal whose fur was used by the locals for payment many centuries ago.)

Language

Good day	Dobar dan
Thank you	Hvala
Goodbye	Do videnja
Yes / No	Da / Ne
Right / Left / Straight	Desno / Lijevo / Pravo
Rock climbing	Slobodno penjanje

Visas & formalities

EU	Other European nationalities	USA / Canada	All other nationalities
No visa for a period of up to 90 days.	Most other European nationalities do not require a visa for a period of up to 90 days.	No visa for a period of up to 90 days.	Most other nationalities do not require a visa for a period of up to 90 days.

Safety

Crime and personal security is not a problem in Croatia and the only thing you still have to watch out for are mines in remote areas, which were placed during the conflict in the 90's. In all tourist areas and on hiking trails in the national parks the mines have been cleared.

Emergency numbers

Police:	92
Fire Brigade:	93
Ambulance:	94

Use of mobile phone

There is an excellent mobile coverage almost everywhere.

Internet access

Internet cafés are springing up everywhere and the connections are usually good for €3 per hour.

Water

Tap water is safe and drinkable throughout the country.

Climbing area Istria

Istria is a region that covers north-western Croatia with a small slice of Slovenia and a tiny area encompassing the town of Muggia in Italy. The landscape of Istria is marked by picturesque towns, fertile fields, rocky mountains and a coast washed by a clear blue sea. The Italian atmosphere, the local artists performing and selling their wares in the narrow streets, and the many authentic cafes and restaurants make Istria a popular tourist destination. Actually it is a perfect family beach destination!

Rovinj, a picturesque fishermen's port, is definitely your best choice to stay when in Istria. It is the perfect spot for combining rock climbing with either water sports or just relaxing on the (rocky) beaches. And in the evening the charming town has more than enough space on terraces to enjoy a good dinner.

Spring   Summer   Autumn   Winter

The climbing in Istria is diverse with many different limestone crags of varying height and size. The Croatian peninsula has 12 diverse crags with over 600 routes of which the vast majority is single pitch (up to 40 metres) sport climbing. The four biggest crags are described in this Rock Climbing Atlas. Istria is a good place for those who have just started climbing but intermediate climbers too have lots to choose from.

Sector Horoskop at Limski Kanal

When to go

Istria boosts a pleasant Mediterranean climate with mild winters and warm summers. The sea is warm enough to swim in from May until the end of September. Due to these favourable conditions, climbing is possible year round. During the day in the summer months the temperatures are high but the sea breeze might cool things down.

Crag

Ⓐ Rovinj

Ⓑ Limski Kanal

Ⓒ Dvigrad

Ⓓ Vela Draga

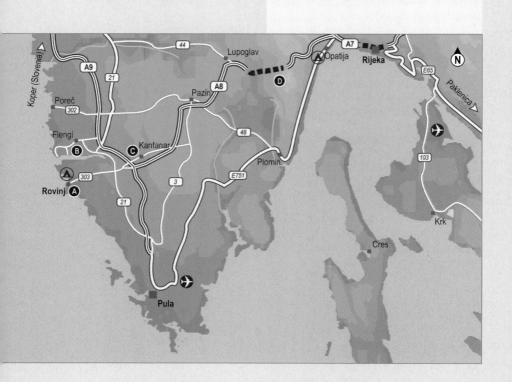

How to get to the area & how to move around

 By car

Rovinj, the most convenient and one of the nicest towns in which to stay, can be easily reached by public transport. Nonetheless, a car would be convenient as it allows to get to a wide range of crags in a short period of time.

 By public transport

There are many options to reach the area from different countries. The best are:

Via Rijeka
Fly directly to Rijeka and then take one of the ten daily buses to Rovinj [3½h, 80Kn]. Buses leave from the central bus station in the centre of Rijeka.

Via Italy
Fly to Trieste or to Treviso (Venice) in Italy. From Treviso you can take one of many trains to Trieste [2½h]. Next to the Trieste train station there is the bus station from where 8 buses daily leave for Rijeka [2½h], starting at 8.30 am with the last one at 7.15 pm. There are two buses at 9 am and 2 pm for Pula stopping in Rovinj [3h] (the 2 pm bus does not go on Sundays and special holidays).

There is also a bus from Venice (P. le Roma) to Rovinj [5h], except on Sundays. Check *www.saf.ud.it* and look under "orari-internazionali" for timetables.

There is also a twice-weekly passenger boat from Venice to Rovinj [3¾h, €94 for a return ticket]. Check *www.aferry.com* for all ferry schedules.

Quite a few climbers rent a mountain bike to get to the crags of Rovinj, Limski Kanal and Dvigrad although getting to the latter two requires some pedalling effort. In Rovinj the company Globtour, at Obala Alda Rismondo 2 (in the centre of town on the promenade) rents (mountain) bikes for about 65Kn per day.

If you plan to climb at Vela Draga you will need a car to get there. There are a few car rental agencies based in Rovinj, for example Vetura on Nazorova bb (Tel: +385 52 815209).

Rovinj is 60km from the border with Slovenia and only 93km from Trieste in Italy. From Munich, in Germany, the drive to Rovinj via Slovenia takes 6 hours.

Where to stay

There are plenty of campsites around Rovinj (watch out in case you end up on a nudist site!) as well as various apartments and hotels. Expect to pay 100Kn to 150Kn for a pitch on a campsite for two people with a car and a tent. Downtown there are apartments for rent: prices start at €35 per day per apartment and are roughly 20% more expensive in the high season.

A very basic, but definitely the cheapest, place to stay is Camping Sport & Relax, near the crags of Dvigrad. Another possibility, if you'd like to be near to the crags of Vela Draga, is to find accommodation in Opatija, which is 15km away from Vela Draga. There is only one campsite in Opatija.

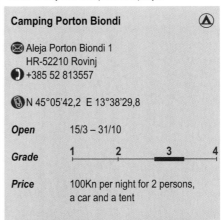

Camping Porton Biondi

✉ Aleja Porton Biondi 1
   HR-52210 Rovinj
📞 +385 52 813557

N 45°05'42,2 E 13°38'29,8

Open	15/3 – 31/10

Grade	1	2	**3**	4

Price	100Kn per night for 2 persons, a car and a tent

Camping Porton Biondi is less than 1km from the centre of Rovinj, situated in an old pine forest. The campsite covers 11 hectare offering plenty of "rocky" places to pitch your tent. Try to find a spot on top of the hill, as far as away from the road, where only the squirrels and the birds will wake you up.

Directions
Follow the signs in Rovinj to get to the campsite.

Camping Sport & Relax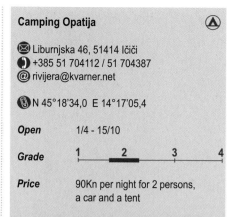

✉ Koreniči
☎ +385 91 7335326

Open   This rather depends on the whims of the eccentric owner, but it should be open from spring until autumn.

Grade   1 ━━━ 2   3   4

Price   No fixed prices so it is better to ask before you pitch your tent

It can hardly be called a campsite, but it is a convenient and cheap option to camp as it is very close to the crags of Dvigrad. The crazy, but friendly, owner will give you a warm welcome and you can use his shower and kitchen for cooking.

Directions
Camping Sport & Relax is located 50 metres after the parking for the crag.

Lovely Rovinj

Camping Opatija

✉ Liburnjska 46, 51414 Ičiči
☎ +385 51 704112 / 51 704387
@ rivijera@kvarner.net

📍 N 45°18'34,0 E 14°17'05,4

Open   1/4 - 15/10

Grade   1 ━ 2 ━ 3   4

Price   90Kn per night for 2 persons, a car and a tent

Camping Opatija, a simple place with no extras, is situated 5km from the centre of Opatija and just a few minutes walk from the beach. It is reasonably clean and offers plenty of space and shelter from the sun.

Directions
Signs in Opatija will take you to the campsite.

Camping Valdaliso

✉ Monsena BB
   HR - 55210 Rovinj
☎ +385 52 805505
@ info@rovinjturist.hr

📍 N 45°06'09,9 E 13°37'21,8

Open   1/4 - 15/10

Grade   1   2   3   4 ━

Price   130Kn per night for 2 persons, a car and a tent

Camping Valdaliso is situated 5km north west of Rovinj. It is a very modern campsite, aimed at holidaying families, with many facilities and its own beach front (no sand). There is a scuba diving and windsurfing school located at the campsite.

Directions
Follow the signs in Rovinj to get to the campsite.

Linda Rutten on Praz, 6a, at Dvigrad

Where to buy groceries

In Rovinj you can find a good discount supermarket called Valalta just outside the centre - there are road-signs for the store. In Opatija there is a small supermarket and if you have your own wheels there's a mega-supermarket along the main road from Rijeka to the highway to Rovinj.

Where to find the local climbing guidebook

All the crags described here are covered in the guidebook "Climbing without frontiers" and in "Climbing guide Croatia". The closest places to buy the guidebooks are in Rijeka and Trieste. The Iglusport shops (www.iglusport.hr) in Zagreb, Split and Starigrad sell the guides as well.

Rijeka - Nova Bookshop
✉ Trpimirova Ulica 3
(around the corner from the bus station)

Trieste (Italy) - Tecnosport
✉ Via Imbriana 5
34122 Trieste
📞 +39 40 306440
@ tecno.sport@virgilio.it
🌐 www.climbingsport.com

What else is there to see & do

Pula
Situated near the base of the Istrian peninsula, Pula is the largest city in Istria. The city has one of the most famous sights in the whole of Croatia - its well

preserved Roman amphitheatre. Built during the 1st century, the three-story amphitheatre is the sixth largest in the world. It hosts the Pula Opera Festival in the summer and is also used for other events during the year. Other impressive sights include the Triumphal arch of the Sergii and the Cathedral.

Poreč
Poreč is one of the most popular holiday resorts in Istria. A visit to the old town (Poreč is 2,000 years old) is a must if you are into historical sights. In particular, the 6th century Euphrasian Basilica (a World Heritage site) is wonderfully preserved and is well known for its beautiful gold mosaics.

Limska Draga Fjord (if you do not go climbing here)
This fjord is considered to be one of the most beautiful in the Mediterranean, which is definitely not an overstatement. It is 9km long and the cliffs rise up to 100 metres above the water. You can take a boat excursion along the canal from where you see oysters being farmed by local fishermen and fellow climbers struggle their way to the top. You can try the wine, liquor or honey sold by the locals along the road to the fjord.

Water sports
The varied submarine world of the Croatian coast provides excellent opportunities for scuba diving. Shipwrecks are a common sight. A 5-day open water diving course for beginners costs around €300. Check www.diving.hr for more information. Furthermore there are possibilities to go jet skiing, windsurfing and sailing. A 4-day windsurfing course consisting of 2 hours instruction per day costs around €110. The Tourist Association in the centre of town (Pina Budicina 12) or plenty of tour operators can tell you where to go to hire gear.

Biking
The coastline and surrounding hills have excellent biking trails passing through beautiful bays and wild spaces. The price for renting a bike is around 60Kn for a whole day.

Boat tours
Most tour operators in Rovinj offer scenic boat tours along the Istrian coast and to the Limska Draga Fjord. Prices are around 130Kn per person for a day trip.

Rovinj

The most popular crags in this area lie close to Rovinj along the Adriatic coast and are situated in one of the most beautiful protected forest parks in Istria. You can climb right on the water's edge and let the sea breeze cool you down. There are even a few routes that allow you to belay your partner while standing in the water itself!

The rock is of good quality, but due to some graffiti it can feel as if you are climbing the Berlin wall! It is a pity that the routes are short, only about 12 metres on average, but they're also generally easy so it is a very suitable place for beginners. There is not much in the way of harder routes (7a and above) here.

The climbing at Rovinj is also perfect for families as there is enough space to let the kids run free. Also, there are lots of easier routes ideal for children.

Marloes on Spigolo istriano (6a+)

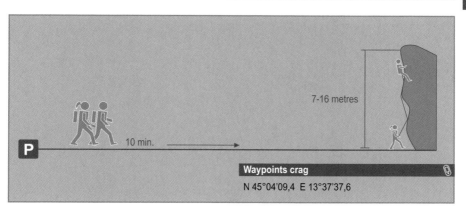

7-16 metres

10 min.

P

Waypoints crag

N 45°04'09,4 E 13°37'37,6

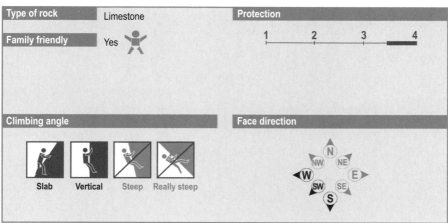

| Type of rock | Limestone |
| Family friendly | Yes |

Protection

1   2   3   4

Climbing angle

Slab   Vertical   Steep   Really steep

Face direction

N NE E SE S SW W NW

Number of routes & Grade range

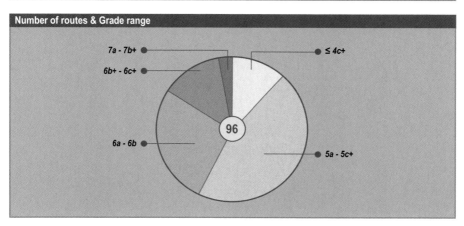

7a - 7b+
6b+ - 6c+
6a - 6b

≤ 4c+
5a - 5c+

96

Having fun at Rovinj

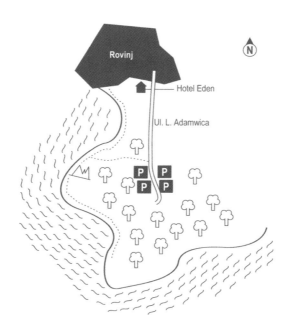

Directions

Off for a swim

► In Rovinj follow the obvious signs for the Hotel Eden and go past this huge hotel (it will be on your right). The name of this street is Ulica L. Adamwica. Continue to the end of the street, where you can park. Follow the hiking trail towards the sea that starts about halfway down the car park. Once you hit the sea turn left and after a few hundred metres you'll find the crags.

Limski Kanal

If you are looking for some tougher routes, Limski Kanal is the place to go. The sectors are situated along the pretty Limska Draga Fjord, guaranteeing excellent views while climbing.

Sector Gavranik is the most easily accessible of all the sectors, as it lies directly next to the road. This sector has some fine routes that are well bolted, though some belay bolts are a bit corroded. Of all the sectors, Sector Horoskop definitely has the best view over the canal. It takes about 10 minutes to get here from the parking. The routes are fine, well bolted and you will see the tourists cruising the canal watching you climb. Sector Krugi lies just below Sector Horoskop and these two sectors are easily combined on one day. Sector Šimije has recently been rebolted and there are now bolts every 1½ to 2 metres.

As it is mostly too hot to climb during the day in mid-summer, most climbers go in the morning or late afternoon. It's worth noting that there are trees at each sector that provide (some) shade while belaying.

Boris Čujić on Crvena tisina (7b), Sector Krugi

View from Sector Šimije

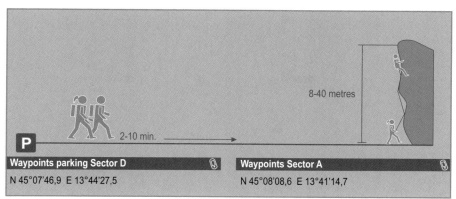

8-40 metres

2-10 min.

P

Waypoints parking Sector D

N 45°07'46,9 E 13°44'27,5

Waypoints Sector A

N 45°08'08,6 E 13°41'14,7

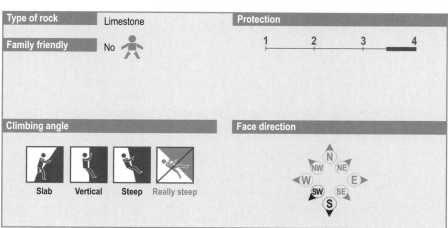

Type of rock

Limestone

Family friendly

No

Protection

1   2   3   4

Climbing angle

Slab   Vertical   Steep   Really steep

Face direction

N
NW   NE
W   E
SW   SE
S

Number of routes & Grade range

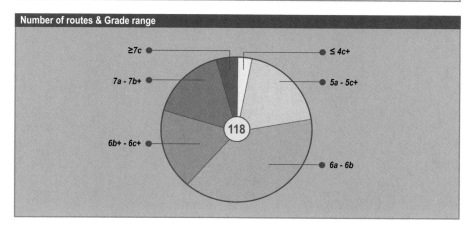

≥7c

7a - 7b+

6b+ - 6c+

≤ 4c+

5a - 5c+

118

6a - 6b

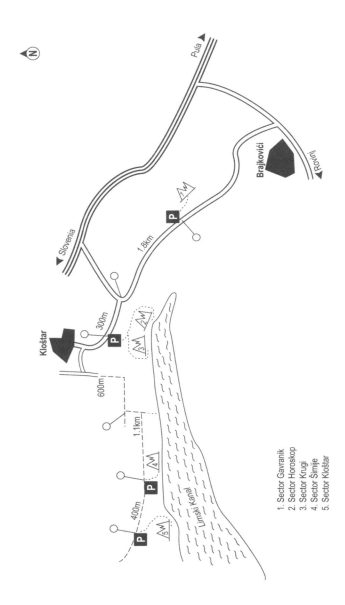

1. Sector Gavranik
2. Sector Horoskop
3. Sector Krugi
4. Sector Šimije
5. Sector Kloštar

Directions

► The sectors of Limski Kanal are 18km from Rovinj and are easily reachable by car and bike. From Rovinj take the road towards the Pula-Koper highway. After Brajkovici turn left at the junction and follow the sign for Limski Kanal. Just after you see the canal on your left you will pass the first sector on your right, which is just above the road. To reach sectors Horoskop and Krugi, turn left for Kloštar at the next junction. There is a car park on your left after 300 metres.

► For Sector Šimije and Kloštar continue along the road after the car park a little further and turn left just after you have passed the turn-off sign for Kloštar. Turn immediately left again and then follow the unpaved stony road for about 1.6km, until you reach the trail that leads to Sector Šimije. A few hundred metres further the trail starts for Sector Kloštar.

Sector Horoskop

Dvigrad

In the Draga valley lie the crags of Dvigrad, named after the long-abandoned mediaeval castle of El Dvigrad. The town itself was deserted in the 17th century after the great plague that swept Europe. The ruins of the castle can be seen from the top of the crag and it's still possible to visit them.

The crag is not only beautifully situated but also consists of excellent rock with very attractive climbing. The routes are technical gems demanding good footwork and the majority of them are in the 5th and 6th grade, although there are some harder ones too.

Marloes looking for crimps on Duga, 6b

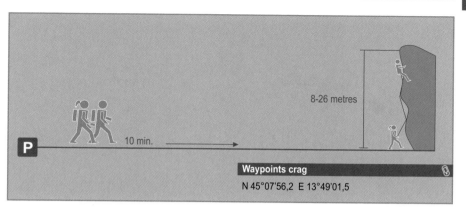

8-26 metres

10 min.

P

Waypoints crag

N 45°07'56,2 E 13°49'01,5

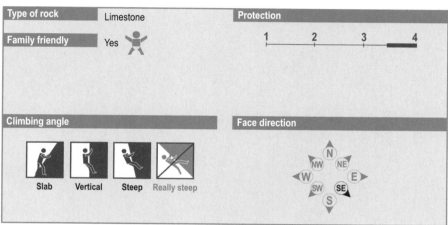

| Type of rock | Limestone |
| Family friendly | Yes |

Protection

1   2   3   4

Climbing angle

Slab   Vertical   Steep   Really steep

Face direction

N NE E SE S SW W NW

Number of routes & Grade range

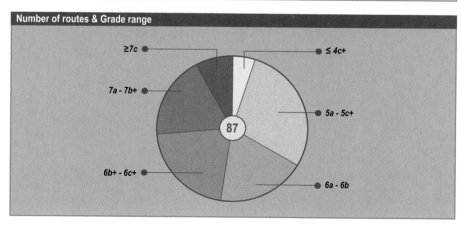

≥7c

7a - 7b+

6b+ - 6c+

≤ 4c+

5a - 5c+

6a - 6b

87

Pure slab climbing on Bukatela, 5a

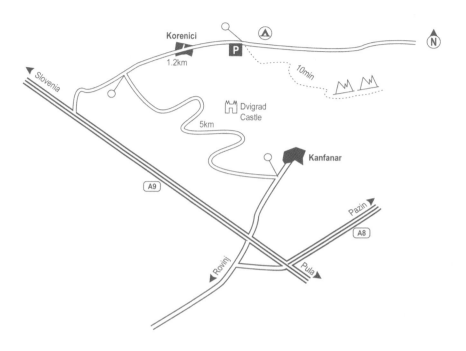

Directions

Camamila (6c) requires for special techniques

▶ Dvigrad is about 20km from Rovinj. From Rovinj head towards the Koper-Pula highway but, instead of turning onto this highway, go straight towards Kanfanar. Just before you enter Kanfanar turn left at the sign for Dvigrad Castle. Follow this road for 5km until you reach a junction where you turn right. From here it is about 1200 metres to the car park and the trail that leads to the crag. This is on the right hand side, 50 metres before Camping Park & Relax.

Vela Draga

Ever since the legendary Italian rock climber Emilio Comici climbed the first route to the summit of Veliki Toranj in 1931, Vela Draga has become well known around the world as an unusual place to climb. Its setting in a canyon, with limestone pillars reaching up to 100 metres high, is extraordinary. Also the stunning sunset is a rewarding and special experience after a good day's climbing.

The place shows a clear history of bolting in Croatia as quite a few of old bolts are still in place. However, as Vela Draga is still being developed, many new routes with proper protection have been recently put up and older routes are being rebolted. Most routes are in the 6th grade on slabs and steep vertical walls.

Vela Draga

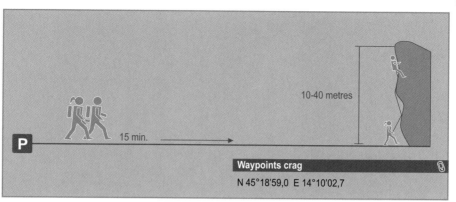

10-40 metres

P ——— 15 min. ————————→

Waypoints crag

N 45°18'59,0 E 14°10'02,7

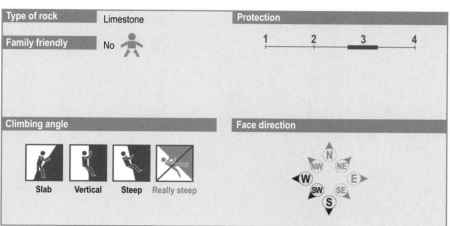

Type of rock	Limestone
Family friendly	No

Protection

1 ——— 2 ——— **3** ——— 4

Climbing angle

Slab Vertical Steep Really steep

Face direction

N NW NE W E SW SE S

Number of routes & Grade range

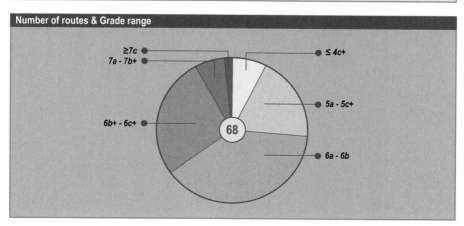

≥7c
7a - 7b+
6b+ - 6c+

≤ 4c+
5a - 5c+
6a - 6b

68

The Veliki Toranj tower

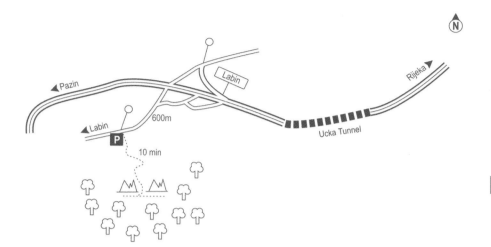

Directions

▶ From Opatija drive towards the highway Rijeka-Pula and take the Učka Tunnel. After the tunnel take the first junction towards Labin. The car park is on this road almost immediately on your left and Vela Draga is signposted. From here a well-marked trail leads to the crag.

Climbing area Split

Split, in central Dalmatia, is the second largest city in Croatia and the main departure point for the islands by ferry. Split, and the other Dalmatian towns around, have lots of interesting old buildings and museums, and there's a fantastic restaurant and cafe culture. Plus, the coastline here is one of the most beautiful that Europe has to offer! The climbing area consists of seven different crags all situated close to the sparkling city of Split. Besides high rising walls with splendid (and well bolted) single and multi pitch sport climbing routes, the area offers a range of other things to do which makes it an ideal and accessible destination. The four most interesting crags in this area are described into detail.

The most southern climbing routes in Croatia are at Brela, where the crags rise high above the village. The majority of the routes are of medium difficulty and simply the view from the top, over the islands, makes it well worth climbing here.

| Spring | Summer | Autumn | Winter |

North of Brela lies the small town of Omiš, that attracts quite a lot of visitors every year. Among the high rising crags in and around the stunning canyon of Omiš, shaped by the river Cetina, there are several crags suitable for climbing. Everyone can find a route to suit them here as it is a diverse area, and there are even three beautiful and well equipped multi pitch routes up to 305 metres. Omiš itself is a lovely place to stay - it has a long beach and charming narrow streets filled with bars and restaurants. Furthermore, the canyon offers plenty of hiking, biking and (easy) rafting opportunities.

Split itself hosts a beautiful crag with almost 70 routes in the city's nature reserve. The sectors all lie

Beautiful climbing in Omiš - Ante Predovic on Dr. Ivan Merz (6b+)

at the western side of this peninsula, called Marjan. About 11 kilometres north east of Split lies another nicely shaped crag, Markezina greda, that only has a few routes, but is worth a visit.

When to go

Spring and autumn is the best time to visit Central Dalmatia. But even in winter temperatures can be quite enjoyable for climbing, although the weather is more unpredictable compared to other seasons. In mid summer it will be too hot for climbing during the day as most sectors face south. Omiš is the best place to go to in this time of the year.

Crag

Ⓐ Brela

Ⓑ Omiš

Ⓒ Marjan

Ⓓ Markezina greda

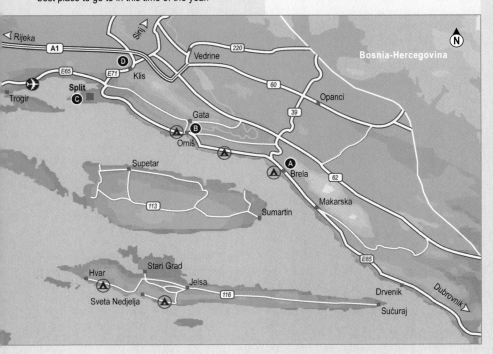

How to get to the area & how to move around

It is easiest to get to the different crags using a car. Without a car you'll need more time, though it is possible to get everywhere except for Markezina greda.

 By public transport

There are various low cost airlines operating direct flights from several cities in Europe to Split. The UK particularly has many inexpensive and direct flights. Amongst others, the low cost airline Sky Europe (*www.skyeurope.com*) handles flights to Split via Budapest and Bratislava.

From the central bus station of Rijeka there are 11 buses daily to Split [8h, 170-250Kn]. From the Zagreb bus station there is a bus almost every half hour to Split [6h, 130Kn].

Another option is to fly to Italy and take the boat to Croatia. See the 'Getting there' section in the introduction chapter for more information.

Moving around between the different towns is possible by bus. There are hourly buses between Split, Omiš and Brela and all crags are close to the centre of these towns. The only crag that is impossible to reach by public transport is Markezina greda.

 By car

Split is about 440km from the Italian border and the journey from there takes around 6 hours by car. The distance from the Austrian-Slovenian border is approximately 560km.

Get yourself lost in historic Split

Split Boulevard with Marjan National Park in the back

There are several car rental companies in Split. Try ITR at the airport bus stop or Avis and Budget in Hotel Marjan at the Obala Kneza Branimirova (southwest of the centre). See the 'Moving around' text in the introduction section for more information about car rental. An alternative is to rent a scooter for a day or more. This is possible in Split and Omiš and costs around 200Kn per day.

Where to stay

Depending on the amount of time you have available, your means of transport and interests, there are several places which could make a good base for exploring the region. You can either choose to stay in one town and visit other crags on daytrips or spend a few days in Split and then move on south to Omiš. If you don't have your own car we would recommend that you make Split or Omiš your base.

The best low cost options in Split itself are private rooms, since the nearest campsite is 20km out of town. There are always women offering sobe (rooms available) at the bus station. Expect to pay around 100Kn per person per night. It is also possible to book a room in advance via for example *www.palmasplit.com*, although rooms booked in this way are usually more expensive.

If you would like to stay near Split and you do have your own transport there is a wealth of cheaper accommodation, especially apartments, right on the seaside along the Split-Dubrovnik road. It will be cheaper to bargain on the spot rather than booking in advance. The price for 2 person apartments range between 180Kn and 360Kn per day if you stay 3 nights or more. The closest campsites to Split are either in Trogir (north of Split - but there's no sense in staying out there) or in Omiš.

If you have your own transport there are a few quiet campsites situated on the coast between Omiš and Brela. We don't recommend staying in Brela as there is not much to do there. Staying in or near Omiš on the other hand gives you the opportunity to experience Dalmatian life (both day and night!) in an attractive town. It is also an option, although not legal, to camp wild along the river Cetina in Omiš.

Camping Sirena

✉ Lokva Rogoznica - Omiš
☎ +385 21 870266
@ autocamp-sirena@st.hinet.hr
🏠 www.autocamp-sirena.com

🌐 N 43°24'22,6 E 16°46'36,1

Open   1/5 - 31/10

Grade   1────2────3────4

Price   100Kn for 2 persons, a car and a tent

Camping Sirena lies between Brela and Omiš, 15km from Brela and 10km from Omiš. Without a doubt this campsite has the best pitches in the whole of Croatia. You can pitch your tent directly next to the sea and have your own private beach. It is not uncommon to see dolphins passing by. Its size makes it an ideal place to escape the bigger, well-known tourist campsites. However, you will need your own wheels to get here. There is a small store that sells cold beer and fresh bread.

Directions
The campsite is signposted along the road from Split to Makarska. When you see the sign for the campsite, turn right immediately after the tunnel.

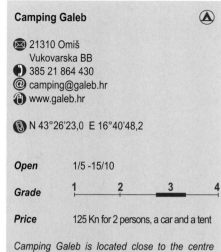

Camping Galeb

✉ 21310 Omiš
   Vukovarska BB
☎ 385 21 864 430
@ camping@galeb.hr
🏠 www.galeb.hr

🌐 N 43°26'23,0 E 16°40'48,2

Open   1/5 -15/10

Grade   1────2────3────4

Price   125 Kn for 2 persons, a car and a tent

Camping Galeb is located close to the centre of Omiš. This super-sized, old, communist-style campsite can take up to 1800 guests. The campsite has a beach and several facilities including a pizzeria and a tennis court.

Directions
Follow the clear signs for Camping Galeb in Omiš, which can't be missed.

Where to buy groceries

There is a huge Mercator supermarket on Split's outer ring road, in the direction of the airport. However to get there you need your own transport. There is a big Mercator sign along the road that can't be missed. Of course, Split itself also has many smaller supermarkets dotted all around.

In Omiš there is a daily market where fresh fruit and vegetables are sold. The two supermarkets along the main road (one close to Camping Galeb and one on the northern side of town) have everything you'll need.

Where to find the local climbing guidebook

The climbing guides "Climbing without frontiers" and "Climbing guide Croatia" can, amongst others, be bought in the following shops:

The maze of tiny streets of Trogir

Iglu Sport Split

✉ Varoški prilaz 4, 21000 Split
📞 +385 21 343423
@ split@iglusport.hr
🌐 www.iglusport.hr

Iglu Sport Zagreb

✉ Grahorova 4, 10000 Zagreb
📞 +385 1 3700434
@ iglusport@iglusport.hr

What else is there to see & do

Split

The most striking part of Split is its old town and Diocletian's Palace, an UNESCO World Heritage site. The old town is fantastic to walk around - it has a gorgeous promenade and many small cafes with supremely relaxing chairs. Also you won't even need to visit any museums to enjoy the work of Ivan Meštrović, Croatia greatest 20th century sculptor, whose work is displayed in the streets.

Trogir

The old town of Trogir, 28km north of Split, is also an UNESCO World Heritage site and draws a lot of tourists each year. In the 3rd century BC, Greeks from the island of Vis founded the settlement of Tragurion before it became part of the Roman Empire. Parts of the city walls, built between the 13th and 14th centuries, are still visible today on the southern side of the city. Also the remarkable city gate, built in 1593, is still standing. The cathedral on the east side of the city is on the main square and dates from the beginning of the 13th century. Although the town is rather small – you'll only need a couple hours of to see it all - it is definitely worth a visit.

Dubrovnik

Dubrovnik, in the far south of the country, is certainly one of the highlights of any trip to Croatia. A thick stone-wall surrounds the old town of the city that was once built to keep the barbarians out. The old town has many nice cafes and restaurants hidden away in well-kept small streets. Dubrovnik is also a cultural delight with its many churches, museums, palaces and monasteries. Although the city (especially the roofs of the houses) suffered a lot during the war, it has been beautifully restored. Even though there is no climbing around Dubrovnik, and it is 190km from Omiš, it is a must-see city in Croatia.

Mostar in Bosnia-Hercegovina

The beautiful city of Mostar suffered tremendously during the war and was literary blown to pieces. It is impossible not to notice the 'scars' of the war when driving into town. Almost all buildings show some damage and the ruins hide secrets of the dark times the city and the civilians had to endure. However times have changed. The well-known historic bridge separating the Muslims and the Bosnian Croats was reopened in 2004. These days, the bridge stands for the 'reunion' of different religions - young men jump off the bridge again into the river 21 metres below, showing off to their (female!) friends. Yet again, it is pleasant to walk around town with its' small souvenir stands and beautifully mosques. Let's hope history will never repeat itself.

It is possible to make a day trip to Mostar from Omiš by car but, as it takes 2½ hours to get there, it is worth considering spending the night in Mostar. Another option is to visit Mostar on your way back from Dubrovnik to Omiš or Split.

Hiking

Makarska, south of Split, is a nice port with some fine swimming and the starting point for some wonderful hiking trails. The best of these climbs the highest peak, Sveti Jure (1762m).

Water activities

In Omiš several agencies offer rafting, canoeing or canyoning trips that take about 3 to 4 hours and which cost around 200Kn per person. Shop around as there are many agencies offering the same activities. It is also possible to take a more relaxed sightseeing trip through the magnificent canyon on the river Cetina by motor boat.

A golden rule, which not only applies to Mostar but all of Bosnia-Hercegovina, is not to go into any abandoned buildings and be careful if you leave the paved road. There are still over half a million land mines in Bosnia-Hercegovina, and abandoned buildings can be booby trapped.

Brela

The massive crag of Brela offers stunning views over the coast and the islands with many routes to choose from. The limestone is of good quality and the bolting is excellent. There are many routes of 40 to 55 meters in length but, since these long routes always have a belay-station halfway, a 60 metre rope is mostly sufficient. The majority of the routes are in the 5th and 6th grade and require precise footwork as the climbing is mainly on slabs. One downside of Brela is that there is not much flat ground under the crag, making it a bit unstable for the belayer sometimes.

Makarska with the crags of Brela

Crag details Brela

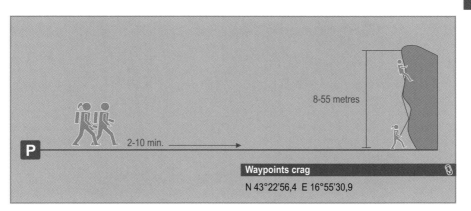

8-55 metres

2-10 min.

Waypoints crag

N 43°22'56,4 E 16°55'30,9

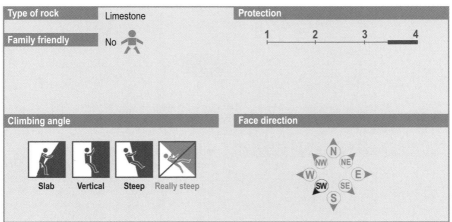

Type of rock Limestone

Family friendly No

Protection

1   2   3   4

Climbing angle

Slab   Vertical   Steep   Really steep

Face direction

N NE E SE S SW W NW

Number of routes & Grade range

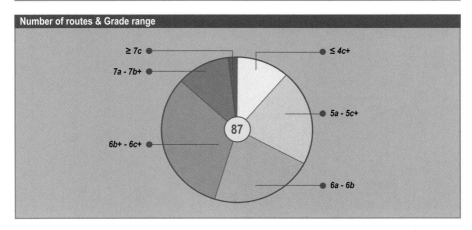

≥ 7c

7a - 7b+

6b+ - 6c+

≤ 4c+

5a - 5c+

6a - 6b

87

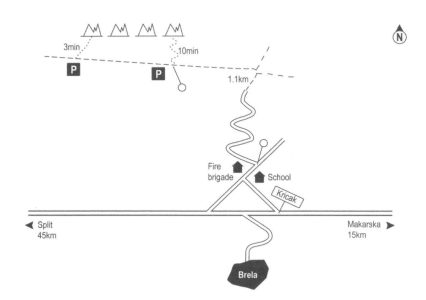

Directions

Brela

▶ The crag is situated above, and is visible from, the Split-Makarska road. Coming from Split, turn left at the sign for Krićak. Turn right at the school and then take the first road to the left. Follow this curvy road up. It becomes a gravelled road that leads to the crag. At the crag it is best to follow the trail starting at the second car park if you want to climb close to sector A.

If you're coming by bus, ask the driver to stop on the main road at the turn to Krićak.

Gorana Jelic on Svemir (6a), Omiš

Omiš

Omiš is one of the best crags of Central Dalmatia. Most routes are of medium difficulty although there are some very tough ones to be found as well. Omiš has several different sectors with one perfectly accessible sector (Sector Planovo) with lots of nice 5th grade routes. This sector is close to where the tourist boats leave for canyon sightseeing trips. During hot summer days you can climb here in the shade in either the morning or late afternoon. The routes are rather sustained with lots of pockets for the hands and the feet. Sector Babina bara and Papa je se vama offer more difficult routes where stamina goes without saying.

Sector Babjača has one bolted multi pitch route and Sector Ilinac has two bolted multi pitch routes. The longest route (6b+) is 305 metres. The other two multi pitch routes are graded 6b and 6a+. The descent is a simple walk down.

If you want to meet other climbers contact the agency 'Active Holidays' (Kezova Kacic b.b.) where the friendly Vicenco Bartulin can get you in touch with the local enthusiasts. Vicenco also gives climbing instructions. The number of the agency is +385 21 861829 and their email address is activeholidays@inet.hr.

Omiš, Sector Planovo

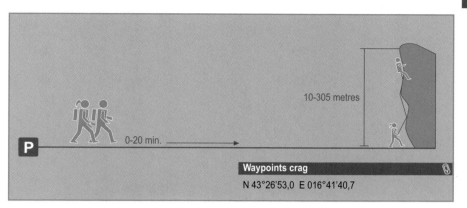

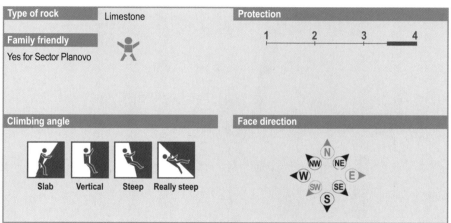

Type of rock	Limestone

Family friendly
Yes for Sector Planovo

Protection

1   2   3   4

Climbing angle

Slab   Vertical   Steep   Really steep

Face direction

N NE E SE S SW W NW

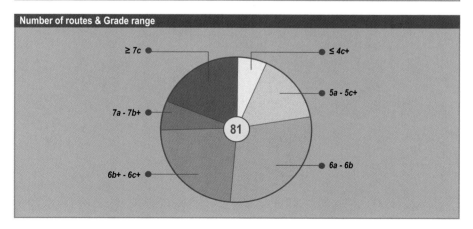

Number of routes & Grade range

≥ 7c
7a - 7b+
6b+ - 6c+
≤ 4c+
5a - 5c+
6a - 6b

81

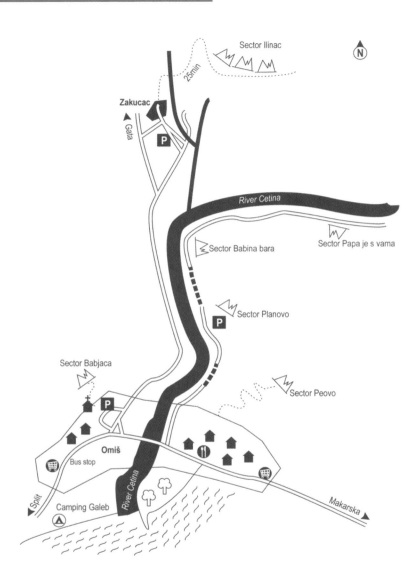

▶ See the detailed plan for the exact locations of the sectors. Sector Planovo, Babina bara and Papa je s vama can't be missed as they are along the road that follows the river Cetina. Sector Peovo is reached through the small streets in the old town of Omiš. Find the street called Jurja Šubica and follow the small path next to house number 4 up to the crag.

Ana Kolovrat on HPD - Imotski (6b+), Omiš

Marjan

Climbing at Marjan is absolutely worth a star due to its beautiful location at the western part of the city of Split. The routes are very diverse, from difficult short routes of 7 metres to easier longer routes of 30 metres. The most famous route is Marulianus (7c+), put up at one of the world's first sport climbing contests. After a days' climbing it is very rewarding to walk or drive down to the Kašjuni cove to swim in the clean blue sea waters of Split. On hot days, forget about climbing here as there is no shade to hide from the sun. On the other hand, on sunny winter days, the climbing could be wonderful here.

Tempting view while climbing at Marjan

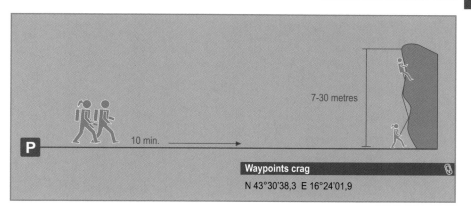

7-30 metres

P → 10 min. →

Waypoints crag
N 43°30'38,3 E 16°24'01,9

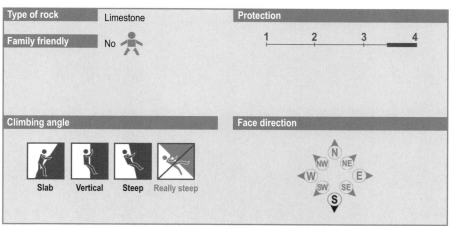

Type of rock		Protection

Type of rock — Limestone

Family friendly — No

Protection: 1 — 2 — 3 — 4

Climbing angle — Slab · Vertical · Steep · Really steep

Face direction — N, NE, E, SE, S, SW, W, NW

Number of routes & Grade range

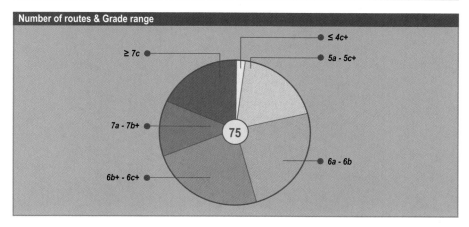

≥ 7c

≤ 4c+

5a - 5c+

7a - 7b+

75

6a - 6b

6b+ - 6c+

Marjan

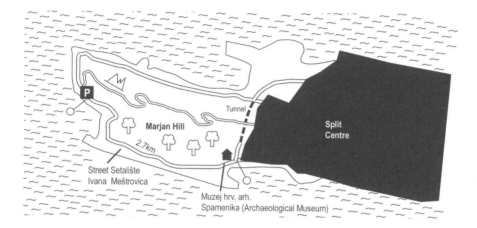

Directions

▶ By car:
In Split follow the signs for Marjan/Muzeji that takes you through the tunnel under Marjan Hill. Turn right at the end of this road at the Archaeological Museum. Continue on this road for 2.7km and park the car at the junction. Walk along the upper road to get to the crags.

▶ On foot:
It is possible to walk to the crag from the centre of Split in about 40 minutes. Follow the shore in the direction of the green peninsula, which is called Marjan Hill. Pass the Archaeological Museum and follow the directions above.

Markezina greda

The crag of Markezina greda certainly looks very impressive when seen from the road. The whole wall is more than one kilometre in length. It is a great crag for those who climb the higher grades - in particular, there are some very good routes in the 7th grade, with a lot of pinches and slopers. Most routes are very constant in difficulty. The single pitch routes go up to 8a+ and there are 5 bolted multi pitch routes up to 100m in length and up to 7c+. This crag definitely has the potential to become one of the bigger climbing locations in the area.

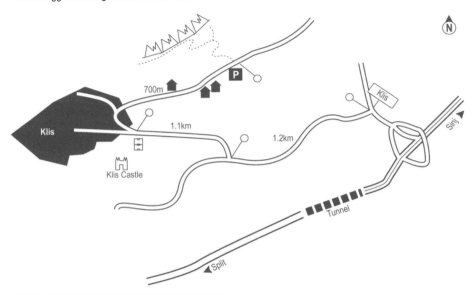

Directions

Markezina greda

► From Split follow the road to Sinj and leave this at the junction for Klis/Drniš after 12km. Follow the signs to Klis. When you enter the village turn right just after a football pitch. Follow the road up and park after 700 metres. From here a trail marked with red stripes leads to the sectors. Watch you don't step on any snakes!

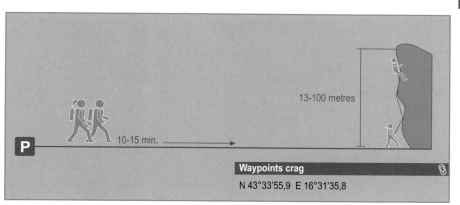

Waypoints crag
N 43°33'55,9 E 16°31'35,8

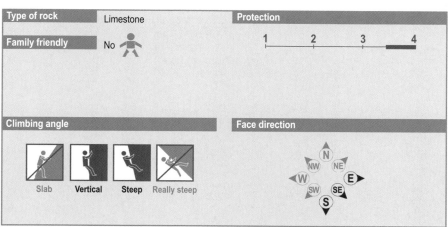

Type of rock	Limestone
Family friendly	No

Protection

1   2   3   4

Climbing angle

Slab   **Vertical**   **Steep**   Really steep

Face direction

N   NE   E   SE   S   SW   W   NW

Number of routes & Grade range

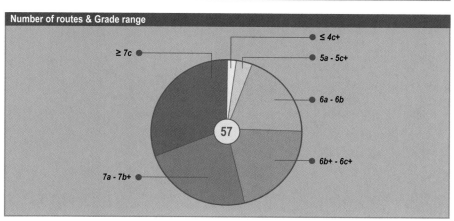

57

≤ 4c+
5a - 5c+
6a - 6b
6b+ - 6c+
7a - 7b+
≥ 7c

Climbing area Hvar

Hvar, the lavender island, boasts the most visitors of all the Croatian islands because of its pretty harbours, small charming villages, peaceful coves, lush vegetation and fine weather. With more than 2700 hours of sunshine per year it gets the most sun in all of Croatia!

Spring   Summer   Autumn   Winter

The island, only 1½ hours by boat from Split, has been an important seafaring place since ancient times due to its geographical position. Over time, different cultures have interweaved and influenced each other, and left their traces for the present day. Hvar town is a great place to spend some time and it has some of the best nightlife of the Adriatic coast!

There are actually three crags on Hvar: Cliffbase, also referred to as Šuplja Stina, is by far the biggest one and is the main reason to visit Hvar. The other two are small and not particularly worthwhile. Cliffbase, hidden away in the former harbour of the small village of Sveta Nedjelja, was once Croatia's best kept secret. Not any more! The owner of Cliffbase, Miroslav Stec, has already put up over 100 routes. Some climbers also call it "Little Thailand" and it truly is!

Spot the climber on the beautiful Sarga bogre (6c+) at Cliffbase

When to go

Climbing on Hvar island is actually possible throughout the year. In winter the south facing crags are sheltered from the Bura wind and sunny days are frequent. Although it gets very hot during summer, the Maestral wind keeps the temperature rather pleasant. Nevertheless, the best period remains spring and autumn.

Crag

 Cliffbase

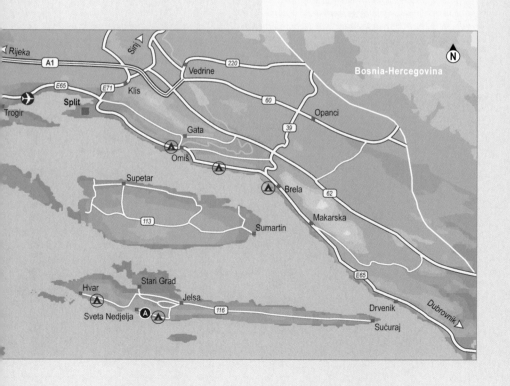

How to get to the area & how to move around

As there are taxis on the island to get you around when there are no buses, it is not necessary to have a car.

 By public transport

Jadrolinija operates ferries between Split and Hvar (Stari Grad and Jelsa) several times daily [1½h, 27Kn pp, 180Kn for a car]. There are also ferries between Dubrovnik and Stari Grad, and between Drvenik and Sučuraj. You can also get to Hvar via Ancona in Italy, this route is being operated by Jadrolinija and SEM, among others.

There are a few daily buses from Stari Grad and Jelsa to Hvar Town during summer that leave from the ferry dock. They go less frequent in winter and on Sundays.

To get to Sveta Nedjelja, the small town near the crags, it is possible to ask Miroslav to send a car for you. To get there by taxi costs around 200Kn from Jelsa, and 250-300Kn from Stari Grad. From Sveta Nedjelja it is a 15 minute walk to Cliffbase.

If you prefer to stay in Hvar Town you can rent a scooter or a mountain bike to get to Sveta Nedjelja. During summer these can be hired in the centre of Hvar Town, near the cathedral. A scooter costs 250Kn per day. Try to get a discount when renting for a week or longer.

 By car

Split is the main ferry port for Hvar. See the 'How to get to the area & how to move around' section in the 'Climbing area Split' chapter for how to get to Split.

Once on the island, follow the main road from Hvar town or Stari Grad to Jelsa. In Jelsa continue in the direction of Pitve and Zavala. After having passed the freaky tunnel - once inside you'll know what we mean by freaky! - turn right in the direction of Sveta Nedjelja.

Pakleni Islands

Where to stay

Hvar has plenty of accommodation. It is possible to stay near the crags in Sveta Nedjelja, find an apartment or private room in sparkling Hvar Town or camp close to the sea.

At the time of writing, a road was being built connecting Hvar Town with Sveta Nedjelja. When this road is finished Hvar Town will be a good place to stay if you don't plan on climbing every day. There are numerous apartments and private rooms for rent in this lively town. For a simple 2-person apartment expect to pay €50 per day or, for a double private room, €28 in the high season. Outside of the high season, discounts of up to 50% can be negotiated. As Hvar Town is a very popular tourist destination, it can be difficult to find accommodation during the high season and you'd be advised to book in advance. Check www.hvar-croatia.com.

In the village of Sveta Nedjelja you can find apartments for rent starting at €7 per person in the low season and €11 in the high season. The friendly owner of Cliffbase, Miroslav Stec, is always willing to provide more details and can help with the booking of the accommodation. See the chapter 'Cliffbase' for his contact details.

There are also a few campsites on the island. The closest campsite to Hvar Town is in Milna - it is located between Cliffbase and Hvar Town. Camping Lili in Jagodna is the closest to Cliffbase.

Camping Mala Milna

✉ Milna
☎ +385 21 745027

📍 N 43°09'45,0 E 16°29'08,3

Open	1/5 – 30/9
Grade	2
Price	80 Kn for 2 persons, a tent and a car

Except for the exceptional location in the small bay of Milna the campsite itself is not that exceptional. Its only positive feature is its beautiful location next to the sea. The village of Milna consists only of a few houses, of which most are picturesque restaurants.

Directions
Milna lies 4km south east of Hvar Town. Milna and its campsite are well signposted.

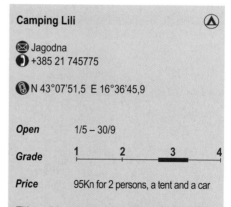

Camping Lili

✉ Jagodna
☎ +385 21 745775

📍 N 43°07'51,5 E 16°36'45,9

Open	1/5 – 30/9
Grade	3
Price	95Kn for 2 persons, a tent and a car

This well kept campsite is an excellent place to stay. It lies close to the sea near the town of Jagodna, about 4km from Šuplja Stina. The owners sell, in their own words, "suberb home-made wine", although superb may not be quite the word for it! Their cheese, however, is simply fantastic, as is their bread.

Directions
A sign along the road to Sveta Nedjelja from Jelsa marks the turn for Camping Lili.

Cliffbase is without doubt one of the most idyllic climbing locations in South Eastern Europe

Hvar town

Where to buy groceries

Hvar Town has the biggest supermarket on the island, located in the town centre next to the main car park. In Milna there is no supermarket or bakery, but there are plenty of restaurants. Camping Lily sells bread and cheese and in Sveta Nedjelja there is a small grocery for daily needs.

Where to find the local climbing guidebook

Miroslav is still developing Cliffbase, and it seems that he will never stop doing so! He sells the latest maps with route information for only 25Kn.

What else is there to see & do

Hvar Town
Beautiful Hvar Town lies safely between its 13th century walls and is guarded by the fortress of Španjol. The town itself is built around a picturesque harbour. The small sparkling cafes and restaurants around the harbour offer a good night out. Besides several artist shops, the town has many things to offer: it has a Renaissance theatre, a Benedictine and Franciscan monastery, museums, palaces and of course the dominating fortress. The town is car free, which makes it wonderful to stroll around.

Stari Grad and Jelsa
Stari Grad is not as pretty as Hvar Town but is still worth a visit. The town has a 16th century castle and a Dominican monastery. Jelsa has a small pleasant port built around a bay where the locals spend their time repairing their boats or simply enjoying a bit of peace.

Pakleni Islands
Those typical holiday photos showing white sand and crystal clear blue water could have been taken on the Pakleni Islands. A trip to this group of islands, or to one of the many small coves on Hvar island itself, is perfect for swimming, snorkelling and sun bathing. Taxi boats to the Pakleni Islands cost around 20Kn per person.

Filip Harna on Gentlemans' agreement direct (7c)

Scuba diving
Scuba diving in the clear blue Adriatic Sea around Hvar is a great experience due to the range of colourful flora and fauna and the many caves and wrecks waiting to be explored. Hvar has a few scuba diving centres. Check *www.diver.hr* for addresses. Expect to pay around €45 for a single dive including equipment and €325 for a PADI course.

Cliffbase

Cliffbase, or Šuplja Stina as it's sometimes called, is a sea-shore based climbing venue located on the south side of Hvar island. Miroslav, a very fanatical climber, has developed the whole place. He has completely dedicated his life to Cliffbase giving climbers one of the most beautiful climbing spots.

The majority of the routes are located directly next to and above the sea, offering the opportunity for deep water soloing. There is even a traverse of 300 metres just above the water. The first 250 metres is 5b/5c climbing, but the last 50 metres goes at around 7a. The only thing is that you will have to swim back....

At Cliffbase there are many long routes, some even up to 60 metres. Those will have belays halfway but there are also many routes of 40 metres for which you need a 80 metre rope. At the time of writing, Miroslav was also developing routes above the village Sveta Nedjelja next to the cave with the monastery inside, called Sector Pazucha. The routes here would then perfectly suit the more advanced climber, as currently the majority of the existing routes only go up to around 7a.

As the land underneath the cliff is private property, contact the owner and developer of all routes before you go climbing: Miroslav Stec (tel: +385 91 7648182 or email: *cliffbase@cliffbase.com*). A small donation of €2 per day is asked for.

Which route to choose next?

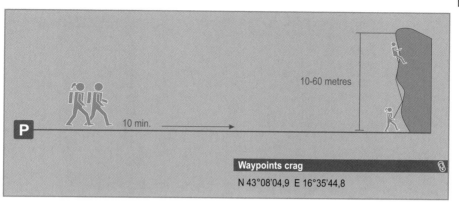

10-60 metres

10 min.

P

Waypoints crag

N 43°08'04,9 E 16°35'44,8

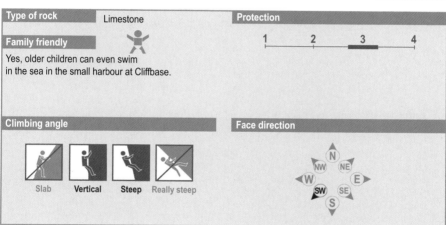

Type of rock		Protection

Limestone

Family friendly

Yes, older children can even swim
in the sea in the small harbour at Cliffbase.

Protection

1   2   3   4

Climbing angle

Slab   **Vertical**   **Steep**   Really steep

Face direction

N
NW   NE
W   E
SW   SE
S

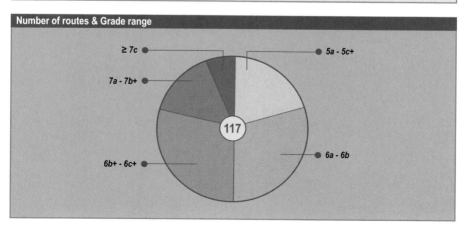

Number of routes & Grade range

≥ 7c

7a - 7b+

6b+ - 6c+

5a - 5c+

6a - 6b

117

Snakes

Despite many people's fear of snakes, less than 10%, of the world's known snake species are venomous and only about 5% are dangerous to humans. Most snakes are not aggressive and will only bite when threatened and only as a last resort - common sense should stop you getting bitten! When walking in an area where snakes are present - virtually every climbing area with a warm climate! - wear boots and long trousers, especially if you can't see your feet for the undergrowth. Snakes will attempt to avoid you if given adequate warning and making noise helps to scare them off. Develop a habit of watching where you step or place your hands. Avoid areas where snakes may be hiding: under rocks, big holes, logs, etc. If you do see a snake, curb your curiosity and keep your distance. In general snakes do not climb up rocks and are mainly nocturnal, coming out during the day to sunbathe.

If you are bitten by a snake, the most important thing to do is to stay calm and try to avoid moving the affected limb, which should be kept below the level of the heart. Seek medical help immediately. Antivenin is the only direct treatment, but it must be given under experienced medical supervision. Sucking the venom out, cutting around a bite or applying ice to a bite are not recommended first-aid measures. Bring in the dead snake only if this can be done without risk of further injury. Do not waste time hunting for the snake, and do not risk another bite if it is not easy to kill the snake. Be careful of the head when transporting it -- a dead snake can bite from reflex.

Sea urchins

The sea urchin is a spiny, hard-shelled animal that lives on rocky seafloors; both in shallow waters and at great depths. Although the spines of sea urchins can inflict a painful wound on the feet when stepped on, most are not seriously dangerous. There are very few venomous sea urchin species.

The best protection against them is to wear sandals while stepping into the sea.

If you step on a sea urchin and some of its spines break off and remain in the sole of your foot, remove them carefully.

Scorpions

Another dangerous animal that lives in all the countries described in this book is the scorpion. Although a scorpion bite will only be fatal to babies, it can leave you feeling extremely ill if left untreated - seek medical attention for all scorpion bites. Scorpions like cool, damp places and they hunt at night. They are very rarely seen during the day.

Ticks

There are more than 800 different species of ticks throughout the world. They are responsible for carrying different diseases of which Lyme disease is most common. Ticks wait for host animals from the tips of grasses and shrubs. When an animal or person passes by, they quickly let go of the vegetation and climb onto the host, burying themselves into the skin. Ticks are common in many places of the world, so always check for them on yourself and your children after having been outdoors. Most ticks seldom attach quickly and rarely transmit diseases until they have been attached for four or more hours. If you spot one, remove it promptly: the best method is to grasp it firmly with tweezers as close to the skin as possible and gently, but firmly, pull it straight out. Whatever you do, do not burn the tick with a match or lighter. If tweezers are not available, grasp the tick with a piece of tissue or cloth or some other barrier between your fingers and the tick. Try not to use bare hands to remove the tick because its secretions may carry disease.

Tick bites are generally painless and may not be noticed and, if the tick falls off after biting, its sojourn with you pass undetected. Small ticks, like the deer tick that transmits Lyme disease, are so tiny they are nearly undetectable. The actual bite may cause symptoms only after the tick drops off. You may notice local redness, itching, and burning, and, very rarely, intense localized pain. The signs of the illnesses transmitted by ticks often appear days to weeks after the tick is gone. If you suspect a tick bite, always consult a doctor – tick-borne diseases can be treated with antibiotics.

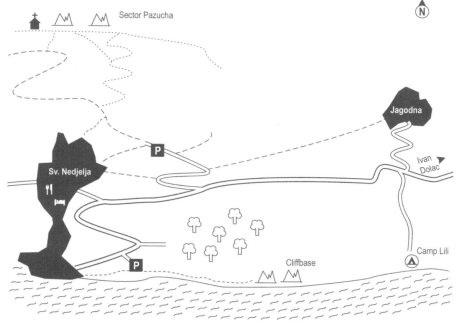

Sector Pazucha

Jagodna

P

Ivan Dolac ▶

Sv. Nedjelja

P

Cliffbase

Camp Lili

Directions

▶ There is a path from Sveta Nedjelja to Cliffbase; see the detailed map for further details.

The routes at Cliffbase are up to 60 metres in length

Climbing area Paklenica National Park

It is absolutely true that Paklenica can be considered as one of the most attractive European climbing areas! Paklenica is the second National Park in Croatia, set-up in 1949, and covers an area of 95 square kilometres. It is famous for its rich flora and fauna and numerous caves. Thanks to its two majestic canyons –Velika and Mala Paklenica- the area has become Croatia's number one climbing venue. The steep sides of the canyons go up to 400 metres and boast incredible sport and trad climbing routes.

Spring   Summer   Autumn   Winter

The climbing record here goes back to 1938, when the first attempt was being made to climb Anića Kuk, the biggest and most important wall in the park. Ever since then, a lot of people have followed and the area has become a very challenging climbing spot. The Paklenica National Park offers excellent hiking trails too, and there is more than enough to see. It's home to many different species of deer and also boars, lynxes and wolves.

The proximity of the sea makes it a very welcoming area, especially during the hot summer months. It is a perfect climbing holiday destination both for keen climbers, as well as for those who come with children and who also want to do other activities.

The mighty Anića Kuk

Crag

Ⓐ **Paklenica**

When to go

The main climbing season in Paklenica begins in spring and lasts until late autumn. In July and August it can get very hot but, fortunately, there are plenty of routes in the shade during the morning and late afternoon and some even throughout the day.

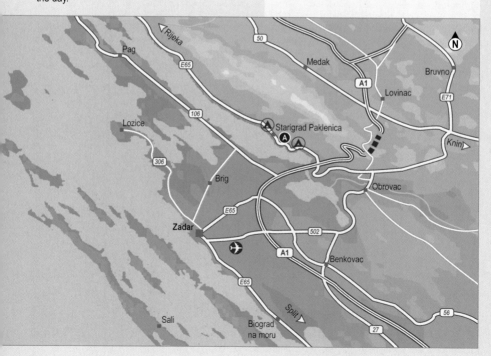

How to get to the area & how to move around

Since several campsites are close to the entrance of the National Park, you don't need to have your own transport. It is a 30 to 40 minute walk to the entrance of the National Park from the campsites near the sea. Unfortunately, from the entrance it is another 2km to the parking and the first routes. However hitchhiking is common, so it shouldn't be a problem to get there without too much effort.

 By public transport

Via Split
From Split there are daily buses heading for Rijeka that stop at Starigrad-Paklenica, but check beforehand to make sure they do actually stop [3h, 165 -210Kn].

Via Rijeka
There are 12 buses daily from Rijeka to Zadar passing Starigrad-Paklenica [3½h, 110 -200Kn].

Via Zagreb
From Zagreb there are 20 buses daily to Zadar that stop in Maslenica [4-5h, 100-170Kn]. From there you will have to hitchhike to Starigrad-Paklenica (about 20 minutes).

Via Italy
Fly to Trieste or to Treviso in Italy. There are trains frequently from Treviso to Trieste. From the bus station, which is next to the Trieste train station, a daily bus leaves for Dubrovnik at 5.30 PM passing Starigrad-Paklenica [6h].

 By car

It takes 3½ hours from Rijeka to get to Starigrad-Paklenica by car. It is about 7½ hours from Munich in Germany as well as from Milan in Italy.

Where to stay

Starigrad-Paklenica is a perfect place to stay - the entrance to the park is only about 2km north of this town. There are several campsites here along the coast. The locals also offer various apartments and rooms for rent. Some cheaper campsites and apartments are located very close to the entrance of the park, but these are a bit further from the sea. Prices for a two person apartment start at €18 per day per apartment in the low season and €23 in the high season. A four person apartment starts at

Camping National Park in Starigrad - Paklenica offers great spots to pitch your tent

€26/€31 (low/high season). Double rooms in private houses start at €12 per night. The tourist office, on the road opposite the small harbour, provides accommodation information.

Camping National Park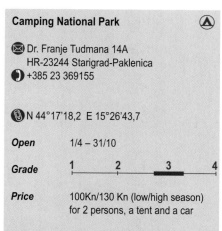

✉ Dr. Franje Tudmana 14A
HR-23244 Starigrad-Paklenica
☎ +385 23 369155

🧭 N 44°17'18,2 E 15°26'43,7

Open   1/4 – 31/10

Grade   1———2———3▬▬▬4

Price   100Kn/130 Kn (low/high season)
for 2 persons, a tent and a car

This campsite is popular with climbers and hikers and is relatively small and quite charming. The campsite is by the sea, offering idyllic spots to pitch a tent. Reservations are not possible.

Directions
The campsite lies on the main road through Starigrad-Paklenica and is well signposted.

Camping Paklenica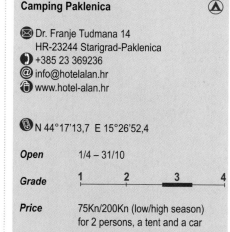

✉ Dr. Franje Tudmana 14
HR-23244 Starigrad-Paklenica
☎ +385 23 369236
@ info@hotelalan.hr
🖥 www.hotel-alan.hr

🧭 N 44°17'13,7 E 15°26'52,4

Open   1/4 – 31/10

Grade   1———2———3▬▬▬4

Price   75Kn/200Kn (low/high season)
for 2 persons, a tent and a car

This campsite is the big brother of the Camping National Park. It has the advantage that guests can make use of the many facilities of Hotel Alan such as its tennis -and volleyball courts, restaurants and swimming pool. Hotel Alan also offers various excursions.

Directions
The campsite lies along the main road through Starigrad-Paklenica and is well signposted.

Paklenica National Park

The small harbour of Zadar

KRKA National Park

Where to buy groceries

Starigrad-Paklenica has a few small supermarkets that are open daily and sell fresh bread and other basics such as beer and wine. There are also a few women selling fruits and vegetables along the road in summer. If you have your own transport, a drive to Zadar to shop at one of its mega supermarkets will save you some money.

Where to find the local climbing guidebook

The "Climbing guide Paklenica" can be bought at the entrance of the park or at many of the kiosks in Starigrad-Paklenica. The climbing shop Iglu Sport (www.iglusport.hr) also sells the guide. The Nova bookshop in Rijeka sells the guide as well.

Iglu Sport
Franje Tudmana 14 (near the petrol station)
23244 Starigrad-Paklenica
+385 23 369889

Nova Bookshop
Trpimirova Ulica 3
(around the corner of the bus station)
Rijeka

What else is there to see & do

Zadar
Zadar is another city in Croatia to have grown from a Roman settlement and has become the main city of northern Dalmatia, with over 82,000 inhabitants. At various points in time, it has also been under Venetian and Austrian rule, the effects of which are still clearly visible on its architecture. The old town is located on the tip of a narrow peninsula and most of the town is surrounded by city walls with towers. The two city gates are of particular interest: The Kopnena vrata (Mainland Gate), to the east of the Old Town, was built in 1543 and has the city coat of arms engraved on it. Close to this is the Five-Sided Tower, dating from the 13th century, and the five wells which used to be the water supply for the city. The other gate is the Lucka vrata (Port Gate) to the north, built in 1573. In the centre of the old town is the Sveti Donat Church, which was built at the beginning of the 9th century and stands 27 metres high. Zadar is a 40 minute drive from Starigrad-Paklenica.

Daytrip to the Kornati Islands
The breathtaking Kornati National Park consists of 147 uninhabited islands of rough rock formations with rugged cliffs and the bluest sea ever seen! A boat excursion to the islands is a rip off (270Kn), but includes unlimited wine and fresh fish. If you can spare the money, it makes for a memorable daytrip. The boat leaves from Zadar at 9am and returns at 5pm. Employees of the agencies organising the excursions visit the campsites regularly to distribute leaflets. The tourist office in Starigrad-Paklenica also provides information.

Daytrip to the KRKA waterfalls
A visit to the KRKA National Park makes a good daytrip due to its wonderful waterfalls, beautiful hiking trails, Franciscan monastery, interesting flora and fauna and the chance to have a refreshing swim. The entrance is 50/60Kn (low/high season) including the 30 minute boat trip to Skradinski Buk, the highest waterfall. If you have your own car you could drive there yourself, otherwise many agencies offer the excursion.

Hiking
The majority of the visitors to the Paklenica National Park are there for the very attractive hiking. There is an excellent map of the Paklenica National Park, covering countless hiking trails. These include strenuous multi day hikes, as well as easy shorter routes. The map can be bought at the entrance of the park. The park is at its most beautiful in autumn and spring.

Paklenica

The Paklenica National Park is the most visited Croatian climbing area and is well known both in Croatia and around the world. The park offers a tremendous variety of rock climbing with routes ranging from those suitable for beginners, with many multi-pitch routes in the 3rd grade, to hard-core adventure routes that will whet the appetite of the best!

The single-pitch routes are located at the beginning of the park in a gorge with crags reaching up to 40 metres. In the morning there is shade at one side of the gorge and in the afternoon there is shade at the other side. The routes tend to be technically interesting and the rock is generally good, however on easier routes it can be very polished in places.

Then there are numerous exceptionally nice multi-pitch routes ranging from 80 to 350 metres. Anića Kuk is the most popular, as well as the biggest and most imposing, crag with 100 different routes leading to the top. If you plan to climb one of the longer multi pitch routes make sure you start early in the morning and bring enough water: it can get very hot here. The amount of fixed protection differs per route – some routes are completely bolted whereas others require the full complement of trad gear. The guidebook gives clear information about the gear needed for each route.

The entrance fee for the park is 30 KN for one day, 60 KN for 3 days or 90 KN for 5 days.

Unknown climber on Domžalski (6a,120m) at Anića Kuk

Directions

▶ The entrance of the park lies north of Starigrad-Paklenica in the direction of Zadar. Turn left at the sign and follow the road until the entrance of the park. This is where the park rangers sell the entrance tickets. Continue for another 2km until a parking lot. The first crags are found straight at the car park. If you don't have your own car you can either walk or hitchhike.

Tips for extreme vertical emotions

What are a climber's real backpack essentials? Without a doubt equipment used – from head to toe – must be as lightweight as possible, easily packable, and exceptionally breathable to provide the ultimate protection. In one word: highly technical.

Step one: the backpack. Aim for the optimal mix of design, performance and functionality [check out the new Arc'teryx range].

Step two: apparel. One tip is to pack the best layering system according to predicted weather conditions, with contingency for surprises. Using technical fabrics is crucial if you are to ensure state-of-the-art protection is guaranteed. American brand Polartec® has a range of over 250 fabrics [divided into three categories: "Next-to-Skin", "Thermal Insulation", "Weather Protection"] and offers fabrics targeting the specific needs of the climber.

Starting with the first layer or next-to-skin protection, Polartec® Power Dry® is one of the most advanced fabrics on the market. Ensuring excellent breathability, lightweight, comfort, and sun protection from ultraviolet rays it offers all the features relevant to climbers who often spend hours on the wall.

The second layer – we recommend Polartec® Power Stretch® - needs to provide unrestricted freedom of movement. Polartec® Power Stretch® does this thanks to its body-hugging four-way stretch. It also keeps skin dry even under extreme physical effort and provides wind and abrasion resistance.

The third, exterior layer is perfectly provided by Polartec® Power Shield® and is recommended by professionals as one the most advanced soft shell solutions on the market [offering resistance to the elements, thermal efficiency and compressibility, lightweight and stretch].

Step three: the feet. International footwear brand, SCARPA, offers a new climbing line which is extremely innovative in terms of design and technical details.

NEW MUST FOR ADVENTURE - Rho Top - launched by Arc'teryx, famous for outdoor apparel and high-tech backpacks - are made of Polartec® Power Stretch® [stretchy, breathable, wind and abrasion resistant]. "Men's Apex Freeline jacket" - Created by TNF and made of Polartec® Power Shield®, at the moment the most advanced soft-shell standard.

Sport climbing at Paklenica

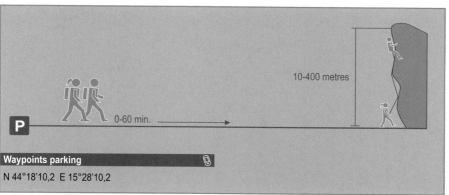

10-400 metres

0-60 min.

Waypoints parking

N 44°18'10,2 E 15°28'10,2

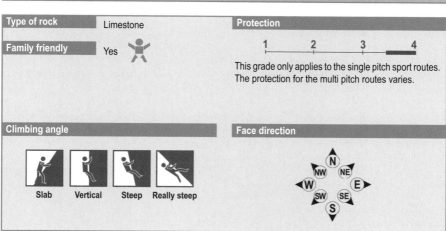

Type of rock	Limestone
Family friendly	Yes

Protection

1   2   3   4

This grade only applies to the single pitch sport routes.
The protection for the multi pitch routes varies.

Climbing angle

Slab   Vertical   Steep   Really steep

Face direction

N   NW   NE   W   E   SW   SE   S

Number of routes & Grade range

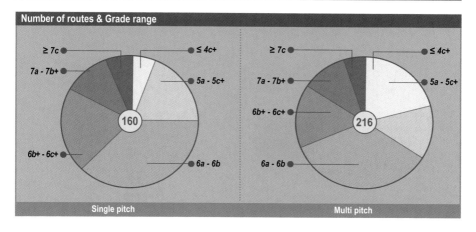

≥ 7c   ≤ 4c+
7a - 7b+   5a - 5c+
   160
6b+ - 6c+   6a - 6b

Single pitch

≥ 7c   ≤ 4c+
7a - 7b+   5a - 5c+
6b+ - 6c+   **216**
6a - 6b

Multi pitch

...a cultural and historical wonder...

Hungary

Keeping your balance at Tardos on Tablas Dune (6c+)

This wonderful country, full of cultural heritage, great plains and hills, rare birds, excellent wines, and with one of the most attractive capitals of Europe, is justifiably a popular holiday destination.

However, as Hungary lacks high mountains and only has a few natural crags, it is not a climber's paradise.

Hungary is located in the geographic centre of Europe and has a long history, enriched with a strong culture and folk traditions. Gypsy music, paprika, Roman ruins, baroque cities, ancient castles and spa resorts are all present in this wonderful country. Geographically speaking, the country is mostly flat – this applies to as much as 50% of the country's territory, with rolling plains and some hills and low mountains on the Slovakian border. The two most important rivers, the Danube and the Tisza divide the country from north to south.

Although the climbing potential here is limited, Hungarian rock climbers are very creative and resourceful – they have put up routes in abandoned quarries and use every crag, no matter how small, for bouldering. Despite this, Hungarian climbers head for Croatia to go climbing whenever possible. And that just about sums things up!

So, it is probably unlikely that you'll want to choose Hungary as the favourite destination for your next climbing trip. However, if you're here as a tourist – Budapest is really beautiful and the countryside has a large number of picturesque historic towns, and it's a justifiably popular tourist destination! – and you fancy a spot of climbing, read on and find out where to go.

Minorite church of Eger

Climbing information

Hungary has 42 different climbing areas scattered throughout the country, although it pays to pick your spot wisely: most of the crags contain just a few routes, climbing's forbidden at some and others have unreliable protection or are simply not worth visiting. Fortunately, there are a couple that are good and they serve as excellent training venues. One small boulder area worth mentioning is Ezüst-hegy near Budapest. Here you'll find a few rose-stone sandstone blocks of 4-10 metres high in an old quarry. Oszoly is a favourite place for beginning Hungarian climbers but not in particular interesting for others. The two most interesting climbing areas are Tardos in the Geresce Hills and two crags in the Mátra Hills. These two areas are fully described in this Rock Climbing Atlas.

Climbing area Geresce Hills

This area only includes the crag of Tardos, probably the best in Hungary, according to the locals. And indeed it is the place to be for the best climbing in the country. There are numerous other crags in the Geresce Hills surrounding Budapest but most of these are rather small, of poor quality and are mainly used for bouldering.

Climbing area Mátra Hills

This is the largest climbing area in Hungary, situated in the forest of the Mátra Hills, with around 140 routes on Andesite, or better known as volcanic, rocks. The two crags of Csőka-kő and Bárány-kő are among the best in the country. Almost all routes are of a moderate level.

Tardos

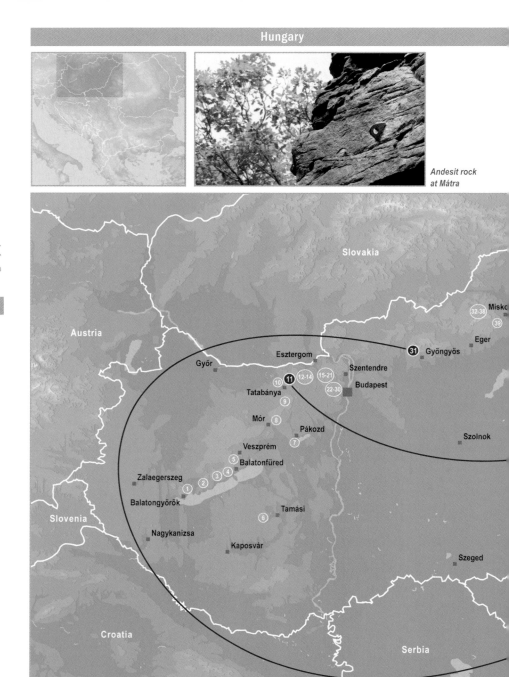

Andesit rock at Mátra

Slovakia

Austria

Miskolc

32-38

39

Eger

Esztergom

31 Gyöngyös

Győr

12-14 15-21 Szentendre

10 11

22-30 Budapest

Tatabánya

9

Mór 8

Pákozd

7

Veszprém

Szolnok

5

Balatonfüred

Zalaegerszeg 1 2 3 4

Balatongyörök

Tamási

Slovenia

6

Nagykanizsa

Kaposvár

Szeged

Croatia

Serbia

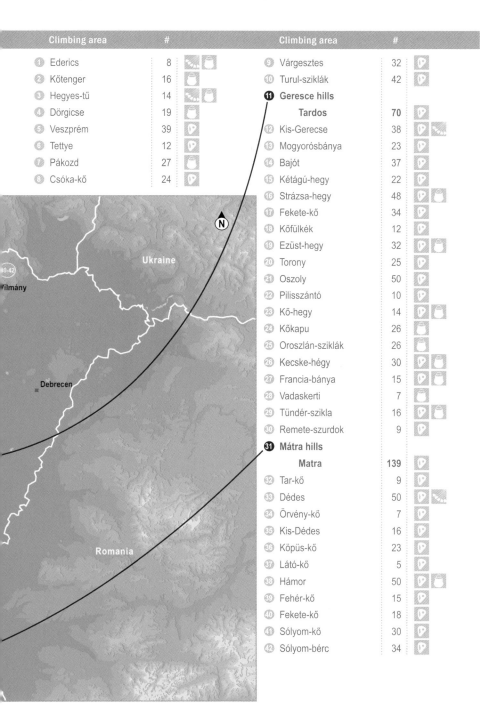

Climate

Summers or winters can vary quite considerably from one year to another. In general winters are cold and snow is common. Spring and the start of summer are generally the wettest times of the year and much of the rain comes in heavy showers. In summer Hungary receives around 9 to 10 hours of sunshine during the day. Even though most days are pleasantly warm, it can get hot as well. On these days it is better to climb in the morning or late afternoon.

The climbing season in Hungary starts in April and lasts until the end of September. The best climbing season is summer, although spring can be very nice too if the rain stays away.

Month	Average temperature (°C)	Average rainfall (mm)
Jan	-1	36
Feb	1	42
March	6	39
April	12	44
May	16	70
June	20	68
July	22	55
Aug	21	46
Sept	16	35
Oct	12	57
Nov	5	70
Dec	1	44

Climate table Hungary

Horse riding is a popular activity in Hungary

Getting there

 By plane

Hungary's biggest international airport is Ferihegy Airport in Budapest. Malév Hungarian Airlines (*www.malev.hu*) connects Budapest directly with many other capitals in Europe, as well as with North America and the Middle East. There are several low cost carriers that fly to Budapest as well. Return tickets from London, Munich or Copenhagen to Budapest cost less than €200. Among others, the following low cost carriers fly to Budapest: *www.wizzair.com, www.skyeurope.com, www.airberlin.com.*

 By train

Budapest has direct railway links with 25 European capitals. There are more than 50 international connections each day. For example, trains depart every three hours between Budapest and Vienna, with a travel time of less than three hours [€29]. Check *http://plannerint.b-rail.be* for international train schedules.

 By bus

Eurolines, or its Hungarian partner Volánbusz, runs buses between Budapest and other European cities. Check *www.eurolines.com* for up to date information. All international buses arrive and depart in Budapest at the Népliget bus station in Pest.

 By boat

From Vienna an alternative route is to take the daily hydrofoil boat on the Danube to Budapest via Bratislava [5½h, €78].

 By car

Budapest is 240km from Vienna, 700km from Munich, and 1400km from Amsterdam. Crossing the border into Hungary with your car is generally no problem.

Wheat fields are everywhere

Moving around

To get to the crags in the Geresce hills you won't need to have your own car. But for those in the Mátra Hills your own wheels are essential as there is no public transport.

 Budapest airport information

From the airport there is an minibus service to the centre. To get to one of the train stations, or to the Népliget bus station, take bus number 93 from the airport to the Kőbánya-Kispest metro station. All the other stations are linked by metro.

 By public transport

Hungary's transport system is efficient and inexpensive. The train network in particular is extensive and is an ideal way to move around the country. Intercity trains running between the capital and the major towns are very popular and this is a comfortable mode of transport. Check *www.elvira.hu* for information about national and international train schedules. Second-class train fares are around €4 per 100km.

Budapest has three major train stations: the Eastern Railway Station (Keleti Pályaudvar), the Western Railway Station (Nyugati Pályaudvar) and the Southern Railway Station (Déli Pályaudvar). The metro line 2 links 'Keleti pu' and 'Déli pu' - as the stops are called - and 'Nyugati pu' can be reached by metro line 3.

The bus can sometimes serve as a good replacement for the train, especially for short trips. Fares are slightly more expensive than second-class train fares.

By car

Road conditions are rather good in Hungary. A few major highways connect Budapest efficiently with other parts of the country. Drivers in Hungary are obliged to purchase a motorway vignette for motorways M1, M3, M5 and M7 (obtainable at border crossing points and major petrol stations). A 10-day vignette costs €9.20.

The usual international car rental agencies - Avis, Budget, Europcar and Hertz - are located at the arrivals hall in Ferihegy Airport in Budapest. Prices start at €280 for an economy car for one week. A cheaper alternative is Fox Autorent, who also let you take your car abroad. Prices start at €250 per week. See *www.fox-autorent.com* for more

Hungarian dish

Bouldering at Ezüst-Hegy

information or call +36 1 3829000. The price of a litre of petrol or diesel in Hungary is less expensive compared to most Western European countries but it doesn't differ much.

The telephone number to dial in case you need car assistance is 188.

Accommodation

Hungary still remains a bargain destination for travellers as regards food and transport. However the costs for staying at a campsite can vary a lot. Large campsites in touristy areas may charge around €16 for two persons, a car and a tent, whereas smaller campsites off the beaten track will only charge €7. Camping in the wild is prohibited, although a lot of the local climbers simply ignore this.

Besides hotels, Hungary has a lot of pensions that offer budget accommodation, starting at €25 for a double room. In a mid range hotel or pension expect to pay around €50 for a double.

Hungarian village

Food & Drinks

No country in the world has such variety in paprika (peppers) and where so many different dishes are made with this kind of vegetable. Nevertheless, traditional Hungarian food is heavy, fatty and always contains meat. The good news is that in all tourist places there are many restaurants serving vegetarian dishes.

Sausages - typical Hungarian food

In general an excellent 3-course meal goes for only €8. A bowl of soup is around €1.75 and a decent pizza costs €3.50. Half a litre of beer in a bar will cost about €2. On a terrace in the centre of Budapest, for example, next to the Fishermen's Bastion, a cappuccino will cost at least €2.50. In a cosy coffee bar in a side street or in a less touristy town, the same cappuccino will cost no more than € 0.70.

In addition to paprika's, a lot of fruit and other vegetables are cultivated on Hungarian ground and therefore prices are rather low. At the market one kilo of the basic kind of paprika costs no more than €0.20. In any case, the markets are the best places to shop for food, although there are lots of modern supermarkets in Hungary as well. And, don't forget to try the Hungarian wine as it is cheap and some of the wines are very good.

Climbing guidebook

At the time of writing the new climbing guide of Hungary 'Magyarország Sziklamászó Kalauza / Climbing guide of Hungary' was being prepared and almost finished. This guidebook covers all the climbing areas of Hungary. The guidebook will be for sale at the Mountex shops and the Tengerszem stores.

Mountex has 18 shops in Hungary of which 5 in the capital. See *www.mountex.hu* for more information. The addresses of several climbing shops in Hungary are covered in the chapters describing the climbing areas.

Mountex climbing & outdoor shop
✉ Margit krt. 61-63
1024 Budapest

Tengerszem-Sport
✉ Budapest, VII. ker., Dohány utca 29.

Oszoly

Facts & figures

Population:	10 million
Religion:	Roman catholic (65%)
Capital:	Budapest
Time zone:	GMT+1
Telephone code:	+36

Money

Currency:	Hungarian Forint (Ft)
Exchange rate:	€1 = 271Ft
ATM machines:	widespread

Language

Hungarians speak Magyar (Hungarian), which is not an easy language to learn. Even saying thank you takes some practice. Most people speak some German and younger people speak a few words of English as well.

Good day	*Jó napot!*
Thank you	*Köszönöm*
Goodbye	*Viszontlátásra*
Yes / No	*Igen / Nem*
Right / Left / Straight	
	Jobbra / Balra / Egyenesen
Rock climbing	*Sziklamászás*

Visas & formalities

EU	*Other European nationalities*	*USA / Canada*	*All other nationalities*

Almost all nationalities planning to visit Hungary
for a period no longer than 90 days (in some cases 30 says) do not need a visa.

Safety

Hungary is not a violent or dangerous country and people are always very friendly and helpful to travellers. As in any other big city, be aware of pickpockets and car thieves in Budapest and never leave anything of value in the car.

Emergency numbers

General:	112
Police:	107
Fire brigade:	105
Ambulance:	104

Use of mobile phone

Excellent coverage almost everywhere.

Internet access

There is no shortage of internet cafés in Budapest. Internet is available in most major towns as well. Costs are €1.50 to €3 per hour.

Water

Some foreigners drink water from the tap (as do the locals), but others swear by bottles of mineral water - it is debatable whether it is ok to drink tap water or not. A bottle of mineral water costs €0.75.

Climbing area Geresce Hills

The scenic Geresce Hills are situated north west of Budapest. Many people from Budapest come here at the weekend to enjoy the numerous hiking trails in the dense woods, for bird watching or for horse riding. This is also the place where one of the best crags in Hungary, Tardos, is found.

Since Tardos is only 75km from Budapest, and close to other interesting towns as Esztergom, a climbing trip can be easily combined with a few days of sightseeing in and around the capital. The Danube River is nearby, providing the visitor with great views and the option for canoeing.

Spring Summer Autumn Winter

When to go

In April and May it can rain, but normally spring is an excellent time. Mid-summer is also fine since there are always parts of the rocks in the shade.

Climbing at Tardos

Crag

Ⓐ Tardos

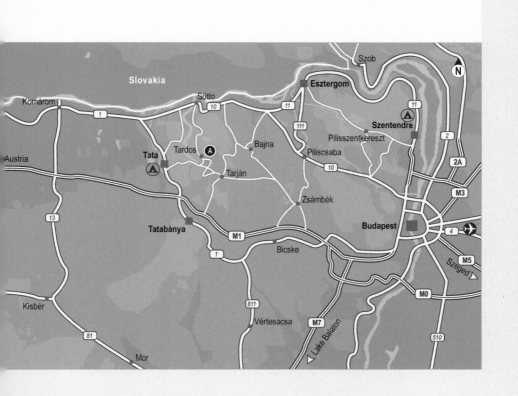

How to get to the area & how to move around

Although it is convenient to have your own wheels, it's not essential.

 By public transport

From the Déli pu or Keleti pu train station in Budapest several trains per day head for Tata [1h, 588Ft].

By car

Tata, the recommended place to stay, lies 70km west from Budapest. Follow the M1 towards Tatabánya. Leave the M1 just after this industrial town. Tata is clearly signposted from here.

Where to stay

Tardos itself is a small, quiet town, but Tata nearby makes a good base to explore the region. From here it is also easy to get to Budapest and other towns by train or bus.

There are a few campsites in Tata, as well as pensions and hotels. Expect to pay around 7500Ft for a double room. Reservations are not necessary, just have a look around to see what suits you best.

It is also possible to camp wild near the crags in Tardos, as many local climbers do in summer.

The Esztergom Bazilika

The old quarry of Tardos offers good climbing

Fényesfürdő Camping

✉ Fényes Fasor
2890, Tata

☎ + 36 34588144

@ fenyes@fenyesfurdo.hu

🏠 www.fenyesfurdo.hu

🌐 N 47°40'00,5 E 18°18'28,7

Open	Open: 1/5 - 15/10

Grade 1   2   3   4

Price 3700Ft in the low season for 2 persons, a car and a tent. In the high season costs are 4400Ft.

This large recreation complex has camping and bungalow facilities. Furthermore, it has a 25m swimming pool, a separate large pool for children and a beach volleyball and soccer court.

Directions
Coming from the centre follow the road Fényes fasor. The campsite is indicated.

Where to buy groceries

In Tata there are a few large supermarkets along the Május ut close to the Fényesfürdő Camping. In Tardos there is a small supermarket.

Where to find the local climbing guidebook

The closest outdoor shop near Tata is in Tatabánya.

Mountex climbing & outdoor shop
✉ Komáromi út 28/a
2800 Tatabánya

Canoeing on the backwaters of the river Tisza

Budapest – one of Europe's most beautiful capitals

What else is there to see & do

Budapest

Budapest really is one of the most beautiful capitals of Europe. Separated by the river Danube, the two parts of the capital, Buda and Pest, hide many interesting buildings, churches, museums, and narrow streets, and there are numerous Unesco World Heritage Sites. Buda, on the right hilly band of the Danube River, is the older part of the city and contains the historic centre. Here on Castle Hill important buildings such as the huge Royal Palace and the Fishermen's Bastion dominate the scene.

Several bridges connect Buda with Pest, but definitely the most famous one is the Chain Bridge. When crossing the Chain Bridge from Buda, you will soon get to Roosevelt Square on the other side. The area around this square marks the centre of the capital. Buda might be older, but Pest is definitely more vibrant and has an exciting nightlife. Almost all of the administration buildings, banks, shopping malls, and bars concentrate in and around Pest.

Be aware that a weekend is simply not enough to get more than a glimpse of Hungary's capital!

Tata

The picturesque town of Tata is located between two lakes and offers, besides recreational activities, some history too. A visit to the remains of the medieval Tata Castle is one of your cultural options. A more relaxing alternative is to have a swim in the lake!

The Chain Bridge at Budapest

Esztergom

Esztergom, 66km north west of Budapest, marks the western entrance to the Danube Bend. The town is clearly dominated by the giant cathedral on the top of a hill next to the river. The cathedral, also referred to as Hungary's largest church, will be the main reason to go to Esztergom. The church itself is 118 metres long and the main dome is 100 metres high.

Hiking

There is excellent hiking in the hills surrounding Budapest. Tardos is a very good starting point for the Gerecse Hills. A good map entitled Geresce (scale 1:40,000) gives an overview of the area and is published by Cartographia.

Horse riding

Horses and Hungary are synonymous with each other. Horse riding plays an important part in Hungarian life and there are many stables, riding schools and courses around the country. Check *www.equi.hu* for more information. In particular, there are two horse riding schools in Tata.

Canoeing

The Danube and Tisza rivers provide perfect opportunities for (multiple day) canoeing trips. You can take part in organised tours or rent a canoe yourself in one of the towns along the river.

Bird watching

Hungary has some of the best bird watching sites in Europe. The Tata's lake attracts a wide variety of species and is a popular bird watching spot.

Danube-bend panorama

Tardos

Tardos is the most popular crag in the vicinity of Budapest. The crag is actually an old abandoned red marble quarry. This definitely makes climbing at this place quite a special experience.

There are around 70 routes on vertical limestone that will be a technical treasure for some, although strong fingers are required as well. The majority of the routes are in the low 6th grade, but 7th grade climbers will also find interesting challenges. Although the first bolts in each route are rather high, most routes are well equipped with a bolt every 2 metres. However, on some routes the bolts are a bit more spaced, with one every 3 to 4 metres. It's a good place to accumulate some air-time!

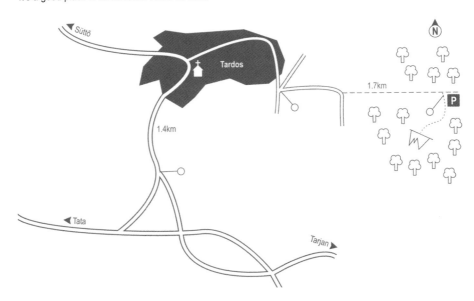

Directions

▶ *By public transport*
From Tata bus station there are a few daily buses to Tardos. Get off at the church. From here it is a 20 min walk to the crag. See the 'By car' text how to get to the crag.

▶ *By car*
From the M1 take the turning to Tardos. Once in Tardos, turn right off the main road just after you pass the church. When the road bends to the right, carry on straight - after a few hundred metres this road becomes unpaved. After 1.7km, park at the right side of the road. Just before the parking spot there is a trail on the right that leads up the hill to the crag in a few minutes.

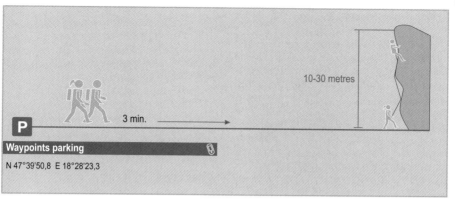

Waypoints parking

N 47°39'50,8 E 18°28'23,3

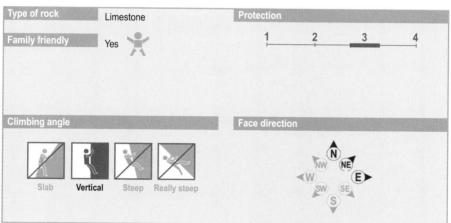

Type of rock Limestone

Family friendly Yes

Protection

1   2   3   4

Climbing angle

Slab **Vertical** Steep Really steep

Face direction

N NE E SE S SW W NW

Number of routes & Grade range

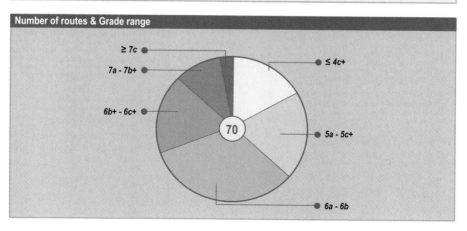

≥ 7c
7a - 7b+
6b+ - 6c+

70

≤ 4c+
5a - 5c+
6a - 6b

Climbing area Mátra Hills

The Mátra Hills in the northern uplands belong geologically to the largest young volcanic zone of Europe. They are situated between the valleys of River Tarna and River Zagyva. The two highest peaks in Hungary can be found here: Kékes rises to 1014 metres and Galyatető to 964 metres. The Mátra is the home of the red deer, the roe deer and the wild boar. The hills are a popular destination both for Hungarian nature lovers and for foreigners. In winter it also serves as a skiing destination. Cities as Eger and Gyöngyös are close by and make for pleasant day trips.

Climbing is possible on the crags of Csóka-kő and Bárány-kő that are found right in the middle of the Mátra Hills, in a dense forest. After Tardos, this is the most popular climbing spot in Hungary.

| Spring | Summer | Autumn | Winter |

When to go

In theory, climbing in the Mátra Hills is good from spring to autumn, but this part of Hungary receives loads of unpredictable rain. The best time to go is in the middle of summer. It won't be too hot to climb, because the crags lie in a forest.

Lorand Istvan on Régi út, 5c

Crag

Ⓐ **Mátra**

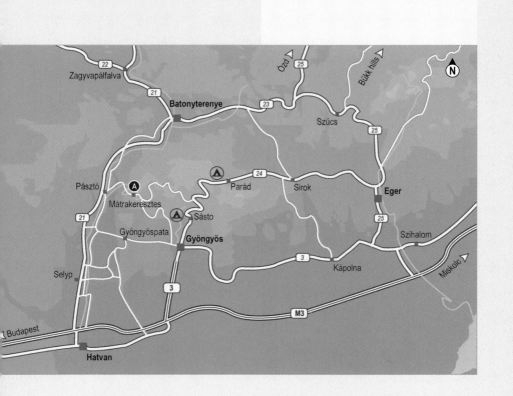

How to get to the area & how to move around

Since there are no good accommodation options close to the crags and, as getting there at all by public transport is difficult, a car is absolutely essential.

 By car

Gyöngyös is 80km east from Budapest and by car it takes one hour to get there. From Gyöngyös take the small road that winds its way up through the hills to Sásto and Parád.

Where to stay

You can camp wild near the crags, but this is not a very attractive choice. The best option is to stay either in Parád or in Sásto - however, both towns are 30km away from the crags and there is little to do.

Camping Mátra (Sásto)

✉ H-3232, Mátrafüred – Sásto, Farkas u.4.
☎ +36 37 374025
@ sasto@elpak.hu
🏠 www.sasto.elpak.hu

🧭 N 47°50'40,0 E 19°57'29,5

Open   20/4 -15/10

Grade   1ㅤ   2ㅤ   3ㅤ   4

Price   2950 Ft for 2p, tent and a car

Camping Mátra is situated near a small lake. The campsite is a popular choice for locals, although it is nothing fancy. In the weekend it can get very noisy due to the nearby bar.

Directions
From Gyöngyös follow the road to Sásto and Parád. The campsite is located at the left side of the road.

Eger, Dóbo Square

Camping Tura

✉ 2340 Parád, Külterület
☎ +36 36 364079
@ turacamping@freemail.hu
🌐 www.szallasinfo.hu/tura_camping_parad

🌐 47°55'02,8 E 19°59'36,9

Open   1/5 – 1/10

Grade   1   2   3   4

Price   2100Ft for 2p, tent and a car

Camping Tura in Parád is both closer to Eger and a bit quieter than Camping Mátka.

Directions
From Gyöngyös follow the road to Parád. The campsite is located on the left-hand side of the road.

Where to buy groceries

Both Sásto and Parád have a small shop that sells basics but, if you plan on cooking yourself, it is better to bring your groceries from Gyöngyös. The food served in the restaurant at Camping Mátka in Sásto is good and inexpensive.

Where to find the local climbing guidebook

The nearest outdoor shop in the area is in Gyöngyös.

Mountex climbing & outdoor shop
✉ Püspöki út 2
3200 Gyöngyös

Mátra, Sector Csóka-kő

Lorand Istvan on Disszertáció, 6a

What else is there to see & do

Eger

There is no other place quite like Eger in Hungary. It is strongly characterised by its beautiful baroque architecture, Mediterranean feeling and excellent wines. This city has one of the most magnificent baroque buildings in the world, the Minorite church. For wine tasting head to the valley of the women, south west of town, and visit the many wine cellars. Here you can drink a glass of wine for only 80Ft or buy 2 litres for 900Ft. You might opt to stay here for the night...

Gyöngyös

If you still haven't seen enough churches, visit Gyöngyös. Here you will find the largest gothic church in the country. It is a pleasant town to stroll around and drink a glass of wine or two.

Hiking

The Mátra Hills offer well marked, easy, hiking trails. Cartographia has a 1:40,000 map of the area called "A Mátra map". Mátrafüred is a popular starting point, as is Sástó and Parád.

Every village has its own church

Mátra

The Andesite rocks of the Mátra Hills are the leftovers of a once volcanic area. The dark forest hides two rock formations on opposite side of the valley. The sectors are pretty well bolted and suit the moderate climber perfectly. On hot summer days the crags heat up quickly but the trees provide enough shade to hide from the sun. After rainfall the Csóka-kő side dries faster than the Bárány-kő side. The latter has unfortunately more moss due to the lack of sun on some parts. The crags are not very challenging but they will keep you busy for a short while.

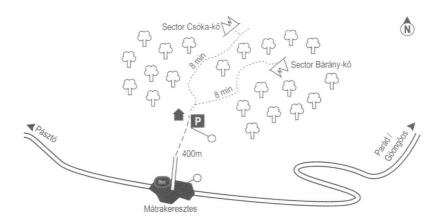

Directions

▶ Mátrakeresztes is the village close to the crags and lies along the road connecting Parád with Paszto. The turn for Mátrakeresztes is halfway along this road. Coming from Parád, follow the road for 24km until you reach the village of Mátrakeresztes. Turn right in the village after you have crossed the small stream just before the bus stop. Follow this road for 400m and park the car. On foot, carry on straight and take the trail with the white-red-white marking for Csóka-kő. For Bárány-kő follow this trail until the first junction and take the path that goes right, pass the small stream (which can dry up after a period of no rain) and climb the hill to the crags on your right.

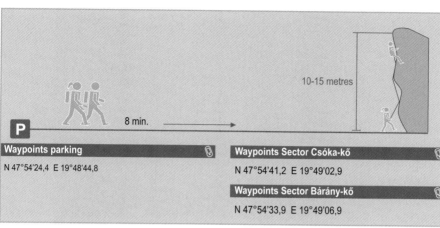

Waypoints parking

N 47°54'24,4 E 19°48'44,8

Waypoints Sector Csóka-kő

N 47°54'41,2 E 19°49'02,9

Waypoints Sector Bárány-kő

N 47°54'33,9 E 19°49'06,9

10-15 metres

8 min.

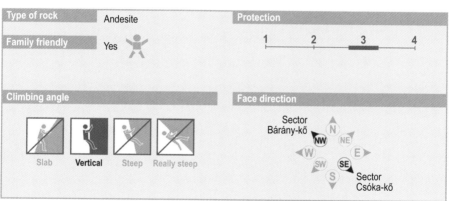

Type of rock	Andesite
Family friendly	Yes

Protection

1   2   3   4

Climbing angle

Slab   **Vertical**   Steep   Really steep

Face direction

Sector Bárány-kő

N NE
NW
W   E
SW SE
S

Sector Csóka-kő

Number of routes & Grade range

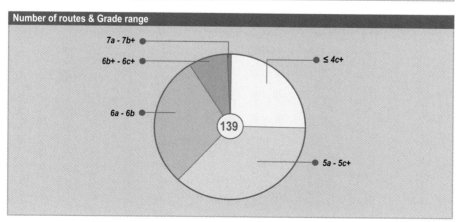

7a - 7b+
6b+ - 6c+
6a - 6b

≤ 4c+

139

5a - 5c+

...a country full of surprises...

Macedonia

Ilija Ristovski on Three Lions (7a+) at Demir Kapija

The Republic of Macedonia is a small natural paradise with mountains, forests, lakes and rivers, situated in the heart of the Balkans. Besides a brilliant mix of natural wonders, including some fantastic limestone crags, you'll find here a special blend of history and culture.

Macedonia - or "The Former Yugoslav Republic of Macedonia", as it's officially known - is the historic birthplace of Alexander the Great. This famous king of Macedonia left behind an empire that stretched all the way from the Mediterranean to India after his death in 323BC. Today, Macedonia is merely as big as Belgium but still serves as a geographical and cultural crossroads between Christian Europe and the Islamic Orient.

After the troubles in its neighbouring countries in the 1990's life moves to a different rhythm, overcoming its obstacles from the past. The economy is showing a slow recovery but the country still has to deal with some significant problems and has one of the lowest average incomes in Europe. Despite this, a warm and welcoming country waits to be explored by tourists and climbers. Its most important sightseeing attractions are Lake Ohrid - a real tourist mecca with some 30 cultural monuments around the lake - its medieval monasteries scattered around the country, huge vineyards that produce some of the best inexpensive wines of Europe, lively Turkish bazaars and classical Orthodox churches. Furthermore the whole country is unbelievably green and, where it is not green, the landscape is coloured blue by the many lakes.

Macedonia boasts a few climbing areas with well protected sport routes in splendid settings. A journey to Macedonia will certainly be very rewarding, not just for the climbing but also for the experience of discovering the mountainous heart of the Balkans.

Sv Jovan at Kaneo (13th century church) at Lake Ohrid

Climbing information

There has been sport climbing in Macedonia since the 1980's and the first competition in which Macedonian climbers competed was held in Split in Croatia in 1985. In 1990 the first sport route was bolted in Macedonia in Matka, named Jumbo Jet (7a). Now, there are around 400 sport climbers and the number of routes already exceeds 200. We're pretty sure that in the next two years this number will at least double, due to the strong focus sport climbing has within the national climbing federation.

Besides the sport climbing there is one bouldering area that has an enormous potential for the future. Around the small village of Prilep there is an area of some 7000 square metres packed with granite boulders. At the present time this area only attracts very few boulderers, mainly coming from Greece. There is no topo available and so this area is still one big play ground! It is not included in this Rock Climbing Atlas because we feel the area first needs to be developed before being worth a visit.

In this edition two climbing areas are described:

Matka and Demir Kapija. The third climbing area in Macedonia is around Lake Ohrid but at the time of writing there were only 35 routes there. However, serious plans exist for developing about 50 more sport routes at the end of 2006 at a crag next to the lake. Keep an eye on our website for updates!

Climbing area Matka

The Matka Canyon is a favourite place for Macedonians to escape the busy life of Skopje. In this wonderful setting traditional and sport climbing routes can be found. Bring your camping equipment and be prepared for a small hike to get to a wonderful camping spot next to a monastery.

Climbing area Demir Kapija

This is without doubt the best place in Macedonia for climbing with an enormous amount of high quality limestone, a rustic setting, a large number of routes and great potential for further development. Enjoyable wild camping is possible in the gorge near the crags.

Enjoy the tranquil environment at Matka Canyon

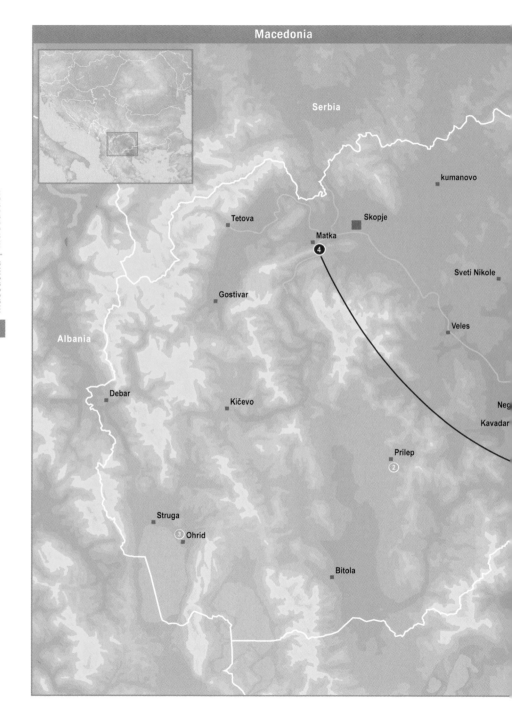

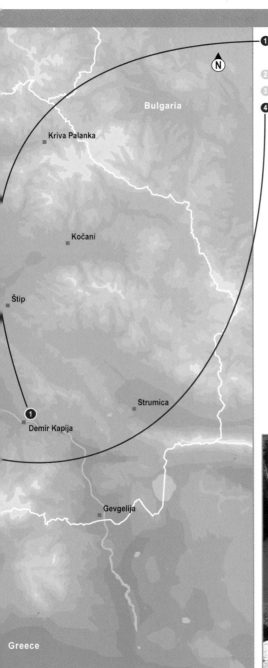

Climbing area	#	
1 **Demir Kapija**		
Demir Kapija Gorge	120	
2 Prilep	95	
3 Lake Ohrid	35	
4 **Matka**		
Matka Hut	45	

Bulgaria

Kriva Palanka

Kočani

Štip

Strumica

1
Demir Kapija

Gevgelija

Greece

Vesna Talevski at Matka

Climate

As a landlocked country, Macedonia has a predominantly continental climate with very cold winters and hot and dry summers. Heavy snowfall and extremely low temperatures - minus 20°C is not unlikely - characterise winter. The temperatures in summer range between 25°C and 40°C. Spring is a very unpredictable season, especially in April, whereas autumn tends to be drier.

Month	Average temperature (°C)	Average rainfall (mm)
Jan	1	39
Feb	3	31
March	7	37
April	12	39
May	17	53
June	20	45
July	23	28
Aug	23	28
Sept	18	36
Oct	11	61
Nov	6	53
Dec	1	53

Climate table Skopje

Getting there

 By plane

Macedonian Airlines (*www.mat.com.mk*) is the national carrier with connections from Western Europe to Skopje and Ohrid although direct flights to Ohrid are scarce and therefore the cheapest option is to fly to Skopje. At the time of writing Skopje was not served by any of the low cost carriers but flight tickets are still very reasonably priced. The best fares are actually offered by Alitalia (*www.alitalia.com*). They connect most European cities with Skopje via Milan for about €300.

For those with more time than money, a cheap flight to Thessaloniki in Greece is a very good option. Thessaloniki is connected with Skopje by train and this journey takes 4 to 5 hours. Another alternative is to catch a flight to Sofia in Bulgaria, though this probably won't work out a lot cheaper.

Trpejca village at Lake Ohrid

By train

There are a number of international trains heading to or passing through Skopje. These include trains from Thessaloniki [4h], Belgrade [9h] and Ljubljana [18h]. Check *www.reiseauskunft.bahn.de* for exact schedules.

 By bus

There are frequent daily buses running to Macedonia from its neighbouring countries. The journey to Skopje from Sofia takes six hours and about the same from Belgrade.

Bouldering at Prilep

 By car

Driving to Macedonia is no problem as the roads are well kept, the same being true for Serbia through which you'll need to pass. From Zagreb it is 825km to Skopje and from Vienna 1050km.

Moving around

 Skopje airport information

Skopje's Petrovac Airport lies 20km east of the centre, and is small and efficient. There are no buses connecting the airport with the centre and a taxi is your only option. A taxi to the centre of Skopje should cost 800MKD (€13.20).

 By public transport

Depending on the destination there are either buses or trains to choose from and both networks are reasonably well developed, efficient and inexpensive. The new modern bus station in Skopje is located next to the train station south of the Vardar River. All international and domestic buses leave and arrive from here.

An alternative to travelling in an overcrowded damp bus is to take a shared taxi, which is around double the price of a bus ticket per person. Travellers interested in this option will find dozens of taxi drivers standing around the entrance of the Skopje bus station, shouting out the name of their destination.

Legitimate taxi companies should have metres and are recognized by their four-digit phone number starting with a 9, printed on the car door. Taxis are rather inexpensive and are a good way of covering short distances.

 By car

The road infrastructure in Macedonia is good with a fast highway running from Skopje to the border with Greece. A toll has to be paid on this main highway, which costs €4 for the full distance. Fuel prices are quite similar to those of Western European countries. Diesel is slightly cheaper than petrol.

Rental car prices in Macedonia generally range from €35 to €40 per day. A few international rental companies are located at Skopje Airport. Reservations can be made via their websites. Other cheaper, local rental companies are found in or near the centre of Skopje. These usually don't have websites so ask around and shop for the best deals.

Accommodation

Every kind of accommodation is available in Macedonia, from luxury five star hotels to beautiful camping spots. Locals tend to rent apartments or rooms next to or inside their private home. This kind of private rental can be found by looking out for signs with the word, 'Sobe'. In Ohrid in particular, this is the way to go with prices of around €10 per person per night. Accommodation in Skopje is more expensive and budget choices are unfortunately very limited. Campsites in Macedonia can only be found around Lake Ohrid for approximately €4 per person per night.

Food & Drinks

Macedonian cuisine is similar to that of Turkey and Greece. Different types of kebab can be found almost everywhere, as can dishes such as moussaka (aubergines and potatoes baked in layers with minced meat). If someone invites you for a real typical Macedonian dinner, expect to get large amounts of meat either grilled or on baked bread like a kind of pizza. Make sure to order a shopska salad to keep your vitamin levels in check!

Sobi for rent

A typical breakfast consists of burek (cheese, spinach, potato or minced meat in filo pastry) and a yogurt drink.

Prices for eating out are extremely kind to your budget - for less than €8 you can get a complete meal. Even in Skopje's more western-style restaurants prices remain relatively low. A cappuccino usually costs €1 whereas a good glass of Skopso Pivo, the local beer, costs €1.25.

Self-caterers can buy all they need in Macedonia and low priced vegetables, fruit and white cheese are abundant in every town.

Climbing guidebook

At the time of writing there was neither an official guidebook nor a good internet site providing complete route information. Fortunately, at Demir Kapija there is a notice board with all the route information. Route names are clearly written on the rock. Also, there are plans to publish a comprehensive guidebook for Macedonia. This is expected to be published mid 2007. Until then, the website of the national federation, *www.climbing. org.mk*, provides the best information available. You could also contact them for further information via contact@climbing.org.mk or +389 23 165540.

Climbing at Ohrid

Facts about Macedonia

Facts & figures

Population:	2 million
Religion:	Orthodox (66%), Muslim (29%)
Capital:	Skopje
Time zone:	GMT +1
Telephone code:	+389

Money

Currency:	Macedonian Denar (MKD)
Exchange rate:	€1 = 60.50MKD
ATM machines:	widespread

Language

Good day	*Zdravo*
Thank you	*Blagodaram*
Goodbye	*Do gledanye*
Yes / No	*Da / Ne*
Right / Left / Straight	*Desno / Levo / Pravo*
Rock climbing	*Sportsko kacuvanje*

Visas & formalities

EU	Other European nationalities	USA / Canada	All other nationalities
No visa for a period of up to 90 days.	Other European nationalities do not require a visa for a period of up to 90 days, except for: Czech Republic, Estonia, Hungary, Latvia, Lithuania, Poland, Slovak Republic and Slovenia. They can obtain a visa via the consular offices.	Americans do not require a visa for a period of up to 90 days. Canadians do require a visa, obtainable via consular offices.	Most other nationalities do not require a visa for a period of up to 90 days.

Safety

Macedonia is a very pleasant and safe country to travel around in. Besides taking normal precautions there is nothing specific to be worried about.

Emergency numbers

Police:	92
Fire Brigade:	93
Ambulance:	94

Use of mobile phone

There is good coverage in the whole country.

Internet access

Almost every larger town has an internet café with prices of about €1 per hour.

Water

Water fountains can be found everywhere in Macedonia and this water is good to drink. The water coming from the tap is also safe to drink but doesn't always taste good. A bottle of 1.5 litre of water costs about €0.40.

Climbing area Matka

Spring   Summer   Autumn   Winter

Matka is one of the many outdoor gems in Macedonia and is a popular place to spend the weekend, being located only 13km west of Skopje. The wild River Treska splits the Suva Mountains into two parts giving rise to the Treska Canyon. Nearby, dozens of caves are to be found making this a great playground for speleologist. The whole area is great for hiking and the Treska River has a world-renowned wild water canoe course.

About 15 minutes upstream from the busy car park lies the dilapidated Matka Hut at the small artificial Lake Matka. This mountain hut once must have been a fantastic place to spend the night, right in the middle of nature. The huge building still looks great from the outside but the interior hasn't kept pace with time. It's a pity, since now the only other convenient option is camping. Although for sure, the camping spots next to St. Nikola's Monastery (built in 1389), offer more than just a perfect alternative.

In terms of setting, the climbing at Matka is absolutely wonderful - the crags are right in the middle of a lush area with splendid views over monasteries, the Treska River and little, far-away villages. However, in terms of number of sport routes the area is not so big and there are just a few dozen routes that make the journey worthwhile. Trad climbers on the other hand can find more lines of 150 metres to choose from. Traditional climbing has a long history in Matka and the first route was climbed in 1958 by Otmar Hudomalj. Unfortunately he died at the age of 18. The whole crag has been named after Otmar Hudomali and there is a special monument to him next to the Matka Hut, representing a bolt with a karabiner.

The Matka Hut seen from St. Nikola's Monastery

When to go

The best time for climbing in Matka is from mid-April until the end of November. The best sector for sport climbing, sector Trlo, faces south, which makes summer a less attractive time to visit Matka.

Crag

Ⓐ **Matka Hut**

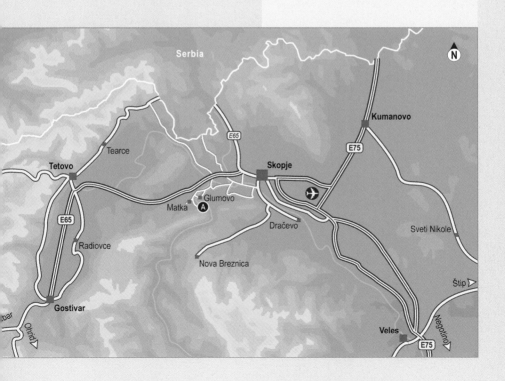

Otmar's rock at Matka

How to get to the area & how to move around

The only form of transport you'll need while at Matka is your feet!

 By public transport

Bus number 60 leaves Skopje's main bus station every 100 minutes starting at 7am [45min, 60MKD]. Get off at the last stop and continue towards the canoe slalom course. See 'By car' for further directions.

You can also take a private taxi for about €15 from the centre; from the airport a taxi should cost around €20.

 By car

From the centre of Skopje, head west towards the E65 following the signs for Ohrid and Tetova. When you are almost out of Skopje there is a sign for 'Ez Traska' to the left. Turn left here and cross the bridge. Continue on this road for 2km until the sign to 'Matka Canoe Slalom' pops up, at which point you turn left. Follow this road, which passes through the village of Glumovo, towards the canyon. Park at the car park of the canoe competition course and continue on foot, following the road next to the river. Turn right just before the dam and at the end turn left onto a well-paved path that leads to the Matka Hut.

Where to stay

The Matka Hut is beautifully situated on the edge of the emerald green river surrounded by the high rising crags of Matka. Seen from afar, the hut looks great, however, the inside is completely worn out and a complete refurbishment wouldn't be too much to ask for. Spending the night here is possible and is the only option, unless you choose to camp. There are around 40 beds in a few different rooms. The bathroom is not too welcoming for a shower but at least there is hot water. Plans to refurbish the Matka Hut exist but there is no firm timetable.

You can pitch a tent at the green grass field near to the Monastery of St. Nicola Shishevski. There is a fresh water source here making this a convenient spot. The only disadvantage is the uphill hike of about 25 minutes from the Matka Hut. The most interesting sectors are within easy reach from here, making camping at this spot very attractive.

Of course it is also possible to stay in Skopje, as it is only a 20 minute drive to Matka. The best and only budget option is the HI Ferijal Hostel on Ul Prolet 25, near the train station. Expect to pay €20 per person including breakfast.

Monument at Matka

Matka Hut

N 41°57'01,9 E 21°17'59,1

Open   Year round but only hot water from 15/2 to 1/11

Price   €5 per person per night

Where to buy groceries

Groceries are best bought in the larger sized supermarkets in Skopje or in the small villages that you pass through on the way from Skopje to Matka.

Where to find the local climbing guidebook

Next to the Matka Hut is an information table with an unclear drawing of the trad routes. Better information can be found at *www.climbing.org.mk* and at *www.srichinmoyraces.org*. Some route names are written on the rock.

What else is there to see & do

Hiking
There are some popular hiking trails around Matka offering great opportunities to explore one of Macedonia's most attractive regions. However, you can't buy a map with these paths marked on it. The best available map is made by 'The Macedonian Mountaineering Sports Federation'. This map can be obtained from them in Skopje: Ull. 11 Oktomvri 42a. Their phone number is: +389 23 165540 and email *spsm@mt.net.mk*.

Skopje
The capital of Macedonia is full of life in the warm months of the year, with plenty of bars, restaurants and outdoor clubs playing host to a young crowd. At other times the vibe calms down quite a fair bit. Things to do include a hiking up Tvrdina Kale, the city fortress, which gives a good view over the town, wandering around the old bazaar and eating typical kebapci, or making a visit to one of the beautiful mosques and churches.

St. Nikola's Monastery

Matka Hut

There are several different sectors with sport climbing in Matka but by far the best sector is Trlo. From the Matka Hut it is a strenuous 1 hour walk uphill. Nevertheless, the 20 routes are definitely worth the hike. This solid crag is slightly overhanging, south facing, and most routes are between 6b and 7b, requiring delicate moves with good footwork.

Another good sector, although containing only 6 routes, is Sector Otmar's Rock close to St. Nikola's Monastery. The views over the Treska River and the monastery are magnificent.

Then there are 15 trad routes on the Big Otmar Rock. Most routes have some fixed protection in place. There is even a 150 metres long route, graded 6a, which is reasonably well protected.

Climbing at Matka

Having a drink a the Matka Hut

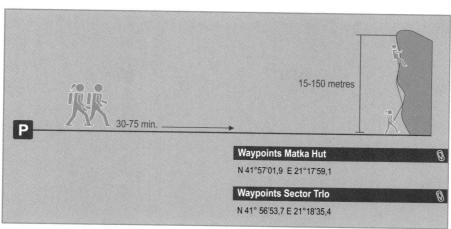

Waypoints Matka Hut

N 41°57'01,9 E 21°17'59,1

Waypoints Sector Trlo

N 41° 56'53,7 E 21°18'35,4

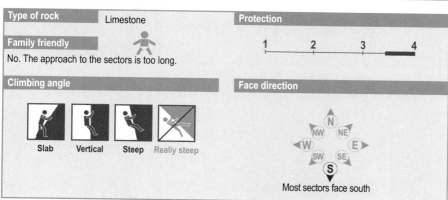

Type of rock

Limestone

Family friendly

No. The approach to the sectors is too long.

Protection

1   2   3   4

Climbing angle

Slab   Vertical   Steep   Really steep

Face direction

Most sectors face south

Number of routes & Grade range

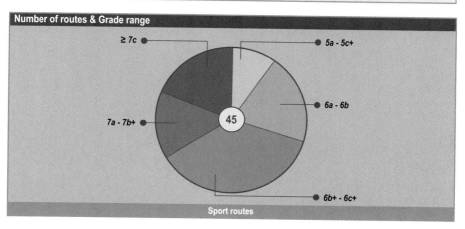

45

≥ 7c

5a - 5c+

6a - 6b

7a - 7b+

6b+ - 6c+

Sport routes

Sector Trlo

100% concentration

The route Charlie Chaplin (6c) at Sector Centrala Rock

Pure trad climbing at Matka

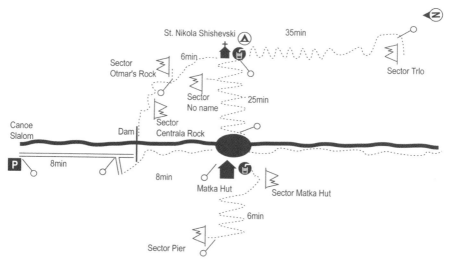

St. Nikola Shishevski

35min

Sector
Otmar's Rock

6min

Sector Trlo

Sector
No name

25min

Canoe
Slalom

Dam

Sector
Centrala Rock

P

8min

8min

Matka Hut

Sector Matka Hut

6min

Sector Pier

Directions

▶ Sector Trlo

Ask the staff of the Matka Hut to take you across the small lake by one of their boats and they will attentively do so. The crossing only takes a few minutes (hit the gong at the other side of the lake to let the staff know to pick you up on the return leg).

Once across the lake, follow the path up to St. Nikola's Monastery. Fresh water can be found at the fountain near the monastery. From the monastery head southeast and follow the path that leads southwards further up the mountain. It is wise to ask the staff at the monastery to point you in the right direction. Once on the path, you'll get to a small field after about 20 minutes where you head to the left and continue on another path. At a certain point blue dots appear on stones to mark the path. Follow these (look carefully for them) until you reach Sector Trlo. The path goes down the last bit and you won't see the crag until you are there.

At the time of writing there were no signs for this path; hopefully the whole path will be sign-marked in the near future. Until then, a GPS device or navigational assistance from other climbers is advised.

▶ Sector No name

Head towards St. Nikola's Monastery and, about three-quarters of the way there, an almost invisible path heads left towards the crag. This path forks off on a sharp hairpin bend to the right at a point where there is a dead tree stump. The sector is only about 20 metres from this point and the shiny bolts are visible.

▶ Sector Otmar's Rock

At St. Nikola's Monastery pass the little gate to the north. Follow the marked path for about 8 minutes until you reach Sector Otmar's Rock.

Climbing area Demir Kapija

Macedonian climbers in Demir Kapija excitedly asked us if we found the routes to be as good and the quality of the bolting to be as high as in France. For them our answer was very important – they are keen for international recognition and want to be considered part of the climbing world. Indeed, they had nothing to fear! The climbing here is of very high quality and there are some challenging routes in the great setting of this refreshingly cool limestone gorge.

Demir Kapija is a small town along the highway running from Skopje to Greece. It has a few restaurants and mini markets, and the people are friendly and open to climbers. But this is about all that Demir Kapija has to offer - a journey to Macedonia's best climbing area is purely for the climbing. This is not a problem at all considering that there were already 120 routes at the time of writing and the area is being very actively developed!

Demir Kapija is also a great place to stop over for a few days on your way to Greece. (If you're keen to go climbing in Greece, check out the Rock Climbing Atlas Greece & The Middle East!)

When to go

Even when all other places are too hot to climb in summer, the Demir Kapija gorge will always stay cool. Due to the narrow gorge, the trees and the small brook running through it, and the fresh wind that seems to be always there, the climate is very agreeable even on the warmest days. Spring and autumn are also fine but always take some warm clothes in case the wind is strong.

Spring   Summer   Autumn   Winter

Tetka Biberce (6b) at Demir Kapija, a very nice route!

Crag

Ⓐ Demir Kapija Gorge

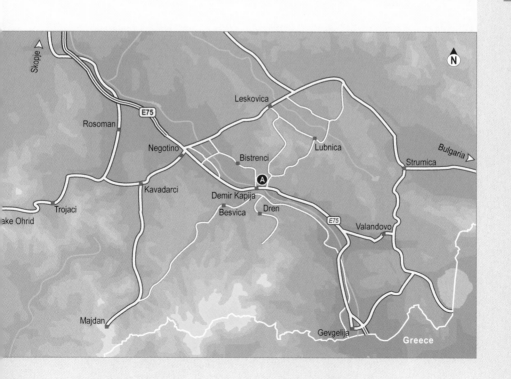

Demir Kapija

How to get to the area & how to move around

You don't need a car to move around or to get to the crags.

 By public transport

Demir Kapija is a stop along the railway line running between Skopje and Thessaloniki and is served by at least three trains each day [2h, 300MKD] from Skopje. From Thessaloniki there is an early morning train and one in the early evening leaving the main train station [3h].

 By car

Demir Kapija lies 110km south of Skopje and it takes a bit over an hour to get there.

Tufa's spotted at the beautiful Sector Arena

Where to stay

At the time of writing there was no other choice than to wild camp in the gorge, although there were initiatives to set-up a campsite in the near future. See the detailed map for the best camping spot - a nice little flat grass field just 5 minutes from the crags, besides a small gentle brook which in mid-summer is nothing more than a tiny flow of water. The water is pretty clean but you are strongly advised to boil the water before drinking.

The brook that runs through the gorge at Demir Kapija

Where to buy groceries

In the town of Demir Kapija several small shops can be found as well as a daily market for fresh fruit and vegetables.

Where to find the local climbing guidebook

There is an information board at the car park that details all the routes. All route names are written on the rocks so bring a pen and a sheet of paper or a good memory along with you.

What else is there to see & do

Unfortunately the area doesn't have any particular interesting things to do on a rest day. Unless you're into wine - Demir Kapija produces the best wines in Macedonia. Make sure you visit one or two wine producers and mingle with the local villagers.

Demir Kapija Gorge

The climbing at Demir Kapija consists of several different sectors, all close to each other, on both sides of the gorge. As this gorge is quite narrow and is full of trees, climbing is possible even during the harshest days in summer. Besides sport climbing, there is also some trad climbing but this is not documented, so put your adventure hat on if you fancy it! The best reason to come here is the excellent sport climbing.

One of the most amazing sectors is unquestionably Sector Arena. Halfway up is a cave that is coloured with dark brown and black stalactites, and is only reachable by a short (and easy) via ferrata. Here some of the best and most difficult routes are to be found, and you'll find yourself dropping Egyptians with regularity. Another good sector where technique is your friend is Sector VDD.

Judith on 'Radar Petra' (7a)

...a journey into the unknown...

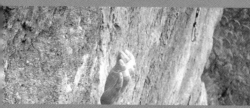

Romania

Cohn Robert in a winning mood during the international climbing competition in 2006, photo by George Stroie

Forget climbing in France, Italy and Switzerland, Romania is the place to be. This wonderful country not only has some excellent climbing but also lets you experience a way of life that is virtually unknown in Western Europe. Here you can still see horse-drawn carts passing by and people working on the fields as if it were 1890. Just travelling round the country and seeing all this gives you the same sense of satisfaction as on-sighting your first 7a. Oh, and we should have said: 7a´s are abundant in Romania!

Despite more than 17 years passing since the revolution of 1989 - as the Romanians call the fall and execution of Ceauşescu - people are still struggling to get the country on its feet again. Many improvements have been made but there is still a lot of work to be done. Romania will join the EU in 2007 and many Romanians see this as a necessary step to reach a higher standard of living.

For travellers Romania has much to offer. There's hiking in the Carpathian mountains or trekking through unspoiled villages in lush valleys - all over the country, the landscape is simply breathtaking. Or there are so many wooden churches, painted monasteries and picturesque castles to see - Romania isn't called Dracula country for nothing and you'll need a lifetime to see it all. In Romania's northern province, Maramureş, time really has stood still - people still use wells to collect water - and spending some time here is an unforgettable experience. But best of all, the local people are genuinely friendly, interested and extremely helpful. The language barrier can be easily overcome with some help of Spanish or Italian (Romanian is a Romance language), a pen and paper and the use of sign language.>>

View from the top of the Suhardul Mic in the Bicaz Gorge

To make a trip complete, Romania has some splendid rock climbing that compares very well with that found in Western Europe. There's fantastic traditional climbing and the better sport climbers will also have plenty to do. The local climbers are very welcoming to foreign climbers and are always happy to show you around.

Climbing information

Romania's climbing history dates back many years and the first routes were climbed in 1934. These days the country has around 27 different climbing areas. Many of these are small and have just a few routes or boulders but there are a few excellent areas with hundreds of routes to choose from. The most popular areas are described in this Rock Climbing Atlas. As Romania is a very big country, the distances between the areas are rather large. You'll need about four weeks if you want to visit them all. Two weeks would allow you to get to one or two areas. However long you decide to spend here, you'll have a great trip!

Some still use a well to collect water

Climbing area Bucegi Mountains

This area covers the crags of Sinaia, which is the place to be for harder sport climbing! Furthermore, the Bucegi Mountains offers lots of trad climbing in the area around Coştila. This whole place is also great for hiking.

Climbing area Bicaz

The Bicaz Gorge is a very nice sport climbing area for those that climb 6c and above – it is the place to find lots of new projects. There are also 73 trad routes of all grades in wonderful surroundings.

Climbing area Turda

The Turda Gorge, close to lively Cluj Napoca, is roughly the fourth largest climbing area in the country. The area is fine for technical climbing, mostly on slabs, or for longer trad routes, but the climbing is not that exceptional.

Climbing area Cerna Valley

This is probably the best sport climbing area of Romania with over 215 well protected sport routes to choose from over a wide range of grades. This is the place where the annual Băile Herculane Open, a popular international sport climbing competition, is held.

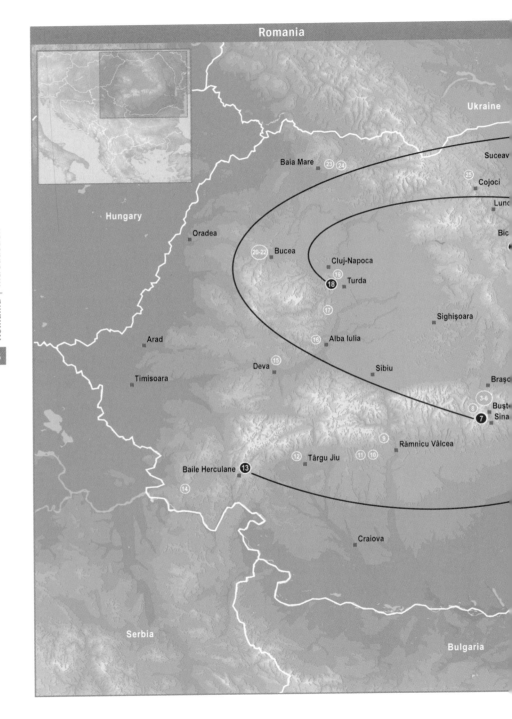

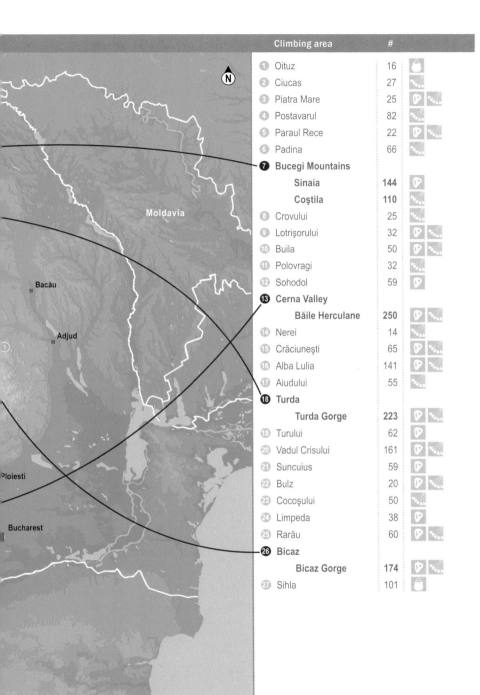

	Climbing area	#	
1	Oituz	16	
2	Ciucas	27	
3	Piatra Mare	25	
4	Postavarul	82	
5	Paraul Rece	22	
6	Padina	66	
7	**Bucegi Mountains**		
	Sinaia	**144**	
	Coştila	**110**	
8	Crovului	25	
9	Lotrişorului	32	
10	Buila	50	
11	Polovragi	32	
12	Sohodol	59	
13	**Cerna Valley**		
	Băile Herculane	**250**	
14	Nerei	14	
15	Crăciuneşti	65	
16	Alba Lulia	141	
17	Aiudului	55	
18	**Turda**		
	Turda Gorge	**223**	
19	Turului	62	
20	Vadul Crisului	161	
21	Suncuius	59	
22	Bulz	20	
23	Cocoşului	50	
24	Limpeda	38	
25	Rarău	60	
26	**Bicaz**		
	Bicaz Gorge	**174**	
27	Sihla	101	

Climate

Romania has a continental climate with cold, snowy winters and warm summers. The weather can vary considerably from one year to another. Still, summers in Romania are generally very warm with an average of nine to ten hours of sunshine per day. In winter it mostly snows. The snow stays for thirty to fifty days a year at low altitudes and up to hundred days in the mountains. The change from winter conditions to those of summer is often rather abrupt. In general spring is a short and changeable season in Romania. Late summer and autumn are often the driest periods and therefore generally the best months for climbing anywhere in the country.

Month	Average temperature (°C)	Average rainfall (mm)
Jan	-2	45
Feb	0	25
March	5	27
April	12	60
May	17	78
June	21	120
July	23	52
Aug	22	45
Sept	18	44
Oct	12	29
Nov	6	35
Dec	1	26

Climate table Romania

Storks are very widespread in Romania

Getting there

 By plane

Romania is quite a big country so it is best to decide which climbing areas you'd like to visit before purchasing a ticket. Bucharest is the most convenient gateway for climbing in the south and north east of the country, in the Bucegi Mountains and the Bicaz Gorge. There are plenty of airlines operating flights to Bucharest from all over the world. All of them arrive at the Henri Coandă International airport, formerly known as Otopeni. However if you are planning on climbing only at the Bicaz Gorge a good option is to fly to Bacău, which is nearby. Tarom (*www.tarom.ro*), the Romanian national carrier, handles flights to Bacău.

If your preference is for climbing in the west - at the Turda Gorge or at Băile Herculane - it is best to fly to Timişoara or Cluj Napoca, which are both served by several international carriers. Expect to pay around €300 for a flight from Western Europe to Romania. Sky Europe tends to offer the cheapest tickets. If you are flexible about your departure dates, it's quite possible to buy a return ticket from London via Bratislava to Bucharest for less than €150.

 By train

A very good option for those with more time than money is to travel to Romania by train. There are connections from most major European cities. From Western Europe the best route is via Budapest. For example, the journey from Vienna to Budapest takes three hours and from Budapest to Arad another five hours. From Budapest to Oradea it is six hours. A one-way train ticket from Budapest to Arad or Oradea costs around €30. From Oradea there are direct daily trains to Cluj Napoca and to Braşov. From Arad there are direct trains to Băile Herculane. Check *http://plannerint.b-rail.be* for all international connections.

 By bus

Eurolines and other private companies operate

A typical Romanian landscape

buses from Vienna, amongst other cities, to different places in Romania, including Timişoara and Braşov. Check *www.eurolines.com* and *www.atlassib.ro* for more information.

 By car

Getting into Romania by car is not a problem, although crossing the Hungarian/Romanian border might take some time, especially at weekends. From Vienna it takes about 6½ hours to cover the 500km to Oradea.

Moving around

You won't need to have your own car in Romania, as it is very easy to get to the climbing areas by public transport and the crags are usually within walking distance from the accommodation. Renting a car is, as ever, an option but it is a rather expensive one.

 *Bucharest airport information*

The bus number 783 departs frequently from the arrivals terminal of the Henri Coandă international airport to downtown Bucharest.

 *Timişoara airport information*

A taxi from the airport to the centre or to the train station (Gara Timişoara Nord) in Timişoara should cost €6.

 *Cluj Napoca airport information*

A taxi from the airport to the centre or to the train station (Gara Cluj) should cost €5.

 By public transport

The Romanian train network is actually rather good and the best way of getting around - the buses are slow, unreliable and uncomfortable. There are five different types of train that vary in speed and levels of comfort. Therefore you'll find different fares for the same destination. Intercity trains are the most comfortable, but aren't any faster than express trains. The price for a first class ticket on an intercity train is around €6 per 100km. A first class ticket for the cheapest category train is around €2.50 for the same distance. Because of these wide price differences, we haven't quoted any prices for trains and buses but it's safe to use these estimates as a rule of thumb. Furthermore price differences between different bus companies exist as well. Be aware that international train tickets and reservations for first class sleeping compartments on domestic trains have to be bought in advance at the offices of the Agenţie de Voiaj CFR. Their offices can be found in every city centre. Check *www.infofer.ro* for all Romanian train schedules.

If you arrive in Bucharest the best option is to travel by train towards your climbing area of choice. Most national and international trains leave from Gară de Nord in northern Bucharest (Bulevardul Garii de Nord 2). Gară de Nord can be reached by metro which is the most convenient and fastest way. However, at the time of writing, the Henri Coandă

Steep walls and small pockets are the main features at Sector HCO in Băile Herculane, photo by George Stroie

International airport was not yet connected to the metro system. Bus 783 takes you to Piața Victoriei, from where you can take the metro to Gară de Nord.

Shorter distances in Romania are best covered with maxi-taxis. These vans can take up to 8 to 10 people on board. The maxi-taxis are run by private companies and mostly leave when they are full and therefore have no (reliable) timetable. At some places they leave from bus stations and at other places from parking lots or lay-bys. Just hail them as regular taxis.

 By car

Driving in Romania is not too far off your worst nightmare. The road conditions are poor and there are all kind of moving objects on the road that struggle to pass for a vehicle. Nevertheless, roads are improving each year and the government is investing heavily. Having a car in Romania certainly gives you more freedom to explore the country.

In the Maramures province almost all houses, churches and monasteries are made from wood

A car vignette is obligatory for every car driving in Romania. These can be bought at the border or at any of the bigger petrol stations and they cost €5 for one month. Keep the receipt you receive with you as the police might check it. Petrol and diesel is less expensive compared to Western Europe but the price difference isn't much.

If oncoming car flash their lights, it's likely that a police speed-trap is around the corner. Speed limits are well signed and are usually 90km/h on major roads and 50km/h inside cities.

The Automobil Clubul Român (*www.acr.ro*) exists mainly for Romanians to renew their licenses but they might provide some information or assistance to tourists as well. Its 24 hour emergency service number is 927.

Various car rental agencies (such as Budget, Hertz and Avis) are located at the International airports of Bucharest, Timişoara and Cluj Napoca. Only Budget does not have an agency in Cluj Napoca. Expect to pay between €35 and €40 per day for a budget class car for a rental period of a week. A price of €30 per day applies for rental periods of three weeks.

 Hitchhiking

Hitchhiking is not recommended since it is never entirely safe in any country of the world. Having said that, hitchhiking in Romania is very common and practised by many. The locals wave down the cars instead of putting up their thumb. It is normal to pay the driver the equivalent of the bus fare.

Accommodation

Camping in the wild is not only permitted but practised almost everywhere in Romania. This is the way many Romanians spend their holidays - they fill their Dacia car with tents, tables, and chairs (not forgetting their barbeque!) and go camping besides one of the many rivers. Consequently, organised campsites are not very common in Romania and those that do exist tend to be extremely poorly maintained and without hot water. They are cheap though, costing around €1 pppn.

There are campsites run by foreigners that are generally good, but there are not a lot of them and they are more expensive. You'll pay around €10 for 2 persons, a tent and a car.

There is a large difference in quality and prices of hotels. The average rate for a budget hotel is €15 to €25 for a double room. For a mid range hotel expect to pay up to €40 for a double room. Hotels in touristy places (like Sighişoara) are more expensive, as you might expect. Romania also has so called villas - big houses that function as a hotel. These villas are often cheaper than hotels and have more ambience as well.

An excellent and frequently offered alternative is to stay in someone's private home. Many families rent rooms, indicated as 'Cazare', as a way of supplementing income, and you'll get to Romanian life first-hand this way. Depending on how touristy a place is, expect to pay between €4 and €10 per person per night. Breakfast and dinner can often be ordered as well.

Food & Drinks

Typical Romanian food is not very special – the favourite dish for most Romanians is barbequed pork in large quantities....Vegetarians will really have a bad time in Romania unless they are able to find a pizzeria or another western style restaurant. Fortunately, in the larger towns these kind of restaurants can be found actually everywhere. In a typical local restaurant the menu consists of different kind of soups (ciorbăs), that are typically meat based. Then there'll be chicken (pui), spicey grilled meatballs (mititei or mici), steak (vacv), pork (porc) or lamb (mile) and a couple of types of salads.

In other words it might be worth it to bring your own cooking gear. Fruit and vegetables are very cheap in Romania and are often sold along the road by locals. Aubergine, carrots, paprika, tomatoes and huge watermelons are abundant. If you cook your own meal you definitely won't spend more than €3 per day per person. Having said that, if you can stand the choice on the menu, the cost of eating out in Romania is also very low. Main courses cost under €1.50 in fast food restaurants, bistro's and

inexpensive café's - in decent restaurants you still won't pay more than €3. Prices are slightly higher in very popular tourist areas, as well as in the bigger cities such as Bucharest and Braşov.

In a bar or restaurant the price for a cappuccino is around €0.75, however, if you are a real cappuccino addict, don't try a Romanian one! The good news is that the local Ciuc beers are fine and half a litre only costs €1.

Wine lovers should bear in mind that unless you specifically order a sec (dry) wine, you'll probably end up getting a sweet red wine that tastes like lemonade - there is usually the choice of sec, demi-sec, dulce and semi-dulce red wines.

Climbing guidebook

Unfortunately there is only one printed guidebook in Romania and this one only describes the traditional climbing in the Bicaz Gorge. However there are several internet addresses where you can download climbing guides for specific areas for free. See the climbing area sections for further details.

All routes in Romania are graded with the UIAA scale.

In Romania the route names are always clearly written on the rock

Facts & figures

Population:	22,4 million
Religion:	Eastern Orthodox (87%)
Capital:	Bucharest
Time zone:	GMT +2
Telephone code:	+40

Money

Currency:	Lei (RON)
Exchange rate:	€1 = 3.5 Lei
ATM machines:	widespread

Language

Romanian is a romance language and has been influenced considerably by the Slavic languages of neighbouring countries. If you speak French, Italian or Spanish you will be able to understand much of the written Romanian, however if it is spoken it is hardly recognizable. English is mostly only spoken by younger educated people.

Good day	*Bună ziua*
Thank you	*Mulţumesc*
Goodbye	*La revedere*
Yes / No	*Da / Nu*
Right / Left / Straight	
	La dreapta / La stânga / Drept înainte
Rock climbing	*Escaladă, Căţărare*

Visas & formalities

EU	Other European nationalities	USA / Canada	All other nationalities
No visa for a period of up to 90 days.	All other European do not require a visa for a period of up to 90 days.	No visa for a period of up to 90 days.	Most other nationalities do not require a visa for a period of up to 90 days.

Safety

Bucharest has the reputation of being a dangerous city with a lot of street crime but in fact it is no more dangerous than any other European city of its size. Outside the capital street crime or other dangers are not much of an issue. Common sense has to be employed: leave your stuff in a safe place instead of leaving it visible in a car. When you camp wild it is best not to leave any valuables in your tent.

Emergency numbers

Police:	955
Fire Brigade:	981
Ambulance:	961

Use of mobile phone

Romania has reasonably good coverage except in very remote areas.

Internet access

Most towns, even smaller ones, have internet connections for a maximum price of €1 per hour.

Water

To be sure it is better not to drink tap water anywhere in the country. There are many places where water comes directly from the mountains and this is generally save to drink.

When you buy bottled water or order some in restaurants it is often carbonated. Water without gas is called 'apa plata'. A 2 litre bottle of water costs €0.50 in a supermarket.

Climbing area Bucegi Mountains

Spring   Summer   Autumn   Winter

The Bucegi mountains are part of the Southern Carpathians, also known as the Transylvanian Alps. Located south of Braşov, this group of mountain ranges have peaks over 2500 metres. The beauty of the nature and the whole setting makes this part of Romania a paradise for lovers of every kind of outdoor sport. From cross country skiing to mountain biking, from hiking to climbing, there is more than enough to do, both in winter and summer time.

There are two main spots for climbing in the Bucegi Mountains. The towns Buşteni and Sinaia are the best places from which to explore the area. If you're into climbing big routes, Coştila is your newly found heaven. The traditionally protected routes here reach up to 400 metres! If you want to spend your days in a bit more relaxed fashion, then head to the crags of Sinaia. Although the word relaxed only applies if a 7a is child play for you!

Salvamont rescue service
In case of a problem in the Bucegi Mountains climbing area, contact the Salvamont rescue team who can be called out at any time of the year. Tel: +40 244 320048.

When to go

The best period to climb here is from mid April to mid September but be aware that the weather can change in a blink of an eye. In summer it can even get pretty cold too.

Trad climbing at Coştila

Crag

A Sinaia

B Coştila

How to get to the area & how to move around

You don't necessarily need a car to move around or to get to the crags.

 By public transport

Bucharest is the best starting point to get to Buşteni and Sinaia. Both are on the Bucharest-Braşov rail line and all express trains, running frequently, stop here. When taking the train to Sinaia from either Gară de Nord in Bucharest or Gară Braşov (Bd. Garii nr.5) in Braşov be careful not to get out at the stop 'Halta Sinaia Sud' which is 2km south of the city centre. Instead, leave the train at Sinaia's main station.

You can also take a maxi-taxi from either Bucharest or Braşov. From Bucharest these leave from the

Brook that flows through Sinaia

centre of Piaţa Gară de Nord. From Braşov they leave from Autogară 1, next to the train station.

By car

Buşteni and Sinaia, the two most practical towns to stay, are situated close to Braşov along the highway E60, only 136km and 126km north of Bucharest. The Bucharest-Braşov road is busy but, as the road condition is good, it takes less than two hours from Bucharest.

Where to stay

For climbing at Sinaia, the best place to stay is in the town itself. Sinaia is a fairly charming city stretching out over a hill and does not get as much traffic as Buşteni (the E60 motorway runs through Buşteni). Sinaia has enough hotels and villas to choose from and there are also several cabanas (wooden mountain huts). Unfortunately there is no campsite in the direct vicinity of Sinaia and good spots in the wild are hard to find.

If you do choose to stay in Buşteni, this town also offers plenty of hotels and villas. On your way to Refugio Coştila, locals offer rooms on Str. Moralui (see "Directions to Coştila")

When climbing at Coştila, high up in the Bucegi mountains, make Refugio Coştila your base for a few days. The hut can only be reached on foot.

Refugio Coştila

📍 N 45°25'52,7 E 25°30'00,7

This simple refugio offers sleeping places comfortably up to 10 people. There are some mattresses, but no blankets. On weekends it can get crowded and unfortunately there are not so many places where you can pitch your tent around the refugio. If it has rained, water can be collected 30 minutes back down from the refugio. Otherwise take water from the village.

Directions
See "Directions to Coştila" for how to get to this refugio.

Hotel Intim

✉️ Carol I Bv 8
Sinaia

📍 N 45°21'18,8 E 25°32'55,3

Price   70 Lei per night for a double room

Halfway up the hill in Sinaia this budget hotel offers good value for your money but, we warn you, it is nothing fancy. Cooking is possible in the parking lot just before the hotel. Ask for a discount if you stay for 3 days or longer.

Cabana Schiorilor

✉️ Drumul Cotei 7, 106100
Sinaia
@ schimont@yahoo.com

📍 N 45°21'31,1 E 25°31'54,3

Price   110 Lei per night for a double room

This popular place, in a perfect location, has some nice rooms and a good restaurant next to it. You will pass this cabana on the way to the crags of Sinaia. It is also marked on the map.

Refugio Coştila

Where to buy groceries

There are many small (super-) markets both in Sinaia and Buşteni selling everything you need, including lots of fruits and vegetables.

Where to find the local climbing guidebook

There is no printed guidebook for Coştila and Sinaia, but there are some good internet sources. Although it is in Romanian, check out *www.costila.go.ro* for routes at Coştila. A simple detailed drawing including the different massifs is also available for download at this site. The PDF file is named 'Schita Zona Coştila. A topo can also be downloaded from *www.roclimbing.net*. The printouts from this site are available in the Refugio Coştila, but please leave these behind for other climbers to use after you. Route names are written on the rock at the start.

Braşov view from above

The latest information on the sport routes in Sinaia can be obtained via *www.escalada.verticon.ro* or via *www.roclimbing.net*. Although both sites are in Romanian, they provide links for you to download a good topo of Sinaia. All names of the routes are clearly written on the crags making it very easy to find the right route.

You can buy a map of the region with hiking trails at the bookshops in Sinaia and Buşteni. The small bookshop in Buşteni on the corner of Str. Coza Voda and the main road sells one called 'Munţii Bucegi; Hartă Turistică', by Octavian Arsene. The price is 7 Lei.

What else is there to see & do

Braşov
If you want to relax after having done some hard climbing in the Bucegi Mountains, head for the city of Braşov. Braşov is the second most visited city after Bucharest and it offers many trendy western bars and modern shops. The city centre has a nice fountain on Piaţa Sfatului where the locals meet and streets bands play different kind of music.

Sinaia monastery

Peleş Castle

It is said that Peleş Castle in Sinaia is one of the most beautiful castles of Romania. It used to be a summer residence of King Carol I. The castle's interior is even more stunning than the exterior, with every room being decorated in a special style. For the entrance fee of 10 Lei you can join an English speaking tour that will tell you all about the castle.

Hiking

The Bucegi Mountains are a dreamland for hikers - there are countless well marked hiking trails and every couple of hours you'll come across a mountain hut (cabana). Those huts are open year round. The website *www.montania.ro* gives an overview of various hikes between 1 to 15 hours.

Buşteni landscape

Sinaia

In the foothills of the Bucegi Mountains lie the different crags of Sinaia, all situated in a forest. In total there are 7 different sectors with 144 sport routes. The climbing here is very popular with Romanian climbers as it isn't far away from Bucharest and easy to get to. However, you do have to choose the right sectors as not all sectors are equally good.

The south facing Sector Surplomba has the hardest routes on a steep overhanging crag. There are several 7th and 8th grade routes to choose from, the hardest being graded 8b+. Here you'll need to combine power with delicate moves to complete the very demanding but wonderful routes. Sector Faleza Francezilor and Sector Sf Ana have some interesting lines as well. Sector Poiana Stanii has easier and shorter routes, but these are not the reason to go climbing in Sinaia.

Pump up your arms at Sector Surplomba

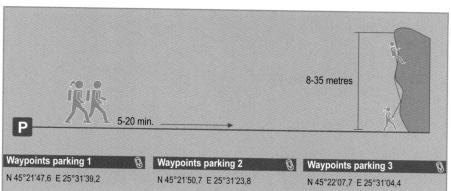

Waypoints parking 1	Waypoints parking 2	Waypoints parking 3
N 45°21'47,6 E 25°31'39,2	N 45°21'50,7 E 25°31'23,8	N 45°22'07,7 E 25°31'04,4

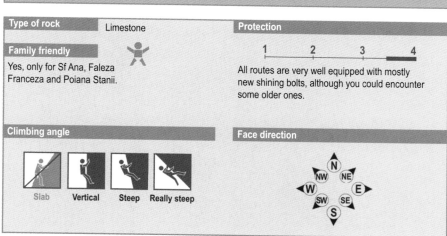

Type of rock

Limestone

Family friendly

Yes, only for Sf Ana, Faleza Franceza and Poiana Stanii.

Climbing angle

Slab Vertical Steep Really steep

Protection

1   2   3   4

All routes are very well equipped with mostly new shining bolts, although you could encounter some older ones.

Face direction

N NE E SE S SW W NW

Number of routes & Grade range

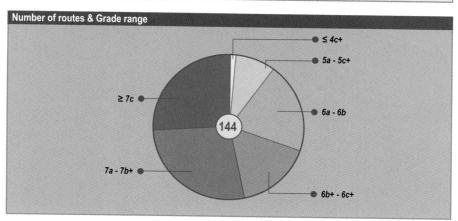

144

- ≤ 4c+
- 5a - 5c+
- 6a - 6b
- 6b+ - 6c+
- 7a - 7b+
- ≥ 7c

Climbing at Sinaia, photo by George Stroie

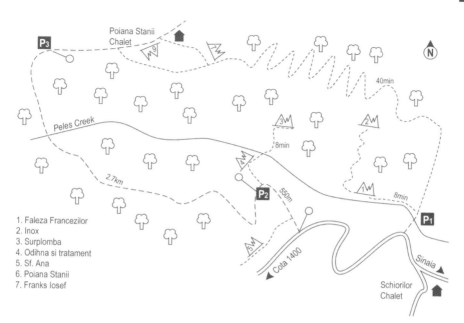

1. Faleza Francezilor
2. Inox
3. Surplomba
4. Odihna si tratament
5. Sf. Ana
6. Poiana Stanii
7. Franks Iosef

Directions

Sinaia

▶ From the centre of Sinaia drive or walk in the direction of the Cota 1400 chalet, which is signposted, and pass the Schiorilor Chalet. See the detailed drawing with further information about how to reach each sector.

Climbing at Coştila will definitely give that special sense of freedom you get being up in the mountains. Once there, you'll wonder why life has to include work! At this wild place the surrounding views are splendid and the rock is simply excellent. As it takes 1½ hours to get from Buşteni to Refugio Coştila on foot, the best option is to spend a few days up there.

The variety of routes, up to several hundred metres in length, is huge and there is something to do in every grade. Although a lot of routes have some fixed protection, you'll need to bring nuts, friends and slings. There are some routes that start right next to the refugio and that area is reasonably well protected. Get the detailed drawing and route information from *www.costila.go.ro*.

Some climbs start directly behind the Refugio

Buşteni seen from Refugio Coştila

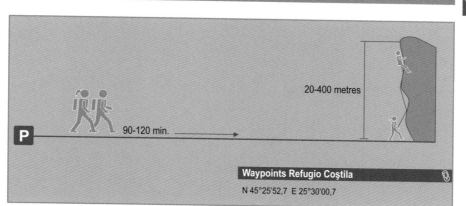

20-400 metres

90-120 min.

P

Waypoints Refugio Coştila

N 45°25'52,7 E 25°30'00,7

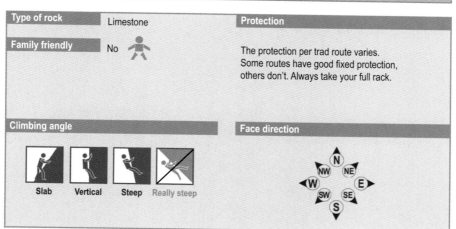

Type of rock Limestone

Family friendly No

Protection

The protection per trad route varies.
Some routes have good fixed protection,
others don't. Always take your full rack.

Climbing angle

Slab Vertical Steep Really steep

Face direction

N NE E SE S SW W NW

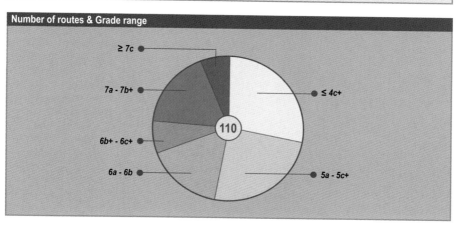

Number of routes & Grade range

≥ 7c

7a - 7b+

6b+ - 6c+

6a - 6b

≤ 4c+

5a - 5c+

110

Superb climbing at Coştila, photo by George Stroie

Directions

Coştila

► The path to Refugio Coştila as described here is not marked on the maps that are for sale at the kiosks in Buşteni and Sinaia. However, with the following directions you'll easily be able to find it.

From the main road in the village of Buşteni turn right into Str. Valea Alba, which is at the northern part of the city. Take the first street on the right (Str. Costi Lei) and follow the road, which becomes Str. Moralui. At the end of Str. Moralui is a junction. Continue straight on and follow the unpaved road which leads to a field (waypoints; N 45°25'21,7 E 25°31'57,5). Go straight until you see a red-white triangle sign. Follow this path for about 900 metres or 15 minutes until you see two paths (waypoints; N 45°25'26,4 E 25°31'25,3), the left one being marked with a red vertical line and the right path with a triangle sign. Take the path on your left and start following the red vertical lines. From here it takes about 1 hour and 15 minutes to get to the refugio. After a while the red line becomes a vertical white-blue-white sign. Continue until you see the refugio, but you won't see the refugio (waypoints; N 45°25'52,7 E 25°30'00,7) until you actually arrive, as the forest hinders your view.

Climbing area Bicaz

Spring   Summer   Autumn   Winter

Situated in the less travelled region Moldavia lies one of the most stunning gorges in Romania, and maybe even in the whole of Europe. In fact the Bicaz Gorge (Cheile Bicazului) is a whole complex of gorges with steep limestone rocks and in some places the distance between the walls is less than seven metres. The mysterious Red Lake, called Lacul Roşu, which is full with dead tree stumps, completes the whole scene.

The road from the small town of Bicaz to the Red Lake leads through the Bicaz Gorge – a stunning 5km despite the traffic. Along this road there are dozens of artisans selling their crafts. The high rising walls of more than 400 metres provide unlimited great climbing opportunities. It will definitely give you an overwhelming feeling! The crag of Piatra Altarului, 160 metres high with the cross on the top, is the most remarkable one.

If you are into long, traditional routes you are lucky as there are 73 routes of different lengths, styles and levels of difficulty to choose from. These routes are spread over 10 imposing massifs in the Bicaz Gorge. The routes can mostly be climbed free, although you'll occasionally need to use some aid. There are also some 100 single pitch sport climbing routes that will suit the more experienced climber. And we warn you, more than half of those routes are graded 7a and higher. If you climb at this grade, you will have a wonderful time! Those that climb less than 7a or are not into traditional climbing can enjoy the wonderful hikes in this area.

The sport climbing routes are very well protected and many routes have only been (re)equipped in 2000 and 2001. You'll find some fixed protection on many trad routes but do not be surprised if this is in the form of antique bolts or pitons - the first route was climbed in 1934 - so don't rely on them!

In case of an emergency call the Salvamont rescue service. Their office is located in Lacul Roşu in the house at the northern side of the campsite across the stream. Phone number: +40 745 979425.

Piatra Altarului

When to go

This is a perfect summer destination although you have to take into account that there can be some rainy periods from the second half of May until the middle or end of July. The driest months are August and September.

Crag

A Bicaz Gorge

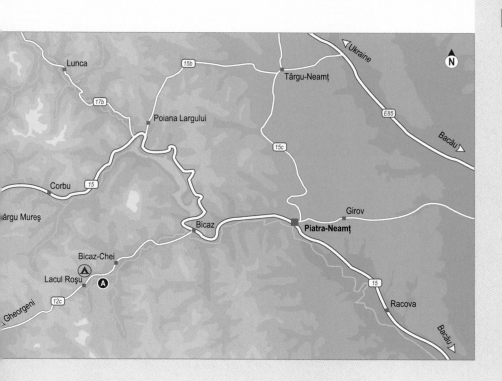

How to get to the area & how to move around

Having your own transport is not necessary since all sectors are within walking distance. Sector 21 can be reached by hitchhiking.

 By public transport

From Gară de Nord in Bucharest there is one train a day to Bicaz [6h]. There are more daily trains to Bacău [4h] from Bucharest. From Bacău there are five trains daily to Bicaz [1½ h - 2½ h]. From Bicaz there are buses towards Gheorgheni, Miercurea Ciuc or Braşov that pass by Lacul Roşu.

 By car

The Bicaz Gorge lies along road number 12c that runs from Bicaz to Gheorgheni. This spectacular road goes right through the gorge. The trip from Bucharest will take about 6 hours covering a distance of 360km. From the Hungarian border at Oradea it will take about 8 hours to cover the distance of 435km.

Where to stay

At Lacul Roşu there is a kind of campsite opposite Villa Andrei where you can pitch a tent. Water is available at the bottom of the stairs to Villa Andrei. In summer this is also a popular spot for holidaying Romanians, so expect some barbeques and loud music. Fortunately, there are plenty of hotels and villas in the Lacul Roşu area to choose from.

Hotel Jasicon

🏨 N 46°47'39,8 E 25°47'47,5

Price   80 Lei for a double room with bath

Hotel Jasicon has some 100 simple, no-nonsense, but clean rooms. The hotel is marked on the detailed map.

Vila Andrei

Villa Andrei

✉ Judetul Harghita,
Lacul Roşu

🏨 N 46°47'40,8 E 25°48'03,3

Price   60 Lei for a double room with bath

The friendly Villa Andrei is a good budget option. Outside there is place to cook and barbeque and you are allowed to make use of their tables and chairs.

Find a spot among the locals at the Bicaz Gorge campsite

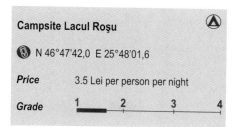

Campsite Lacul Roşu

N 46°47'42,0 E 25°48'01,6

Price   3.5 Lei per person per night

Grade   1 —— 2 —— 3 —— 4

Where to buy groceries

There are a few small supermarkets selling basic things in Lacul Roşu, but they don't sell a lot of vegetables. It's best to buy these on your way to the Bicaz Gorge where fruits and vegetables are sold along the road.

Where to find the local climbing guidebook

The guidebook of the Bicaz Gorge is named "Ghid de alpinism de Cheile Bicazului" and gives good information about each trad route in the area. Yet it is in Romanian, but the most important details of each route are described in one or two sentences in German as well. Unfortunately, the guidebook is

not for sale in Lacul Roşu but you should be able to find it at the following Ascent Mountain shops (make sure to call ahead to check if it is available).

Bucharest
✉ Vasile Lascar street 26-28
✉ Blanari street 10 (tel: +40 213 140781)

Timişoara
✉ Bocsa street 4 (tel: +40 256 437703)
✉ Aristide Demetriade 1 (tel: +40 256 247682) (Inside the Iulius Mall)

Iaşi
✉ Anastasie Panu street 30 (tel: +40 232 278787)

Olivier Batar in action on Fantasmagoria (8a+)

If you weren't able to get the guidebook before arrival, you can try your luck at the house of the Salvamont rescue team, at the northern side of the campsite across the stream. Sometimes team members are willing to lend you a spare guidebook.

Wynand climbing Stynx (6b+), sector Faleza Raza Soaralui

Sector Faleza Raza Soaralui

What else is there to see & do

Hiking
The Bicaz Gorge is rich with numerous fine walking trails, most of them going through canyons with lots of refreshing waterfalls. There are also trails that lead to the top of the crags from where the views are marvellous. Other trails go through the forest and open fields where deer, wolfs and maybe even brown bears can be seen. Ask for a map of the region at one of the kiosks at the Lacul Roşu.

Rowing on Lacul Roşu
At the western end of town lies the lake Lacul Roşu, also called the Killer Lake. The lake itself is a bizarre phenomenon - lots of dead tree stumps stick out of the water. The locals rent rowing boats if you want to have a closer look.

Mythical Lacul Roşu

In total there are 21 different sectors. Sport climbing is possible on 11 of them and the majority of the climbing is in the 7th grade and above. For some difficult climbing in the public view, head for Peretele Polițele Bardosului and Gâtul Ladului. These are the sectors right behind the craft stands along the road. Faleza Raza Soarelui boasts beautiful easier routes in a more quiet part of the Bicaz Gorge. Fantastic difficult routes are found at Lângă Turnul Negru and Faleza "K2" that have beautiful vertical and overhanging crimpy walls.

The new Sector 21 has been opened shortly after our visit. It is supposed to have good routes, also in the easier grades.

The 190m trad route Creasta Estică (4a) on Piatra Altarului is a recommended route to start with as this route is easy and relatively safe with some fixed protection.

Most of the route names and grades are clearly written on the crags in red at the beginning of each route. This goes for both the sport routes as well as for the trad routes, making it easy to find your way around.

Sector Turnul Negru (at the right side)

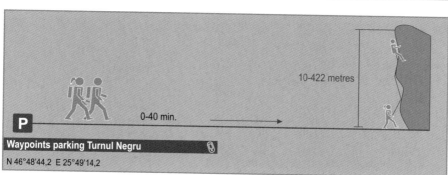

Waypoints parking Turnul Negru

N 46°48'44,2 E 25°49'14,2

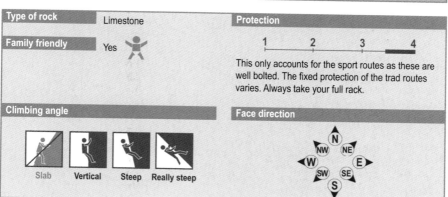

Type of rock	Limestone
Family friendly	Yes

Protection

1   2   3   4

This only accounts for the sport routes as these are well bolted. The fixed protection of the trad routes varies. Always take your full rack.

Climbing angle

Slab   Vertical   Steep   Really steep

Face direction

N NE E SE S SW W NW

Number of routes & Grade range

The routes in the "Ghid de alpinism de Cheile Bicazului" are graded according to the Romanian classification.
3: Slightly difficult
4: Difficult
5: Very difficult
6: Extremely difficult

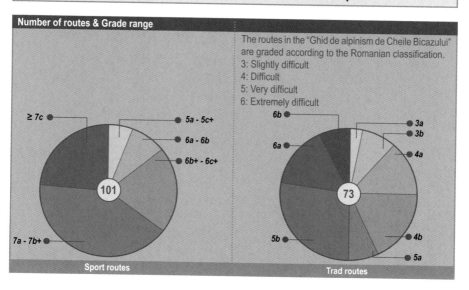

Sector 1 - 20

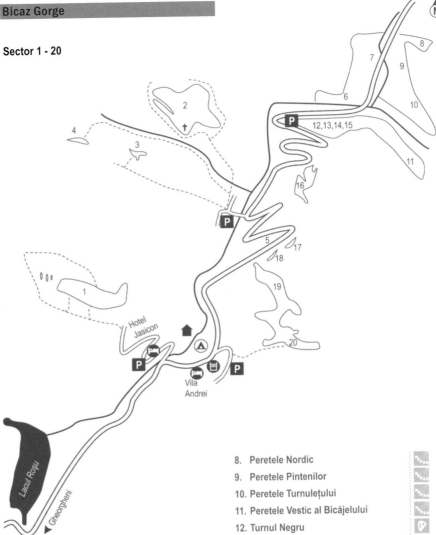

1. Peretele Sudic al Suhardului Mic
2. Piatra Altarului
3. Cuşma Lapoşului
4. Peretele Lapoşului
5. Faleza Ascunsă
6. Peretele Poliţele Bardosului
7. Gâtul Ladului

8. Peretele Nordic
9. Peretele Pintenilor
10. Peretele Turnuleţului
11. Peretele Vestic al Bicăjelului
12. Turnul Negru
13. Bolovanu' lu' Culiţă
14. Lângă Turnul Negru
15. Faleza "K2"
16. Peretele Mariei
17. Faleza Scorpion
18. Faleza "Hornul cu Fereastră"
19. Peretele Nord Vestic din Făgetul Ciucului
20. Faleza Raza Soarelui

Sector 21

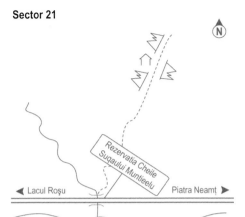

◀ Lacul Roşu   Piatra Neamţ ▶

Directions

▶ Once in the Bicaz Gorge, the sectors can't be missed. See the map for more details about the location of each sector. The new Sector 21 lies close to Bicaz town.

Some of the hardest routes are just behind the craft stands

Climbing area Turda

Spring   Summer   Autumn   Winter

The Turda Gorge (Cheile Turzii) is located in the Apuseni mountains, south of the charming university city Cluj Napoca and west of Turda. This is one of the first places that developed free climbing in Romania. The gorge is not only attractive for climbers, but also for hikers.

The climbing takes place in the gorge itself. There are long traditional climbing routes and shorter sport climbing routes at different sectors. Most of the equipping was done in the mid eighties and again in 2004/2005. Although the Turda Gorge is one of the favourite climbing areas for Romanian climbers, we found the beginning of the sport routes a bit dirty with lots of grass and moss - it feels as if not much climbing is done. On the other hand, once you're past this barrier you'll discover that most of the routes on the slightly fallen facades are surprisingly ok. The majority of the sport routes require technical climbing and need creative solutions in order to reach the top.

The views while climbing the trad routes are amazing and very well worth the climb. There is some fixed protection but you can't always rely on it. Take a set of nuts, friends and some slings.

Salvamont rescue service
In case of an emergency in the Turda Gorge, contact the Salvamont rescue service. Call: +40 744 777867.

When to go

Climbing is possible from spring until autumn. On hot days during summer there is always enough shade to hide from the sun as the gorge is quite narrow. Multi pitch climbing is not recommended during hot days.

Crosing the bridge in the Turda Gorge

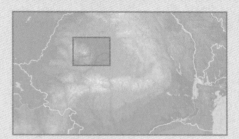

Crag

🅐 **Turda Gorge**

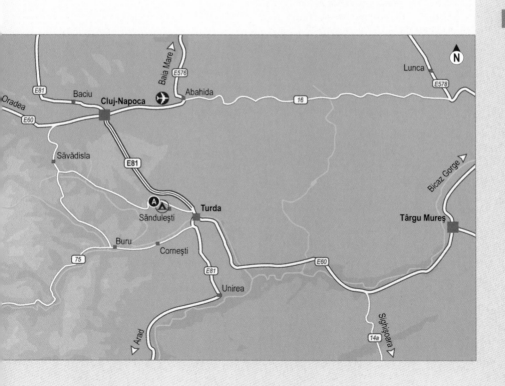

How to get to the area & how to move around

Once you are in the Turda Gorge you don't need your own car, but getting there requires a 5km walk uphill...

 By public transport

First get to Cluj Napoca. There are 7 trains per day to Cluj Napoca from Bucharest [7½ h - 8½ h] as well as from Timişoara [5h -7h]. There are 12 trains per day between Oradea and Cluj Napoca [2½ h- 4½ h].

Once in Cluj Napoca take a bus to Turda. The intercity bus station (Strada Giordano Bruno nr 3-5) in Cluj Napoca is located 5km from the centre. There are seven daily buses from Cluj Napoca to Turda [40min]. From Turda you can catch the bus to Corneşti or the less frequent bus to Câmpeni. Both depart from the Piaţa Republicii in the centre of town. Get off at the junction to Cheile Turzii. From here it is unfortunately a strenuous 5km walk uphill. You could also try to get a lift - the locals are used to hitchhikers.

 By car

The city of Turda lies 30km south of Cluj Napoca. Once in Turda the signs for Cheile Turzii can't be

Turda Gorge

missed. The paved road leads through the village of Sandulesti. After the village the road becomes unpaved. The last part of the road is quite steep and less suitable for mobile homes, especially after heavy rainfall.

Where to stay

Those that love to wild camp are lucky since this is the only option here. Camping is allowed next to the river just before the gorge starts. This flat ground also functions as the parking place. At the weekend it fills up with Romanian day-trippers whose favourite pastime is having barbeques and playing loud music from their sound systems. On other days it is a relaxing spot.

Waypoints campsite and parking:
 N 46°33'41,4 E 23°41'25,5

Where to buy groceries

At the parking / campsite there is a 24 hour (or as they call it themselves) "non-stop" kiosk that sells cold beer and other drinks, as well as a lot of barbequed meat. Groceries are best bought in Turda where many smaller sized supermarkets are found. In Corneşti there are a few very small shops.

Drinking water can be collected in the gorge. Halfway up, on the left side, is a fresh stream running into the brook.

Where to find the local climbing guidebook

You can download a topo for free on *www.roclimbing. net*. This topo gives an overview of the different sectors and shows simple drawings of its routes. All names of the routes are clearly written at the beginning of each route.

What else is there to see & do

Visit Cluj Napoca
This trendy place has everything to offer what you expect from a modern city. From charming neighbourhoods with homely bars and restaurants to churches, ruins of mediaeval times and museums, Cluj Napoca has it all.

Visit the salt mine
A trip to the salt mine of Turda is a fun and interesting thing to do. The impressive mine has salt stalactites up to 3 metres long. The mine is well known for its treatment of people with breathing problems due to its favourable climate. Also the acoustics are great and concerts are given inside.

Hiking
Although the walk through the gorge only takes an hour, there are many hiking trails in the surrounding area. A map, which can be found in front of Cabana Cheile Turzii, shows all the trails. The cost to enter the gorge is 2.5 Lei, which has to be paid at the entrance. The path leading to the entrance starts from the cabana.

Some smooth vertical walls at the Turda Gorge

Turda Gorge

Climbing is possible on both sides of the Turda Gorge. The left side of the gorge faces northwest and has shade in the morning whereas the other side has shade in the late afternoon. The bolts on the sport climbing routes are closely spaced. However, at the time of research, there were some older rusty bolts and pitons on some routes that were equipped a long time ago.

The vast majority of the sport routes is in the 6th grade. The easiest sport routes can be found at Sector Turnul Galben. The most difficult routes are at the cave at Sector Peretele Vulturilor.

Bring the usual equipment for the trad routes.

Neeltje on Gepeto (6a)

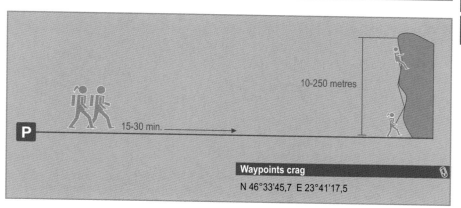

Waypoints crag

N 46°33'45,7 E 23°41'17,5

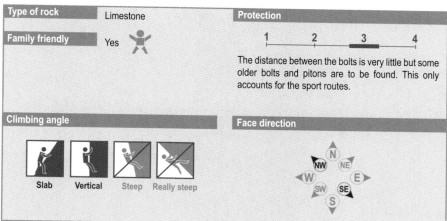

Type of rock	Limestone
Family friendly	Yes

Protection

1   2   3   4

The distance between the bolts is very little but some older bolts and pitons are to be found. This only accounts for the sport routes.

Climbing angle

Slab   Vertical   Steep   Really steep

Face direction

N NE E SE S SW W NW

Number of routes & Grade range

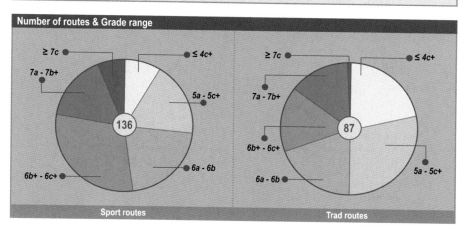

Sport routes

136

≥ 7c
7a - 7b+
6b+ - 6c+
6a - 6b
5a - 5c+
≤ 4c+

Trad routes

87

≥ 7c
7a - 7b+
6b+ - 6c+
6a - 6b
5a - 5c+
≤ 4c+

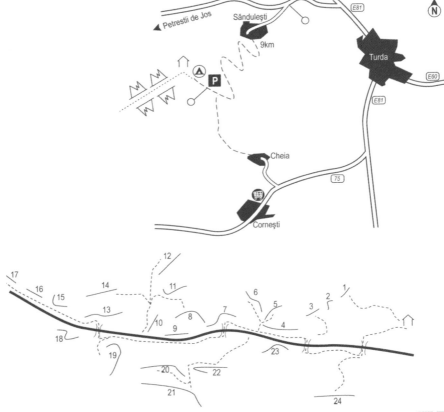

1. Povârnisul Emil Pop (Peretele Cald)
   + Poligonul "Timpuri Noi"
2. Peretele Marac + Turnul Bors
3. Alghinelor
4. Turnul Galben
5. Pripoanelor
6. Peretele Caprelor
7. Peretele Uriaş
8. Peretele Porumbeilor (Gourile)
9. Poligonul de peste apă
10. Turnul despărţitor
11. Zona Turnul Ascuţit
    + Poligonul Unguresc
12. Coasta Călăştur

13. Cetateaua Mică
14. Peretele Aerian
15. Peretele Scoruş
16. Gabor Feri + Colţul Morarilor
17. Moara Petridului
18. Coltul Cetății
19. Creasta Sanşil
20. Zona Coltul Crăpat + Stânca Şoimilor
21. Peretele Suurime
22. Peretele Rotunjit
23. Politele lui Bieltz
24. Peretele Vulturilor
    + Peştera Ungurească

▶ The trail through the gorge, from which all sectors are accessed, starts next to the cabana.

Testing the bolts

Climbing area Cerna Valley

Spring   Summer   Autumn   Winter

Băile Herculane is situated in the Cerna Valley in the southwest of Romania and is mostly known for its Roman thermal baths. The popular town lies beautifully situated along the Cerna River with on both sides high rising impressive limestone crags. Those crags host many excellent well secured routes in splendid surroundings.

Every year in May, an international climbing competition is held in Băile Herculane. If you are planning on going here, try to take part in the event (where the emphasis is more on fun!). Because of this competition, new routes are put up every year, but still only 15% of the crags have been turned into a climbing venue. Most local climbers come from Timişoara and they are always willing to help you to find the latest and best routes. Some of the local climbers also have the habit of taking a thermal bath during the night. So if you are lucky they will also show you the best places to relax after a hard day climbing. Have fun!

Warning: The very poisonous viper snake lives in this area. It is always good to pay attention to snakes but this time be extra careful where to place your hands and feet.

Ane Popa successfully trying a new route at Sector HCO, photo by George Stroie

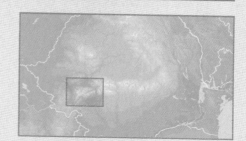

When to go

Climbing is possible from early spring until October. All sectors are either situated on the north, lie in a forest or are in a gorge making it possible to climb here in summer, even on very warm days.

Crag

Ⓐ **Băile Herculane**

How to get to the area & how to move around

A car is not essential to move between the different sectors and your accommodation. You can either walk or take one of the many taxis, which only cost approximately 2 Lei per kilometre.

By public transport

Băile Herculane is on the main Timişoara-Bucharest railway line and has 7 daily trains in either direction. The train from Timişoara to Băile Herculane takes 2½ to 4 hours. From Bucharest it takes about 5 hours to Băile Herculane. The train station in Băile Herculane is near Camping Hercules.

By car

Băile Herculane is situated in the southwest of the country not far from the border with Serbia. The town lies close to the E70 motorway. From Bucharest it is 368km to Băile Herculane and from Timişoara 177km.

Quiet street through the Cerna Valley towards Băile Herculane

Where to stay

Băile Herculane offers many hotels, villas and cazare to choose from. There is one modern campsite and there is a campsite at the Seven Springs with no facilities. Along the Cerna River, next to the road towards Baia de Arama, there are also many places to pitch a tent for free. It gets quieter the further north you go, towards Baia de Arama.

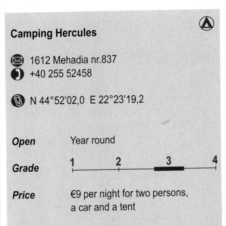

Camping Hercules

✉ 1612 Mehadia nr.837
📞 +40 255 52458

📍 N 44°52'02,0 E 22°23'19,2

Open Year round

Grade
1   2   3   4

Price €9 per night for two persons, a car and a tent

This German run campsite is the best one in the area and the only one with clean toilets and hot water. The campsite lies next to the road to Timişoara and the railway and this makes it quite noisy. Using earplugs is not a bad idea.

Directions
The campsite is located 700 metres from the train station of Băile Herculane along the E70 towards Timişoara.

Sector Cariera, Băile Herculane

Camping Seven Springs

N 44°55'21,3 E 22°26'40,1

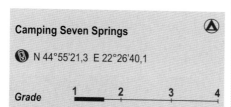

Grade 1 ▬▬▬ 2 ─── 3 ─── 4

During July and August this free campsite is very popular with Romanians due to the thermal waters and nearby 'beach'. So, simply put, it gets overcrowded and noisy during those months, but it is a good place off season.

Directions
The campsite is located at the Seven Springs on the road from Băile Herculane to Baia de Arama.

Vila Jojo

Str. Pecinişca 175
Băile Herculane
+40 255 560965

Price 100 Lei per night for a double room with bathroom

Vila Jojo offers you a bit more comfort. The villa is located at the foot of sector Cariera and has nice clean rooms with a fridge and TV. There is a back garden where you can sit outside and cook your own meal. The owner speaks German.

Where to buy groceries

There are many small supermarkets along the main street that runs from the train station to the old centre in Băile Herculane. Everything is sold at these supermarkets, except for fruits and vegetables. You can buy these at the daily market which is located on the first street on the left coming from the train station.

Where to find the local climbing guidebook

There is no printed guidebook of this area but you can get free downloads of the topo from *www.roclimbing.net*. Once in the area, ask local climbers for the latest routes which might not yet be on the internet. All names of the routes are clearly written on the crags.

Welcome to Băile Herculane

Sector HCO, photos by George Stroie

What else is there to see & do

Taking a thermal bath
Yes it smells bad but, no worries, once you are in you won't notice the odour anymore....Taking a thermal bath is part of the adventure of being in Bäile Herculane and since it is actually good for your muscles, why not try it? There is the choice between the free baths at The Seven Springs and the baths in the hotels, for example in Hotel Roman or Hotel Cerna.

Hiking
The Cerna valley is known for its rich flora and fauna and offers many well marked hiking trails that take you around the whole valley. Information can be found at Camping Hercules or at the receptions of the better hotels in town.

Sighişoara - the Clock Tower

Băile Herculane

Băile Herculane consists of 5 different climbing sectors. Sector Cariera, which is beautifully located, is the largest sector with very diverse and fine routes that will suit every climber. The majority of the routes are single pitch but there are some multi pitch sport routes of 2-3 rope lengths as well as trad routes. The popular Sector Roman and Surplomba, behind Hotel Roman, have the hardest overhanging routes. The newest sector, that is HCO where the international climbing competition is held in 2005 and 2006, offers some of the best moderately difficult routes. Sector Magnolia offers 22 diverse routes. Sector Izvorul Munk is less often climbed and only has 10 routes.

In general it can be said that the routes in Băile Herculane are extremely well equipped with bolts every 1.5 to 2 meters. Many routes have new shiny bolts, although you could encounter a very few rusty bolts and belays.

Lots of fifth grade routes - Marloes warms up on Olive (5b)

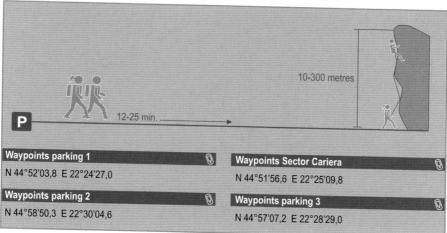

10-300 metres

P 12-25 min.

Waypoints parking 1
N 44°52'03,8 E 22°24'27,0

Waypoints Sector Cariera
N 44°51'56,6 E 22°25'09,8

Waypoints parking 2
N 44°58'50,3 E 22°30'04,6

Waypoints parking 3
N 44°57'07,2 E 22°28'29,0

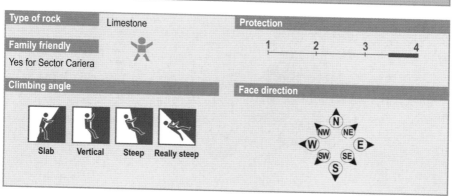

Type of rock Limestone

Family friendly
Yes for Sector Cariera

Climbing angle

Slab   Vertical   Steep   Really steep

Protection

1   2   3   4

Face direction

N NW NE W E SW SE S

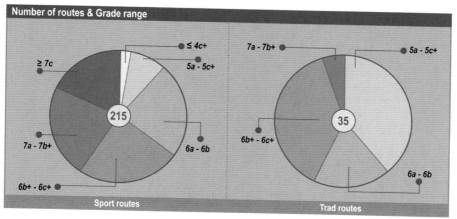

Number of routes & Grade range

≥ 7c
7a - 7b+
6b+ - 6c+
215
≤ 4c+
5a - 5c+
6a - 6b

Sport routes

7a - 7b+
6b+ - 6c+
35
5a - 5c+
6a - 6b

Trad routes

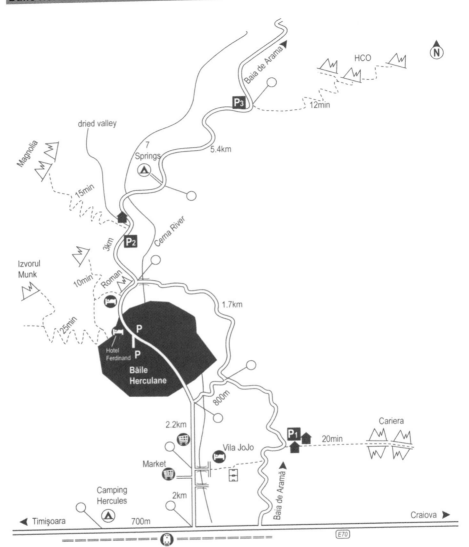

HCO

N

Baia de Arama

P3

12min

dried valley

Magnolia

15min

7
Springs

5.4km

Cerna River

3km

P2

Izvorul
Munk

10min

Roman

25min

Hotel
Ferdinand

P

P

Bäile
Herculane

1.7km

800m

Cariera

2.2km

P1

20min

Vila JoJo

Market

Baia de Aramă

Camping
Hercules

2km

◀ Timişoara

700m

Craiova ▶

E70

▶ Sector Cariera
Coming from the E70 motorway or the train station, go towards the centre of Băile Herculane. After 2km, cross the second bridge on the right where you can park your car if necessary. Walk straight towards the visible crags, passing a soccer field on the right. When you get to the road, follow it to the left until you see some Roma houses on the right. Behind these houses there is a path leading to the crags. Before you start your ascent you can get fresh water from the spring just behind the houses. The path is marked with yellow/white stripes. It takes about 20 minutes to get to the first routes.

▶ Sector Roman
Standing in the centre of Băile Herculane with your back towards the Hercules statue, walk straight in the direction of Hotel Roman. Pass the hotel and you will see Sector Roman and a bit further Sector Surplomba at the left side. Sector Scorpioni and Faleza lie 10 minutes walking from Hotel Roman. Take the path from the rear of Hotel Roman.

▶ Sector Izvorul Munk
To the left of the post office, located on the Hercules Square in the centre of Băile Herculane, a track marked with yellow circles starts with a set of steps. Follow the yellow circles to Sector Izvorul Munk.

▶ Sector HCO
Follow the D67 from Băile Herculane to Baia de Arama. Park the car at the kilometre sign '93' or ask the taxi to stop here. A small white sign indicates the path to the right that goes through the forest. It takes about 12 minutes to get to the crags.

▶ Sector Magnolia
Sector Magnolia is just outside Băile Herculane. Pass Hotel Roman and Sector Roman on your left and head to the main road. Turn left and follow the D67 in the direction of Baia de Arama until you reach an isolated house on the left. There is a small dried up river on the left side of the house. The steep path through the forest to the routes starts on the left bank of the, mostly, dried up river and it takes about 10 minutes to get to them.

Tankball (6b) at Sector HCO

...the green pearl of Europe...

Slovenia

Due to beautiful landscapes, interesting culture and a wide choice of outdoor sports, Slovenia is becoming increasingly popular with active-minded tourists. What's more, this attractive country also boasts over 3,500 perfectly equipped sport routes that are all easy and quick to reach....so a new climbing destination appears!

Slovenia gained independence from the former Republic of Yugoslavia on June 25th 1991 and was one of the first regions to do so. Fortunately Slovenia suffered little ill effects from the Balkan conflicts in the 1990's and, much as Slovenia had always been Tito's most prosperous region, it is now an active and economically vibrant member of the European Union, which they joined on May 1st 2004.

Slovenia is not only a rich country but it is also full of natural riches, situated as it is between the Alps, the plains of Hungary, and the warm Adriatic Sea: it has a truly astonishing range of scenery. Slovenia offers imposing rock climbing areas as well as a multitude of other adventurous activities. Winter sees the country play host to skiing, both cross-country and downhill, snowboarding and ice climbing. Then in summer you can face the rapids of the Soča River and hit the mountains on foot. There are more than enough places to try paragliding and parachuting, and in every region there are countless options for shorter and longer hiking and biking tours. If you are interested in the local culture then Slovenia offers this as well. From the impressive caves, to medieval buildings, interesting museums, and charming smaller towns, Slovenia has it all!

The rock climbing areas in Slovenia are perfect both for those who want to pack in the climbing and also for those who want to make climbing a part of their general holiday. Whatever you chose to do, a trip to Slovenia is guaranteed to be a memorable experience.

Judith van de Geijn on Popajev raz, 6b+, Črni Kal

Bernd Linke on Samsara (8a) at Mišja Peč

Climbing information

A trip to Slovenia gives you the choice of 72 very diverse rock climbing venues. Not all of them are equally big but they all consist of good, well equipped, sport routes on solid rock. The areas are scattered throughout the country, with the majority being in the Alpine region. The largest climbing spots, however, are to be found in the south west of Slovenia and there is also one excellent crag in the east.

We describe the whole of Slovenia split into three main areas and the most exciting, beautiful and largest rock climbing areas are covered.

Climbing area Bled - Bohinj

This area covers the crags scattered between the popular places of Bled and Bohinj in the north west of Slovenia. Due to their fantastic location in the Julian Alps, Bled and Bohinj offer a wide range of other outdoor activities such as hiking, rafting, canoeing, hydro speeding, skydiving and paragliding as well as some very fine rock climbing. The area includes the crags of Bodešče, Bohinjska Bela, Bitenj Potok, Bitnje and Bohinj. It is a perfect destination for those who want to have a generally active holiday in the mountains and it's the perfect place to come with children.

Climbing area Osp - Trieste

The Osp – Trieste climbing area covers the crags around and in the environs of the village of Osp, in the south west of Slovenia, and those around the city of Trieste in Italy. The area has some perfect climbing in an easily accessible location, and also offers a good range of sporting and cultural attractions. This area includes the crags of Osp, Mišja Peč and Črni Kal in Slovenia and Val Rosandra and Napoleonica just across the border in Italy.

Climbing area Celje

This is the best summer climbing destination in Slovenia. Near Celje, in the north eastern part of Slovenia, lie the crags of Kotečnik and the smaller Kamnik, both hidden in a forest. Here you can find excellent single pitch routes, some 272 in total, across the grade range.

Mount Triglav

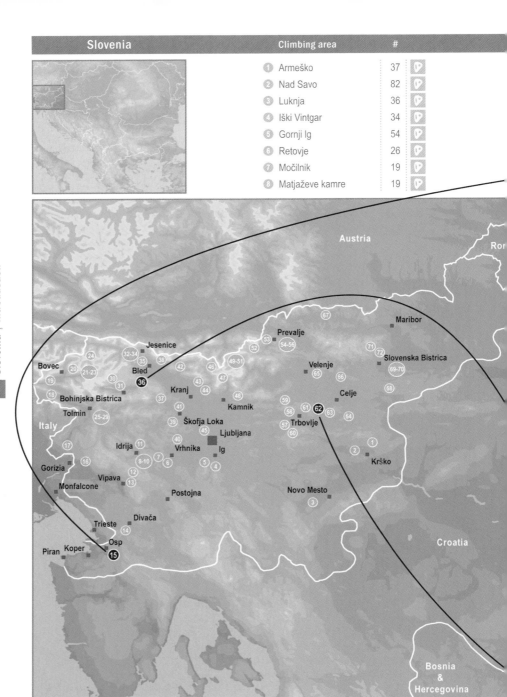

Slovenia	Climbing area	#	
❶	Armeško	37	
❷	Nad Savo	82	
❸	Luknja	36	
❹	Iški Vintgar	34	
❺	Gornji Ig	54	
❻	Retovje	26	
❼	Močilnik	19	
❽	Matjaževe kamre	19	

Climbing area	#
⑨ Gore	38
⑩ Strug	54
⑪ Šnitov rob	20
⑫ Vipavska Bela	129
⑬ Vipava	268
⑭ Risnik	16
⑮ Osp-Trieste	
Osp	**188**
Mišja peč	**181**
Črni kal	**204**
Val Rosandra	**365**
Napoleonica	**178**
⑯ Lijak	29
⑰ Dolge njive	30
⑱ Nadiža	15
⑲ Pri Žvikarju	13
⑳ Kal-Koritnica	28
㉑ Trenta	18
㉒ Pri Pavru	18
㉓ Zadnjiški Ozebnik	5
㉔ Vršič	37
㉕ Pri Čiginju	47
㉖ Senica	37
㉗ Slap ob Idrijci	16
㉘ Lutne skale	55
㉙ Pisano čelo	9
㉚ Peč	31
㉛ Rudnica	12
㉜ Radovna	13
㉝ Blažčeva skala	19
㉞ Kovačevec	22
㉟ Gorje	16
㊱ Bled-Bohinj	
Bodešče	**38**
Bohinjska Bela	**105**
Bitenj potok	**39**
Bitnje	**45**
Bohinj	**83**

Climbing area	#
㊲ Pod Sušo	10
㊳ Završnica	38
㊴ Zminec	28
㊵ Jaklovca	8
㊶ Kamnitnik	46
㊷ Dolžanova soteska	39
㊸ Preddvor	54
㊹ Krvavec	13
㊺ Turnc	82
㊻ Mlinarjeva peč	12
㊼ Kamniška Bistrica	27
㊽ Vranja Peč	8
㊾ Klemenča peč	3
㊿ Logarska dolina	30
(51) Igla	26
(52) Burjakove peči	71
(53) Štenge	28
(54) Matvoz	22
(55) Kot nad Prevaljami	38
(56) Sele	45
(57) Renke	49
(58) Zelenc	9
(59) Vransko	18
(60) Čerjan	24
(61) Pod Reško planino	69
(62) Celje	
Kotečnik	**225**
Kamnik	**47**
(63) Slomnik	20
(64) Sopota	15
(65) Lipje	12
(66) Socka	11
(67) Radlje	15
(68) Boč	22
(69) Šeginov potok	11
(70) Šoder graben	25
(71) Buncove skale	52
(72) Gromberg	12

Climate

The Adriatic coast has a Mediterranean climate with mild winters and warm, sunny summers. Sunshine averages some four hours a day in winter and from ten to twelve hours a day in summer. The coast is backed by hills, and in winter rainfall there can be heavy. The one unpleasant feature of the winter weather is a cold gusty wind, the Bora, which brings cold air from Central and Eastern Europe down to the coast for a few days at a time. Inland climatic conditions change rapidly to become more typical of Eastern Europe, with cold winters and warm summers.

The climbing season starts in April and ends in October. Spring and autumn are nice periods for climbing despite a few rainy days. Summers can be pretty hot but there are usually enough trees to provide shade and, of course, you can always get out of bed early (or, indeed, leave late!).

Month	Average temperature (°C)	Average rainfall (mm)
Jan	-1	88
Feb	1	90
March	5	75
April	10	98
May	15	120
June	18	132
July	20	112
Aug	20	127
Sept	17	143
Oct	10	151
Nov	5	130
Dec	2	114

Climate table Ljubljana

Maja Vidmar on Kindergarten (7a+), Mišja Peč

Getting there

 By plane

Adria Airways is the national carrier and mainly operates flights within Europe. The airline often has special offers and is worth checking out: *www.adria-airways.com*. Also, there are more and more low-cost carriers flying directly to Ljubljana, the capital. Amongst others, Easyjet or Wizzair charge under €100 for a return ticket from London or Brussels, for example.

If you want to climb in the Bled-Bohinj area an alternative is to fly to Klagenfurt in Austria. The low cost airline Hapag-Lloyd Express has direct flights from several destinations in Germany, and Kagenfurt is served by other airlines. If you plan to visit the Osp-Trieste area it is worth checking out the flights to Treviso (an airport near Venetia) or Trieste in Italy. Ryanair and others operate flights to both cities from several European cities. For Celje you are best off booking a flight to Ljubljana.

If you are arriving from outside Europe you will either have to fly to Ljubljana or change flights in Europe.

 By train

Slovenia is well connected to its neighbouring countries by train. There is a daily Viena – Ljubljana service [6½h, €55] and six trains a day head from Munich to the Slovenian capital [6¼h, €63]. The website *http://plannerint.b-rail.be* provides excellent information on international train schedules.

 By bus

Slovenia is also well connected by international bus routes. Amongst others, there are several services daily from Frankfurt to Ljubljana [12h, €80] and from Munich to Ljubljana [6¾h, €38]. Check *www.eurolines.com* for up to date information. From the airport at Klagenfurt there are shuttle buses leaving for Bled.

By boat

Venezia Lines operates catamarans every Tuesday during the summer between Venice in Italy and Piran in Slovenia [2½h, €96 return]. See *www.venezialines.com* for bookings.

 By car

It takes less than a day to drive from most Western European countries to Slovenia. The country is well accessible by car and the border crossings are efficiently organised.

Moving around

If you plan on climbing in Kotečnik and Kamnik you'll need to have a car as getting here by public transport is not possible. For Bled-Bohinj and Osp-Trieste a car is not a necessity, however, it goes without saying that having your own wheels makes your life easier.

Family hiking in the Julian Alps

 Ljubljana airport information

The airport lies 23km north of the capital. There are hourly buses to the centre (less frequent at the weekend). Buses also operate frequently between the airport and the central bus station [¾h, €4]. Tickets are purchased on the bus.

 Trieste airport information

Terravision operates a bus service between Trieste airport and several towns along the Slovenian coast, of which Koper [1¾ h, €15] is one. The bus leaves the airport at 14.40 pm.

 By public transport

Slovenia has an extensive bus network, operated by dozens of private bus companies, with services departing from the central bus station in most cities. The train network is less well developed but is also a very good means of transport. The central bus and train stations are both located next to each other in the centre of Ljubljana (Trg Osvobodilne Fronte 7).

 By car

The country has invested a lot in its infrastructure and the road conditions are very good. Some roads have tolls but, where in place, it is not expensive. It is mandatory to drive with your lights on and be aware that the legal blood alcohol limit is 0%! The fuel prices in Slovenia are only slighter cheaper compared to Western Europe. The AMZS is the automobile association of Slovenia - call +386 1 5305353 for assistance.

Most international car rental agencies, such as Hertz, Budget, and Avis, are located in the bigger cities and at Ljubljana airport. Prices usually start at €50 per day, including unlimited mileage, collision damage waiver and theft protection. Reservations can be made via the internet.

Triglav Lakes

Sometimes cheaper rates for small cars, like a Smart or Ford Ka, are given on the spot.

Car rental in Italy is generally much cheaper, so bear this in mind if you are flying to Italy. Every Italian airport has car rental agencies but some of them will not allow you to take the car into Slovenia, so check carefully. Hertz allows Ryanair customers to drive the rental car into Slovenia and Croatia but only when pre-booked via *www.ryanair.com*. In all cases the trans-border permission should be marked on the hire documents or the car may be refused entry at the border. If you succeed in getting across without the appropriate authorisation, your insurance may well be invalid!

 Hitchhiking

Hitchhiking is fairly common in Slovenia and is also legal, except on motorways and a few major highways. Be aware that hitchhiking always involves taking a certain risk.

Accommodation

There are quite a few campsites spread around the country and the quality is in most cases good. Camping in the wild is illegal in Slovenia and checks are even made, especially around Bled. Prices in the low season are unsurprisingly cheaper than in the high season, being the months of July and August. Expect to pay €14 in the low season and €22 in the high season for two adult persons, a car and a tent.

Renting an apartment is also a possibility and they are widely available in tourist areas. Look out for signs along the roads for 'Sobe'. In the low season booking in advance is not necessary. The average price for a decent two-person apartment in the low season is €35, going up to €50 in the high season.

The price for a hotel depends of course on the location and season. Prices start at around €13 for a youth hostel. Expect to pay about €100 for a two-person room in a mid range hotel in the high season.

Food & Drinks

The best way to describe the food and sort of restaurants found in Slovenia is to say that Italian influences are obvious – pizzerias are abundant! In a bar and a restaurant you'll pay between €0.85 and €1.30 for a good cappuccino and half a litre of local beer costs €1.50. Meals start at €5 for spaghetti or pizza and €10 for a steak. Soup as a starter usually costs around €2.

The range of goods on offer in supermarkets is the same as anywhere else and prices are slightly lower than in Western Europe. Just outside cities, along the highway, you are likely to find huge supermarkets, often belonging to the company "Mercator", selling everything from fruits to washing machines.

Rafting on the Soča River

Climbing guidebook

There is one guidebook, "Slovenija, Športnoplezalni vodnik", published by Sidarta, that describes all rock climbing areas in Slovenia (€30). The latest edition is from 2005. This guidebook gives clear topos and text is written in Slovenian, English, German and Italian.

Another guidebook, "Climbing without frontiers", also published by Sidarta, covers the crags around Osp, in the south, around Trieste in Italy and all the rock climbing areas on the Istrian peninsula in Croatia (€25). This excellent guide is written in Slovenian, English, German and Italian.

At most crags in Slovenia the route names are written on the rock, making for easy route finding most of the time.

Both climbing guides can be bought at:

Pro Montana
✉ Ljubljanska cesta 1
Bled
☎ +386 45 780660
@ info@promontana.si
🌐 www.promontana.si

Annapurna
✉ Krakovski nasip 4
1000 Ljubljana
☎ +386 14 263428
@ info@annapurna.si
🌐 www.annapurna.si

Tecnosport
✉ Via Imbriana 5
34122 Trieste (Italy)
☎ +39 040 306440
@ tecno.sport@virgilio.it

Aventura
✉ Via Madonna Del Mare 21
Trieste (Italy)
☎ +39 040 307325

Steep climbing at Mišja Peč, photo by Hermann Erber

Facts about Slovenia

Facts & figures

Population:	2 million
Religion:	Roman Catholic (82%)
Capital:	Ljubljana
Time zone:	GMT+1
Telephone code:	+386

Money

Currency:	Euro (as of January 2007)
ATM machines:	widespread

Language

Good day	*Pozdravljeni*
Thank you	*Hvala*
Goodbye	*Nasvidenje*
Yes / No	*Da / Ne*
Right / Left / Straight	*Desno / Levo / Naravnost naprej*
Rock climbing	*Plezanje po skali*

Visas & formalities

EU	*Other European nationalities*	*USA / Canada*	*All other nationalities*
No visa for a period of up to 90 days.	Most other European nationalities do not require a visa for a period of up to 90 days.	No visa for a period of up to 90 days.	Most other nationalities do not require a visa for a period of up to 90 days.

Safety

The crime rate in Slovenia is very low and it is a very safe and pleasant country to visit.

Use of mobile phone

There is excellent mobile coverage almost everywhere.

Internet access

There is internet access in most towns and this costs €4 per hour.

Emergency numbers

Police:	113
Fire brigade:	112
Ambulance:	112

Water

The tap water is safe to drink throughout the country.

Climbing area Bled-Bohinj

If you are interested in doing more in the great outdoors than just rock climbing, this is the place to be! The Bled – Bohinj region has some very diverse climbing in a spectacular mountain setting with crystal clear lakes and rivers.

The charming town of Bled lies on a beautiful emerald green lake, and a fantastically situated island with a baroque church on it is justifiably well photographed. Bled itself lies at the edge of the Triglav National Park. The national park is named after Mount Triglav, the highest peak in Slovenia. According to an ancient Slavic legend, Triglav is a three-headed god who keeps a watchful eye over the earth, sky and underworld. The summit is at 2864 meters above sea level and, when viewed from a distance, it clearly dominates the rest of the Julian Alps. In addition to alpine valleys and mountain ridges, other distinctive natural features in the park include high mountain

Spring   Summer   Autumn   Winter

lakes, waterfalls and beautiful gorges. It goes without saying that there is enough trekking and touring to keep anyone happy here.

Water-lovers can enjoy the astonishing Slovene rivers on raft or canoe, and by hydro speeding or canyoning. If you like heights you can also try paragliding. Then there are many easy, moderate and difficult mountain bike routes. If you want to try any of these activities, prices are reasonable and it won't ruin your budget too much.

The Bled-Bohinj area has a wide range of sport routes in various grades and everyone, from beginners to advanced climbers, will find something to suit. The area has five different crags on compact

Gondolas at lake Bled waiting for their first customers

limestone and in total there are around 310 routes. You won't get bored here!

When to go

The weather and climate in this area is very similar to southern Austria. Climbing is possible from April to October, although you can encounter rainy days in spring and autumn. Summer can be really hot but some of the crags have shade provided by the trees in the forest in which they are situated.

Crag

Ⓐ Bodešče

Ⓑ Bohinjska Bela

Ⓒ Bitenj potok

Ⓓ Bitnje

Ⓔ Bohinj

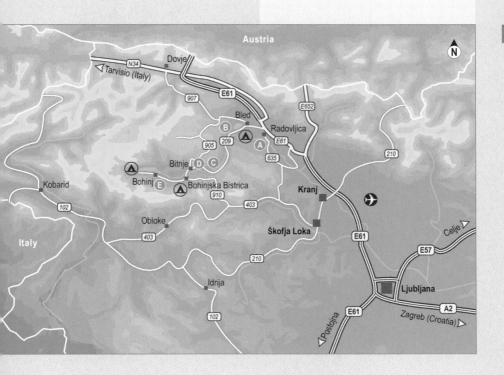

How to get to the area & how to move around

Your need of a car really depends on where you are planning to stay in the area. A car will save you a lot of time getting to the crags, although some of these can easily be reached by other means of transport, by bus or mountain bike.

 By public transport

If you're short of money but long on time then a very good and cheap option is to fly to Trieste in Italy (or even to Treviso and then by train to Trieste [2.5 hours]). There is a daily bus to Ljubljana that leaves at 14.00 pm from the central bus station, except on Sundays [2¾h, €12]. From the Ljubljana bus station (Trg Osvobodilne fronte 4) there are hourly services to Bohinj [2h, €8] via Bled [1¼h, €6].

There are hourly buses from the central bus station of Bled to Bohinj [1h, €3.50]. The bus passes the small villages of Bohinjska Bela, Bitenj Potok and Bitnje before stopping in Bohinj. Ask the driver to drop you at the turn-off for your desired village. To get to the crag of Bodešče a car or bike is required.

 By car

Bled is only 360km from Munich, 400km from Innsbruck, 750km from Frankfurt, 1150km from Utrecht and 1200km from Paris and thus easy reachable in one day by car from these countries!

Those not arriving by car can rent one in Bled - there are several car rental companies based there. The usual agencies are located on Ljubljanska cesta.

If you're feeling active, you can also rent a mountain bike to get around. As the whole area is very popular with mountain bikers you'll find numerous places to rent one. Prices are around €10 per day. Amongst others, the tourist office of Bled (Ljubljanska 4), Camping Šobec and Camping Bled rent bikes. The two crags closest to Bled (Bodešče and Bohinjska Bela) are within easy reach by bike. Bohinj lies the furthest away from Bled and it takes about one hour and a half to get there.

Where to stay

There are many campsites, private rooms, and apartments in this region and all are clearly signposted from the road. All types of accommodation can be booked through the tourist offices in Bled and Bohinj. Expect to pay around €50/€65 (low/high season) for a 4-person apartment with 2 bedrooms. A private room costs around €8.50/€13 (low/high season).

The most interesting place in the area, and hence our recommended base, is Bled. This picturesque village at the foothills of the Julian Alps, just across the Austrian border, receives a lot of tourist traffic during the summer. And this is not without reason as the scenery is almost impossibly romantic and incredibly beautiful. Bled makes an ideal base from where to explore the surrounding crags, and trying your hand at the many other activities in the area from here is easy.

Another option to stay is near the lake of Bohinj Jezero or somewhere in between Bled and Bohinj, in one of the small villages on the way. (The Bohinj valley contains the lake of Bohinjsko

Many houses near Bled offer Bed & Breakfast

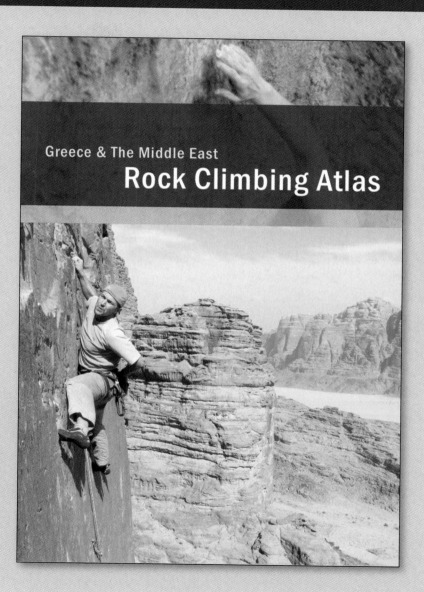

Also available

This edition covers the best climbing areas in:

Egypt, Greece, Jordan, Lebanon, Syria and Turkey

Greece & The Middle East

Rock Climbing Atlas

Jezero - Bohinj is sometimes also called Bohinjsko Jezero.) Bohinj lies 30 kilometres south west of Bled. It is a bit more off the beaten track and less touristy than Bled but still has the full complement of medieval churches and awe-inspiring scenery, being on a magnificent lake surrounded by high mountains. Bohinj has everything you need for a quiet holiday - fresh air, the opportunity for lakeside walks and hikes in wild scenery. There is also a lot to do for the more active minded and there are plenty of mountain biking, hiking and water sports on offer.

Camping Šobec

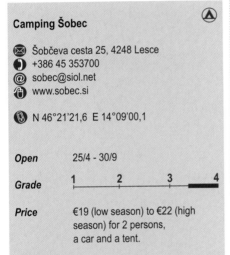

✉ Šobčeva cesta 25, 4248 Lesce
☎ +386 45 353700
@ sobec@siol.net
🏠 www.sobec.si

📍 N 46°21'21,6 E 14°09'00,1

Open	25/4 - 30/9

Grade   1 ——— 2 ——— 3 ——— 4

Price	€19 (low season) to €22 (high season) for 2 persons, a car and a tent.

This is probably the best campsite in Slovenia! Camping Šobec lies next to a river overlooking the mountains. It is a very large campsite and is ideal for families. The campsite is full of trees giving sheltered and quiet camping spots with lots of shade. There is a tennis court, a swimming area in the river, shops, and several clean restroom buildings. There are more facilities than at Camping Bled but it is further away from the centre.

Directions
Arriving from Austria on the A2 in the direction to Ljubljana follow the sign for Bled. The campsite is 4km before Bled and is clearly signposted.

Camping Bled

✉ Kidričeva 10c, 4260 Bled
☎ +386 45 752000
@ info@camping.bled.si
🏠 www.camping.bled.si

📍 N 46°21'41,4 E 14°4'50,2

Open	1/4 - 25/9

Grade   1 ——— 2 ——— 3 ——— 4

Price	€14 (low season) to €20 (high season) for 2 persons, a car and a tent.

The Bled campsite lies in a beautiful location close to the lake, two kilometres from the town centre. This family friendly campsite offers activities for children and has a small grocery and restaurant. It is a clean campsite with modern restrooms.

Directions
Arriving from Austria on the A2 in the direction to Ljubljana follow the sign for Bled. Once in Bled drive towards the lake. Follow the road along the lake eastwards and after 2.5 kilometres you will find Camping Bled on the left.

Camping Šobec

Camping Danica

📧 Triglavska 60
SLO-4265 Bohinjska Bistrica
📞 +386 4 5721055
@ tdbohinj@bohinj.si
🌐 www.bohinj.si/camping-danica

📍 N 46°16'27,5 E 13°56'52,4

Open 1/5 - 30/9

Grade 1 —— 2 —— **3** —— 4

Price Price range: €14 (low season)
to €18 (high season) for 2 persons,
a car and a tent.

This basic but good campsite in the village of Bohinjska Bistrica is situated along the river Sava Bohinjka. Bohinjska Bistrica is a good starting point for a range of activities.

Directions
Follow the campsite sign once you are in Bohinjska Bistrica (a town along the Bled-Bohinj road).

Camping Zlatarog

📧 Ukanc 2
SLO-4265 Bohinsjko Jezero
📞 +386 45 723482
@ alpinum.bohinj@eunet.si

📍 N 46°16'44,4 E 13°50'9,6

Grade 1 —— **2** —— 3 —— 4

Price €12 (low season) to €16 (high season) for 2 persons, a car and a tent.

This basic campsite is nicely located on the shore of beautiful Lake Bohinj. The site is good for caravans but not for tents because of the rocky ground. It is 3.5 kilometres from the crags of Bohinj and the centre of town.

Directions
From the centre of Bohinj follow the road on the left hand side of the lake for about 3.5 kilometres. The campsite is well signposted.

Where to buy groceries

Bled has a reasonably sized supermarket along the main road just before you enter town, coming from the highway. It is located on the right hand side of the road. It has a reasonable selection of food. There is a smaller supermarket next to the tourist office. A few kilometres from Bled along the road leading to the Ljubljana highway there is a big 'Spar' supermarket selling all you need.

In Bohinj, Bohinjska Bistrica and Ribčev Laz there are only small supermarkets.

Church at Lake Bohinj

Lake Bled

Where to find the local climbing guidebook

There is one outdoor shop located along the main road in Bled. It sells the guidebooks 'Slovenija, Športnoplezalni vodnik' and 'Climbing without frontiers'.

Pro Montana

✉ Ljubljanska cesta 1, Bled
☎ +386 45 780660
@ info@promontana.si
🌐 www.promontana.si

What else is there to see & do

Ljubljana
Out of 2 million Slovenians, about 14% live in Ljubljana. Do not let the less attractive view from the concrete suburbs discourage you in visiting the capital. Ljubljana has a very attractive old town centre where you can stroll around and visit the many small cafes. You can visit its castle, museums, galleries, and theatres or just wander along the Ljubljana river and enjoy the local hospitality.

Kranj
South east of Bled the city of Kranj is dramatically situated against the Alps in the Gorenjska region. In the Middle Ages Kranj developed into an important commercial centre and gained city status in the 13th century. Its location and architecture makes a visit to this city a nice day out.

Hiking
Of course the thing to do in Triglav National Park is to climb the mountain itself. The routes to the top are open only between June and October and, although hiring a guide or joining a guided group is not strictly necessary, it is advisable, except for the experienced. There are many trails leading to the top and they start from various points. The easiest way up is from the southern side, from Pokljuka. The northern face of the mountain has some excellent, Alpine style, climbing routes over a range of grades. But there are also some moderate

trails from the north side. One of the best ways to climb Triglav is to start from the north and descend down through the majestic Seven Lakes Valley, to the southwest. Most climbers spend two nights on the route.

The tourist information agency in Bled and Bohinj offers plenty of information if you are planning a hiking trip. They sell good maps of the park, with the trails and mountain huts marked, and they can help you out with hut bookings. There are also private agencies where you can sign up for guided tours. A guided two days tour to the top of the Triglav costs €130 per person (minimum of two persons) and becomes less expensive when more people join the group.

A very popular and gorgeous hike takes in the Vintgar gorge, only 4.5km from Bled, formed by a small mountain river. The gorge is 3km long and is only a few metres wide in places. The beautiful wooden path along the river is mostly fixed directly onto the canyon sides. The Vintgar gorge carves its way through the vertical rocks and is graced by the Radovna with its waterfalls, pools and rapids. The path leads you over numerous bridges, and ends with a sixteen metres high waterfall.

Small village near Bled

Mountain biking

Renting a mountain bike and discovering the beauty of the area via the sometimes hard mountain bike trails is very worthwhile. Maps of those routes are available at the tourist offices and mountain bikes can be rented at many locations (around €10 for a day). It is also possible to take part in an organised mountain bike tour organised by the ubiquitous outdoor activities agencies.

River activities

The Soča River and its challenging rapids has everything to give to the truly adventurous. Here, you can not only test your strength in kayaks, canoes, and rafts but you can also try canyoning through the narrow gorges and small rivers, or plunging over waterfalls into deep pools with hydrospeed boards.

Taking on the challenges of the Soča River

Adrenaline combined with white water is the name of the game on the Sava and the Savinja, as well as many other Slovenian rivers. Many of these adventures can be arranged with experienced guides from sport agencies. They also organize kayak and canoe schools and rent out the necessary equipment. On the more sedate parts of the rivers, family rafting is an option as well. Try Pro Montana (Ljubljanska cesta 1), in Bled, or Pac Sports (Ribčev Laz 50), near the Lake Bohinj. The website *www.pac-sports.com* provides all the information.

Rafting starts at €20 for two to three hours, canyoning costs around €45 for three hours and kayaking starts at €30. All prices include a guide, equipment, and transport.

Skydiving, gliding and paragliding

Mostly the same agencies also offer paragliding flights. You can choose to do a tandem flight or to take a 5-day course. For skydiving or gliding you will have to go to Lesce-Bled Airport (Begunjska cesta 10). They offer several courses for beginners and the more advanced, and offer tandem jumps. See *www.alc-lesce.si* for more information. A guided flight in a glider with a height difference of 1000 metres costs around €70.

Ljubljana

N|H|L
CLIMBING

PROGRESSIVE CLIMBING WEAR

Bodešče

This small local crag with 38 routes lies just outside the village of Bodešče. The crag is next to the Sava Bohinjka, a beautiful alpine river that pours out of the Lake Bohinj. At this point in the river the water flows gently through. The routes on the slightly fallen wall are characterised by pinches as well as slopers - in any case the routes are not easy, with the majority being harder than 7a. There are no route names written on the rock and route finding is a bit tricky here. During hot days the trees provide some relief from the sun. Make sure you bring enough insect repellent to protect yourself from the annoying mosquitoes!

Bodešče

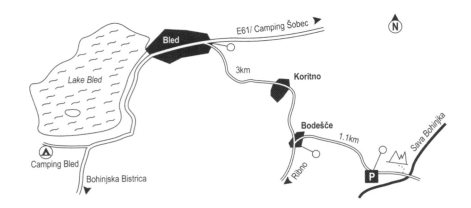

Directions

▶ Bodešče is only 3.5km from Bled. Drive from Bled in the direction of Koritno and Bodešče. In the village of Bodešče turn left for Radovljica and follow the small street down to the Sava River. The small crag pops up after 1.1km on your left, just before the bridge that crosses the Sava River. Park your car here.

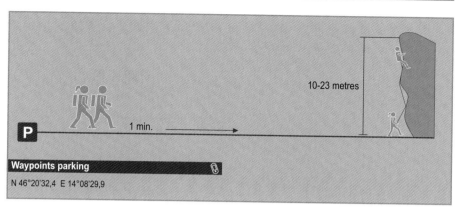

Waypoints parking

N 46°20'32,4 E 14°08'29,9

10-23 metres

1 min.

P

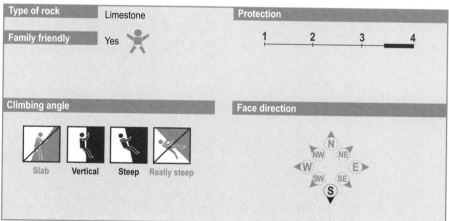

Type of rock	Limestone
Family friendly	Yes

Protection

1   2   3   4

Climbing angle

Slab   **Vertical**   **Steep**   Really steep

Face direction

N   NE   E   SE   S   SW   W   NW

Number of routes & Grade range

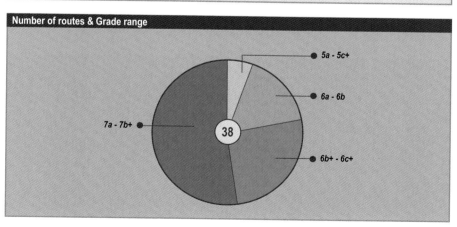

38

- 5a - 5c+
- 6a - 6b
- 6b+ - 6c+
- 7a - 7b+

Bohinjska Bela, just a few kilometres southwest of Bled, definitely has the best climbing in the Bled-Bohinj area. There are three different sectors both on the left and right bank of the Sava Bohinjka.

Sector A lies 1.1 kilometres from the village and is located in the forest. It is an excellent slightly overhanging wall with the majority of the 39 routes graded above 7a, including some very challenging 8a's. Climbing here is comfortable on hot days as the crag faces east.

Sector B lies just in the back garden of the village of Bohinjska Bela. As with everywhere in Slovenia, the routes are well equipped although the first bolt is occasionally placed somewhat high. The rock, with many small pockets, is rather sharp and has good friction. Sector B has 33 routes.

Sector C, actually named Kupljenik, is one of the newest crags around Bled. The slightly fallen wall offers excellent routes of which, again, the majority are graded above 7a. Every route here will, without any doubt, get you pumped to the max as many of the holds are either slopers or pinches! It sure is a tough crag but great if you are into this type of climbing. The crag is hidden in a forest and, as it gets almost no sun, it is the perfect place to escape the heat on warm summer days. There is great potential for new routes and new ones do keep on appearing. All route names and grades are shown on an information board at the crag.

Climbing at Kupljenik

Bohinjska Bela

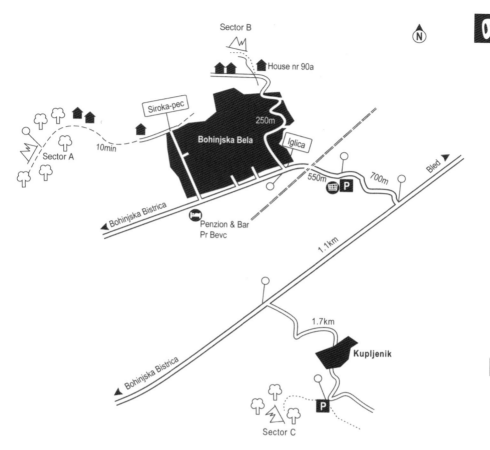

Directions

▶ Bohinjska Bela lies only 4 kilometres from Bled. From the Bled – Bohinjska Bistrica road take the turn to Bohinjska Bela and park at the central supermarket if you intend to climb at either Sector A or B. Don't drive into the village as there is almost no space to park. Follow the sign for 'Iglica' for sector B. The trail starts between the small stream and the house number 90A. It is about a 250 metres walk from the parking and the start of the trail. To get to Sector A don't follow the 'Iglica' sign but continue to the northwest side of the village. Turn left at the sign for 'Siroka-pec' and continue until you see the sector on your right hand side. The last part is a few minutes uphill through the forest.

▶ For Sector Kupljenik don't take the right turn off the Bled-Bohinjska Bela road but continue and take the next road on the left. The small road leads to the village of Kupljenik. There is a car park on the right after the village. Don't follow the big trail up – instead take the small trail into the forest which leads uphill to the crag.

Climbing above the village of Bohinjska Bela

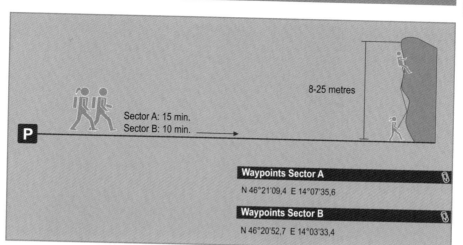

8-25 metres

Sector A: 15 min.
Sector B: 10 min.

P

Waypoints Sector A

N 46°21'09,4 E 14°07'35,6

Waypoints Sector B

N 46°20'52,7 E 14°03'33,4

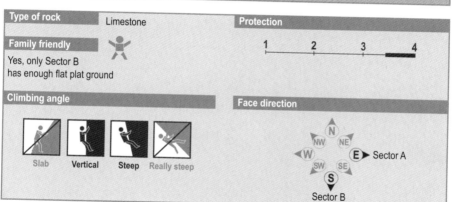

Type of rock Limestone

Family friendly
Yes, only Sector B
has enough flat plat ground

Protection

1   2   3   4

Climbing angle

Slab   **Vertical**   **Steep**   Really steep

Face direction

N
NW   NE
W   (E) ▶ Sector A
SW   SE
S
Sector B

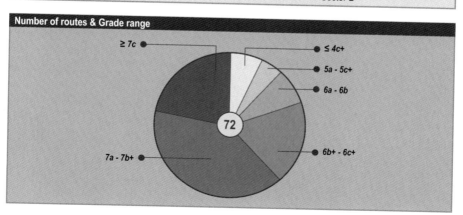

Number of routes & Grade range

≥ 7c

≤ 4c+

5a - 5c+

6a - 6b

72

6b+ - 6c+

7a - 7b+

Maja Vidmar enjoying the shade at Kupljenik

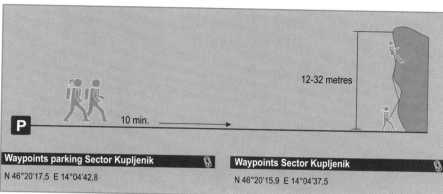

Waypoints parking Sector Kupljenik

N 46°20'17,5 E 14°04'42,8

Waypoints Sector Kupljenik

N 46°20'15,9 E 14°04'37,5

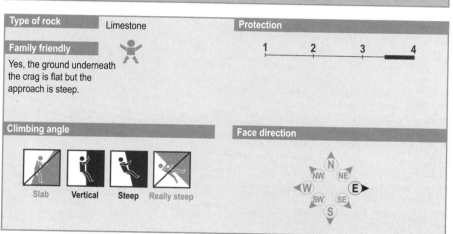

Type of rock   Limestone

Family friendly
Yes, the ground underneath the crag is flat but the approach is steep.

Protection

1   2   3   4

Climbing angle

Slab   Vertical   Steep   Really steep

Face direction

N NE NW W E SW SE S

Number of routes & Grade range

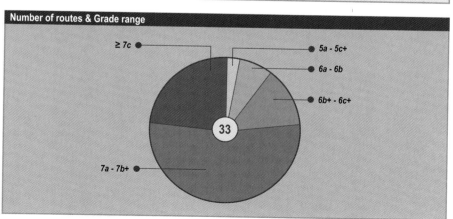

≥ 7c

5a - 5c+

6a - 6b

6b+ - 6c+

7a - 7b+

33

Bitenj Potok

The crags of Bitenj Potok are split by a small waterfall, which gives the place a scenic touch. At the time of writing the crags were still in development but they already contained over 40 really diverse and attractive routes. The majority of the routes fall between 6c and 7b with a strong emphasis on 6c's and 7a's. The climbing is mostly on vertical walls with, every now and then, a few moves on steeper sections. The crag has one three pitch route of 50 metres at 6b+/7a+/6c. Watch out for stone fall!

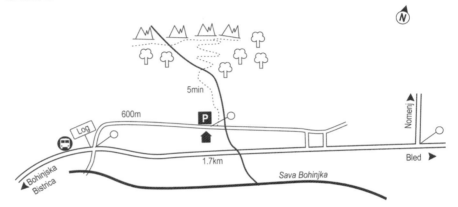

Directions

Local climbers enjoying their weekend at Bitenj Potok

► The crags of Bitenj Potok are about a 15 kilometres drive from Bled. Although the crags are clearly visible from the main Bled - Bohinjska Bistrica road, the waterfall isn't. Turn right just after the village of Nomenj (coming from Bled) at the sign "Log" by the bus stop. Follow the unpaved road and park after you have crossed a stream.

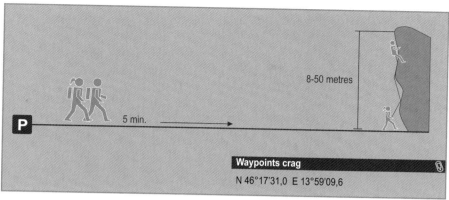

Waypoints crag

N 46°17'31,0 E 13°59'09,6

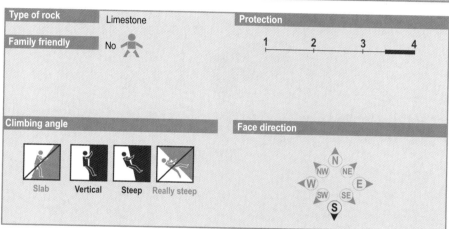

Type of rock — Limestone

Family friendly — No

Protection

1   2   3   4

Climbing angle

Slab   **Vertical**   **Steep**   Really steep

Face direction

N NE E SE S SW W NW

Number of routes & Grade range

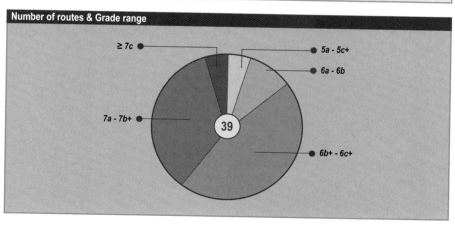

39

≥ 7c
7a - 7b+
5a - 5c+
6a - 6b
6b+ - 6c+

Bitnje

The impressive rock formation above the village of Bitnje offers many fine single pitch routes on beautiful compact rock. There is a lot of variety in the difficulty although, frankly, the fun starts at 6b. Technically proficient climbers will enjoy the routes here - power alone is simply not enough to get you to the top!

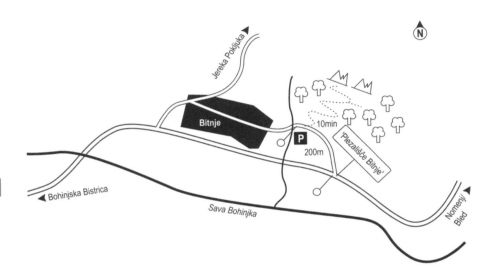

Directions

▶ The crags of Bitnje lie 17 kilometres from Bled and are also situated along the Bled - Bohinjska Bistrica road. Take the road to Bitnje and make another right turn immediately. Park after the stream at a small basketball court. Follow the trail which is indicated by a sign for 'Plezališče Bitnje' up through the forest.

Bitnje

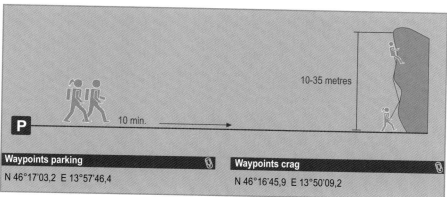

10-35 metres

10 min.

Waypoints parking

N 46°17'03,2 E 13°57'46,4

Waypoints crag

N 46°16'45,9 E 13°50'09,2

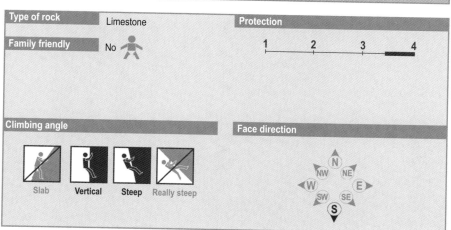

Type of rock	Limestone

Family friendly No

Protection

1 2 3 4

Climbing angle

Slab **Vertical** **Steep** Really steep

Face direction

N
NW NE
W E
SW SE
S

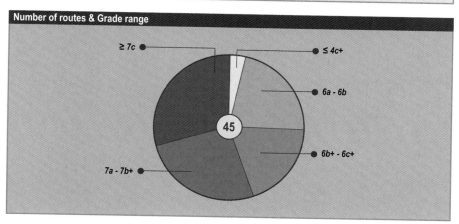

Number of routes & Grade range

≥ 7c
≤ 4c+
6a - 6b
45
6b+ - 6c+
7a - 7b+

There are two different sectors at Bohinj, not too far away from each other. The first one (Sector A) is the ideal crag for beginners and children due to its slabby wall and, as with everywhere in Slovenia, the very well bolted routes. Also, given you can park the car underneath the crags and as there is a small open field, it is a very suitable place to bring young children. Besides the many easy routes at Sector A there are also a few more challenging routes in the higher grades. In total there are 45 routes at this sector.

All of what was said for Sector A also holds true for Sector B, only the routes there are tougher. Sector B is situated directly next to the lake. This imposing vertical and slightly overhanging face, with few jugs, is definitely not the place for beginners. This sector has a few multi pitch routes too. Unfortunately the easier routes are polished. In high season don't be surprised to find a large audience watching you while you struggle to the top, while having a cold drink on the terrace! Sector B has 38 routes.

Bohinj, Sector B

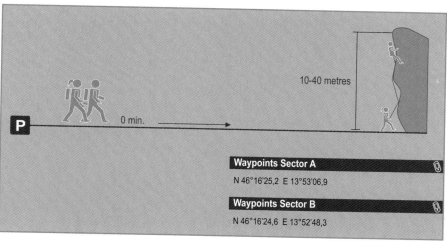

Waypoints Sector A

N 46°16'25,2 E 13°53'06,9

Waypoints Sector B

N 46°16'24,6 E 13°52'48,3

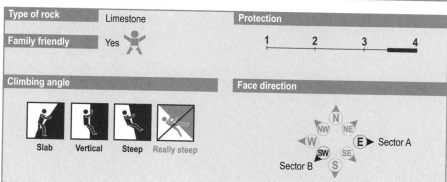

| Type of rock | Limestone |
| Family friendly | Yes |

Protection

1   2   3   4

Climbing angle

Slab Vertical Steep Really steep

Face direction

Sector A
Sector B

Number of routes & Grade range

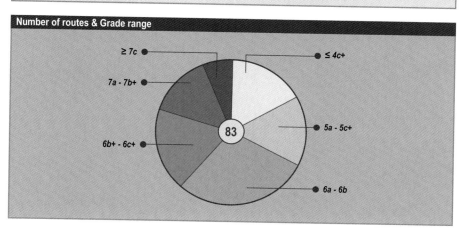

≥ 7c
7a - 7b+
6b+ - 6c+
≤ 4c+
5a - 5c+
6a - 6b

83

The super child-friendly Sector B at Bohinj

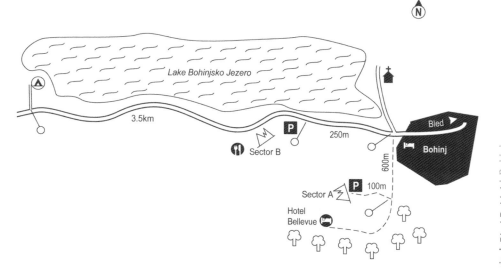

Directions

Relaxed climbing at Bohinj, Sector A

▶ Coming from Bled, follow the signs to Bohinjska Jezero. It is a good 27 kilometres to Bohinj. To get to Sector A follow the road to Hotel Bellevue in Bohinj. Turn right just before the hotel shows up and follow the small, unpaved road. There is a parking directly next to the crag at the end of the road.

For Sector B continue along the lakeside road. The crag appears after 200 metres on your left and can't be missed.

Climbing area Osp-Trieste

Spring   Summer   Autumn   Winter

Undeniably the most popular climbing area in Slovenia is Osp. Osp is a small charming village in the south west of Slovenia, just across the border from Italy. Behind the village are some very beautifully shaped walls of rock. 'Osp' refers to three different crags – the walls behind Osp itself, Mišja Peč just a few hundred meters away, and Črni Kal some 4km from Osp. Together those three crags have 573 routes and across the complete range of grades. If this is not enough for you, or if you'd like to have a change in atmosphere, then it is also very easy to jump over the border with Italy to go climbing at the crags of Val Rosandra and Napoleonica. Those two crags are close to Trieste and only a 20 minute drive from Osp.

The combination of excellent climbing on beautiful rock, the proximity of the sea, which makes for very appealing rest days, the outstanding surroundings, and the mild climate make this area one of the best in Europe.

When to go

The sea nearby tempers the climate and it is possible to climb here all year round, although sunless winter days might be a bit unpleasant. In midsummer it gets too hot to climb around midday, but climbing early in the morning or late afternoon is fine. There are always certain sectors that lie in the shade during parts of the day and at Črni Kal the trees provide extra cover. Definitely the best time to visit this area is during spring and autumn.

Osp

Crag

- Ⓐ Osp
- Ⓑ Mišja peč
- Ⓒ Črni kal
- Ⓓ Val Rosandra
- Ⓔ Napoleonica

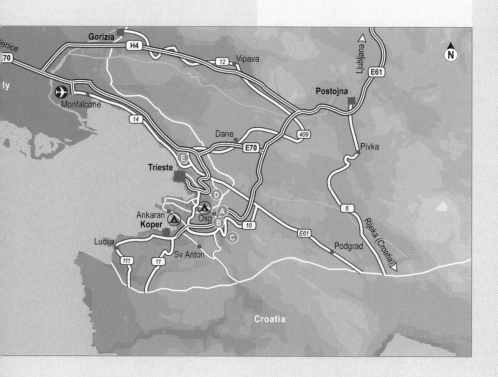

How to get to the area & how to move around

If you don't have your own car, you can reach the area in several ways but you'll find it difficult to move between the different crags described here. Then again the crags of Osp and Mišja Pec are within easy walking distance of the Osp campsite and you'll find plenty of routes there to keep you busy for a week.

 By public transport

You can either fly to Treviso in Italy and take the train to Trieste, or fly directly to the latter. Next to the Trieste train station is the bus station from where there are frequent services to Koper [50 min, €3]. Check *www.saf.ud.it* (look under orari-internazionali) for schedules.

From Koper you can get an infrequent bus to Osp. However, you are better off taking the number 11 bus to Črni Kal, which goes more frequently [20 minutes]. To get to the campsite in Osp ask the driver to drop you at the junction of Črni Kal/Osp. From here it is a 15 minute walk.

From Ljubljana the best option is to take a bus to Koper, which goes 10 times daily [2.5h, €11]. Koper is also well connected by bus with Croatia (Rovinj, Rijeka and Pula).

 By car

If you enter Slovenia in the north from Austria, it only takes 2 hours to get to Osp from the border since the road is a dual-carriageway for most of its length. Osp is only 20 minutes from Trieste by car and 4 hours from Milan.

Where to stay

If you have your own transport there are many accommodation options to choose from. You can either stay at the campsite in Osp or along the Adriatic Coast near either Koper, Izola, Piran or Portorož. There are several campsites around but the one is Osp is definitely the most conveniently located, especially for those who don't have a car. From here it only takes a few minutes to walk to the crags of Osp and Mišja Pec. It is even possible to

Piran

walk to the crags of Črni Kal if you don't have any other means of transport. This would take about an hour. It takes 20 to 30 minutes to drive to the crags in Italy from Osp.

If you are after an apartment there are many to choose from. The most inexpensive apartments for rent are situated along the Piran-Portorož road.

Camp Adria

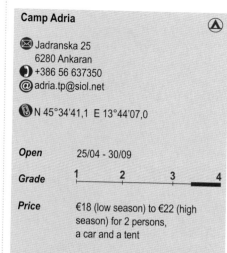

✉ Jadranska 25
6280 Ankaran
📞 +386 56 637350
@ adria.tp@siol.net

🅝 N 45°34'41,1 E 13°44'07,0

Open	25/04 - 30/09

Grade 1 — 2 — 3 — **4**

Price €18 (low season) to €22 (high season) for 2 persons, a car and a tent

Situated in the southern part of Slovenia along the Gulf of Trieste this large family campsite is only 14km from Osp. Camp Adria has pitches with plenty of shade as well as on open fields. There is no real beach since the coastline is covered with concrete! Fortunately there is a large swimming pool filled with seawater since the sea itself is not really that inviting to swim in. The campsite also has a tennis court, minigolf, supermarket, and even a bar.

Directions
Take the Koper-Trieste coast road to Ankaran. Along this road you'll find signs for Camp Adria.

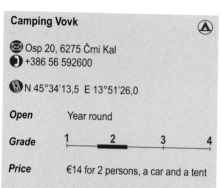

Camping Vovk

✉ Osp 20, 6275 Črni Kal
📞 +386 56 592600

🅝 N 45°34'13,5 E 13°51'26,0

Open	Year round

Grade 1 — **2** — 3 — 4

Price €14 for 2 persons, a car and a tent

The campsite is basic and not too big. There are toilets and good showers with warm water, but no separate bathrooms for men and women. It is mainly used by climbers and is a good place to find climbing partners. If it rains there is a sheltered area in which to cook and the strong looking owner has even build a small boulder area to keep you busy on rainy days. It gets pretty busy during the weekends and on bank holidays.

Directions
Take the exit for Črni Kal off the A1 Ljubljana-Koper highway. After a few hundred metres turn left for Osp. The village shows up just after the village of Gabrovica. In Osp follow the sign for the campsite, which is well signposted.

Coming from Trieste, in Italy, the shortest and quickest route is to cross the Italian-Slovenian border along the small road that leads to Caresana. There are signs for this town along the Trieste-Koper road. Follow these signs which take you to the road to Osp. The other route, but one with more traffic and slow sections, is to cross the Skofije border and follow the highway towards Ljubljana. Take the exit for Črni Kal. From here Osp is well signposted.

View on Camping Vovk

Apartments near Piran-Portorož

There is plenty of choice of apartments along the coast. Prices for an apartment start at €30 a day for 2 persons.

Apartments Horvat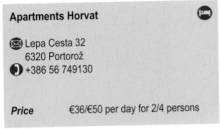

✉ Lepa Cesta 32
6320 Portorož
☎ +386 56 749130

Price   €36/€50 per day for 2/4 persons

Apartments Marjan

✉ Postajališka 2
6320 Portorož
☎ +386 56 740306

Price   €33/€61 per day for 2/4 persons

Apartments Villa Ana

✉ Letoviška 2
6320 Portorož
☎ +386 56 740261

Price   €88 for 6 persons

Piran and other towns along the coast offer lots of accommodation

The amazing stalactites and stalagmites in the Postojna caves

Where to buy groceries

If you are staying in Osp you'll have to go to Koper to find a supermarket. It will take you 15 minutes to get there but, when there, you'll find a huge French-style hypermarket. This is located close to the highway, just follow the signs. There is also a mini-market-on-wheels that stops in the village in the morning.

Camping Vovk and some of the houses in Osp sell home made wine. Just stop at the signs along the road, knock on the door and ask for the vino – it's very basic but worth a try. Prices are around €2.50 per litre.

Where to find the local climbing guidebook

The nearest place to buy the guide is in Trieste.

Tecnosport
✉ Via Imbriana 5
34122 Trieste
@ tecno.sport@virgilio.it
🌐 www.climbingsport.com

Aventura
✉ Via Madonna Del Mare 21
Trieste
☎ +39 040 307325

What else is there to see & do

Most climbers will need one or more rest days in this area as the routes prove rather tiring. Fortunately there is more than enough to do.

Piran

This small picturesque port with its colourful houses, beautiful waterside, and Italian atmosphere is wonderful to stroll around. Even with all the tourists in high summer, it is a quiet place as cars are not allowed inside the town. It's 16th century walls, the lighthouse, and the stunning sunset makes Piran very photogenic. Piran is also a popular place to relax on the beach, though this is rather small and rocky.

Koper

Once an important island stopover on the route from Aquileia east, Koper is now part of the mainland and the most important city on the Slovenian coast. The city is a major port for central Europe. Koper offers some interesting cultural attractions. Among these is Tito Square in the old centre with its symbols of church and secular authorities. There is also the former Venetian palace to visit.

Postojna cave

Slovenia has more than one thousand caves. It is said that these caves are the most beautiful of the underground world. The most famous one is the Postojna cave at the city of Postojna and about 50km from Osp. This cave is a network of 20 kilometres of passages, galleries and chambers. You will be dazzled by the beautiful calcite formations, stalactites, and stalagmites in an abundance of different shapes, colours, and ages. The start of the tour in the cave is by electric train. Although the whole setup is extremely commercial and touristy it is nevertheless worth the visit.

Lipizzaner horses

The birthplace of these famous snow-white Lipizzaner horses is Lipica in Slovenia. In the scenic countryside around Lipica visitors are offered riding courses. Furthermore there is a show of the classical riding art and dressage. Lipica is located south of Sezana, about 35km from Osp.

Trieste (Italy)

The city of Trieste is full of life and has many nice, small Italian restaurants. It takes only 20 minutes by car from Osp to get there.

Relaxing at the sea shore of Piran is an excellent way to spend the afternoon on hot summer days

The imposing walls behind Osp offer something for everyone's taste. Within a few minutes walk from the campsite you'll find Sector Banje that offers tough routes on the overhanging wall, where stamina is your best friend. The next sector, Sector Babna, offers the easiest climbs in Osp with many razor-sharp positive holds but some tougher routes as well. The most famous wall of Osp is the big wall, Sector Stena, where routes go up to 140 metres in length. These routes are not for the faint of heart as most involve at least a pitch in the 7th grade due to some very steep passages. In total there are 61 multi pitch routes.

Max Käser redpointing Jonathan Livingston (7a)

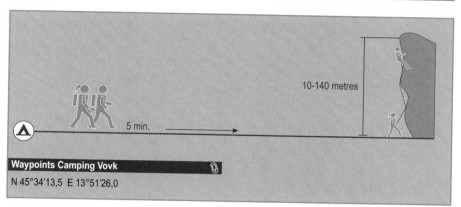

10-140 metres

5 min.

Waypoints Camping Vovk

N 45°34'13,5　E 13°51'26,0

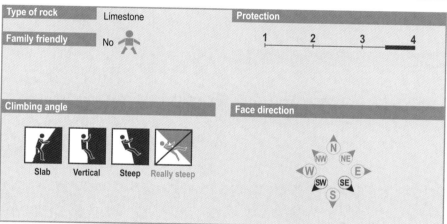

Type of rock — Limestone

Family friendly — No

Protection

1　　2　　3　　4

Climbing angle

Slab　Vertical　Steep　Really steep

Face direction

NW　N　NE
W　　　　E
SW　S　SE

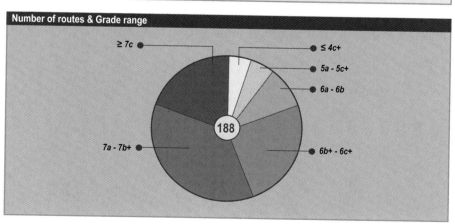

Number of routes & Grade range

≥ 7c

≤ 4c+

5a - 5c+

6a - 6b

7a - 7b+

188

6b+ - 6c+

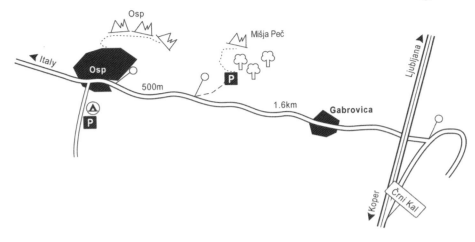

Directions

▶ See the directions to Camping Vovk. There is a car park in front of the campsite for non-guests. You are not allowed to park your car anywhere else in the village. For Sectors Banje and Babna walk up into the village and turn right just before the church. There is a path that leads behind the houses to the first routes. For Sector Stena first follow the road to Mišja Peč and then the path starts after the small bridge to the left.

Climbers on Sector Stena

Jorg Verhoeven sending Sanski par extension on his fourth attempt (9a)

Mišja Peč

Just between the villages of Osp and Gabrovica lies the wonderful Mišja Peč. Shaped like a horseshoe this is the place to be if you are feeling fit and strong as it is almost exclusively a steep route fest. Mišja Peč definitely has some of the best and most challenging routes in Slovenia and it is one of the very few places in Europe where you can find 9a's (in plural!).

The easiest route here is a 6b+ but, honestly, this place is only fun if you can climb at least 7a. The wall at the back takes your breath away and makes you want to come back here over and over again!

Climbing in the cave at Mišja Peč

Climbing at Mišja Peč, route Kravica (7a+)

Directions

▶ From Camping Vovk head in the direction of Koper and take the small road to the left after 650 metres. From the car park it is an easy 5 minute walk uphill to the first route.

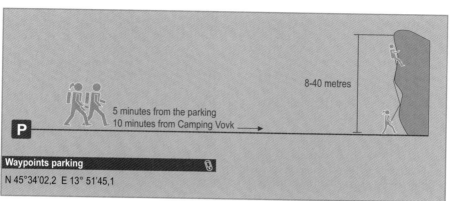

8-40 metres

5 minutes from the parking
10 minutes from Camping Vovk

P

Waypoints parking

N 45°34'02,2 E 13° 51'45,1

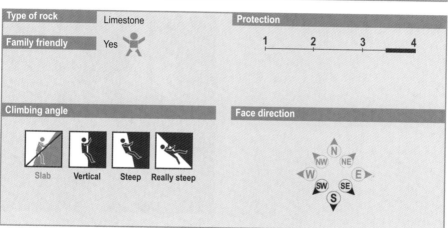

| Type of rock | Limestone |
| Family friendly | Yes |

Protection

1   2   3   4

Climbing angle

Slab   Vertical   Steep   Really steep

Face direction

N NE E SE S SW W NW

Number of routes & Grade range

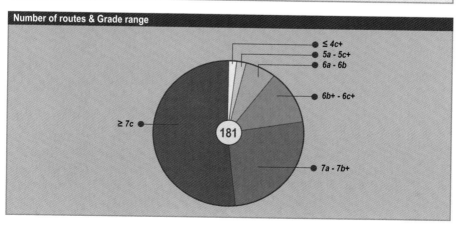

≤ 4c+
5a - 5c+
6a - 6b
6b+ - 6c+
≥ 7c
181
7a - 7b+

The wide stretch of wall above the picturesque village of Črni Kal is clearly visible from far away. The climbing here is not at all similar to that of Osp or Mišja Peč and stands on its own right. The routes here are shorter - a maximum of 35 metres high - and there are more routes in the 5th and 6th grade range. Most routes are on vertical walls that have a lot of natural features and cracks but there are some technical beauties with small holds too.

The view from the top of the crags to the Gulf of Trieste, and the flat ground at the bottom, which enables parents to take their children with them, makes this an enjoyable place to climb. And, as it really gets hot in summer, the trees provide some shelter from the sun while belaying.

When climbing at Osp is too warm, try the shady routes at Črni Kal

We will thoroughly update each Rock Climbing Atlas as often as possible. Between editions, up-to-date information is available on our website www.rockclimbingatlas.com. We genuinely value your feedback and we will read every email and letter we receive. We will use your feedback in an appropriate way.

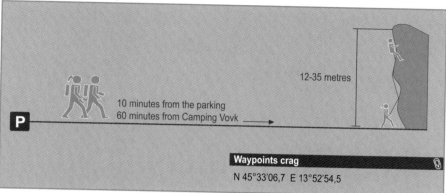

12-35 metres

10 minutes from the parking
60 minutes from Camping Vovk

P

Waypoints crag

N 45°33'06,7 E 13°52'54,5

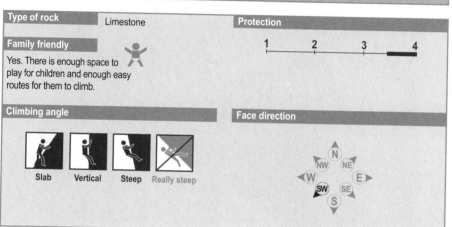

Type of rock   Limestone

Family friendly

Yes. There is enough space to play for children and enough easy routes for them to climb.

Protection

1   2   3   4

Climbing angle

Slab   Vertical   Steep   Really steep

Face direction

N   NE   E   SE   S   SW   W   NW

Number of routes & Grade range

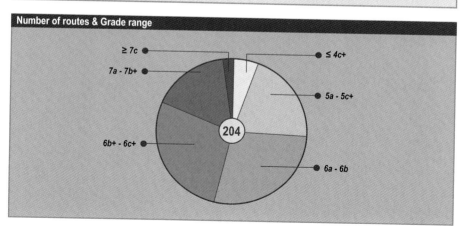

≥ 7c

7a - 7b+

6b+ - 6c+

204

≤ 4c+

5a - 5c+

6a - 6b

Judith van de Geijn on Leve sirove luknje (6c) Črni Kal

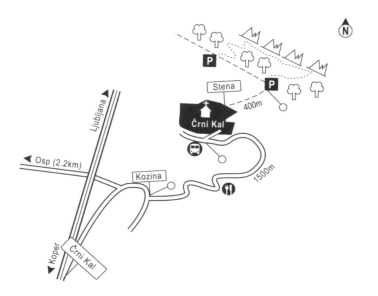

- Ljubljana
- Osp (2.2km)
- Kozina
- Stena
- Črni Kal
- 400m
- 1500m
- Koper
- Črni Kal
- P
- P

Directions

Levicarka (5a)

▶ Leave the Ljubljana – Koper highway at the Črni Kal junction or leave Camping Vovk in Osp to the right (eastwards). Follow the sign to Kozina on the left. Follow the curving road up and after 1500 metres turn right at a bus stop and steer into the village of Črni Kal. Then follow the narrow main road up past the church and follow the sign "Stena" all the way. Continue on an unpaved road where you can park after 50 metres.

The Val Rosandra divides the Triestine Karst (Monte Stena) from that of the Alta Istria (Monte Carso) and has a morphology which is directly related to its geological complexity. The folds and faults have brought to the surface various rocks which have been eroded and dissolved in different ways through the years. This makes the crags of Val Rosandra one of the older ones around. The gorgeous valley of Val Rosandra spreads out behind the village of Bagnoli and attracts climbers and a lot of hikers. This quiet valley with superb views and its easy accessibility makes it a popular place to visit.

Val Rosandra offers numerous routes spread out over different sectors which lie apart from each other. Most of the classic routes have been recently re-bolted. Those who climb 5th and 6th grade routes will find enough to do as the majority of the 365 routes are graded less than 7a. Do not be surprised if you have an audience watching you as a hiking trail goes directly past some of the sectors!

Val Rosandra

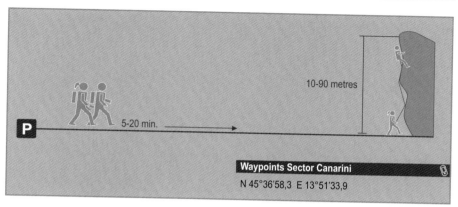

Waypoints Sector Canarini

N 45°36'58,3 E 13°51'33,9

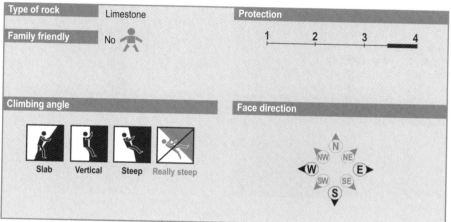

| Type of rock | Limestone | Protection |
| Family friendly | No | 1   2   3   4 |

Climbing angle: Slab, Vertical, Steep, Really steep

Face direction: N, NW, NE, W, E, SW, SE, S

Number of routes & Grade range

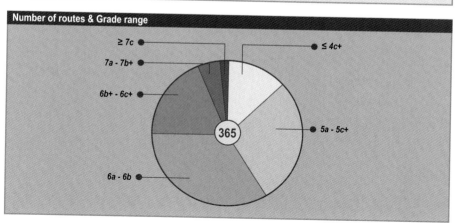

≥ 7c
7a - 7b+
6b+ - 6c+
6a - 6b
≤ 4c+
5a - 5c+
365

Val Rosandra, Sector Falchetti and Falchi

Fulvio Bertos climbing in his back garden at Val Rosandra, Sector Canarini

Sector Canarini is just above Bagnoli

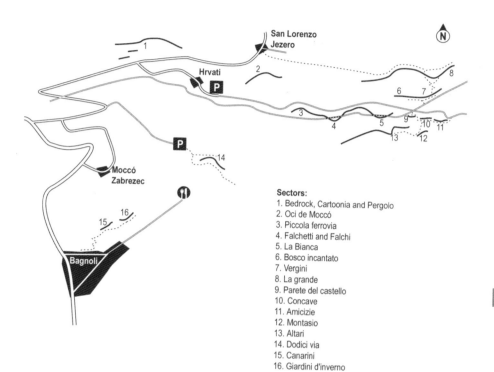

Sectors:
1. Bedrock, Cartoonia and Pergolo
2. Oci de Moccó
3. Piccola ferrovia
4. Falchetti and Falchi
5. La Bianca
6. Bosco incantato
7. Vergini
8. La grande
9. Parete del castello
10. Concave
11. Amicizie
12. Montasio
13. Altari
14. Dodici via
15. Canarini
16. Giardini d'inverno

Directions

▶ From Camping Vovk

Leave the campsite and turn left to the direction of Italy. Pass through the village of Caresana after the border. When you reach the Skofije-Trieste road follow the signs for Trieste Centro until you see the sign for Dolina and Strada del Rosandra. Follow the road towards Dolina where the signs for Val Rosandra and the village of Bagnoli will start to show you the way. Follow these to reach Bagnoli. See the map that shows the different sectors in the area for further details. The village of Bagnoli is about 14 kilometres from Osp.

Napoleonica is an extremely popular climbing spot in the weekends for the many Italians living in Trieste - it is very close to the city centre. If they don't come here to climb, it is to walk, run, or just to relax and enjoy the view over Trieste and the sea. The different crags provide routes of different difficulties and lengths. There is also some very good bouldering at the base of the crag and this is what many locals come to do after a day at work. The easier routes are a bit polished in some places but are still very enjoyable. The routes are also very well bolted. All sectors are sheltered from the "Bora", a cold north wind that is typical of the area especially in winter, making it relatively pleasant to climb here on a sunny winter's day.

Napoleonica is a popular evening bouldering venue for climbers from Trieste

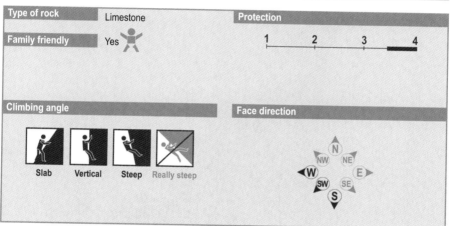

Waypoints crag
N 45°41'51,0 E 13°44'33,5

Type of rock
Limestone

Family friendly
Yes

Protection
1　　　2　　　3　　　4

Climbing angle
Slab　Vertical　Steep　Really steep

Face direction
N　NE　E　SE　S　SW　W　NW

Number of routes & Grade range

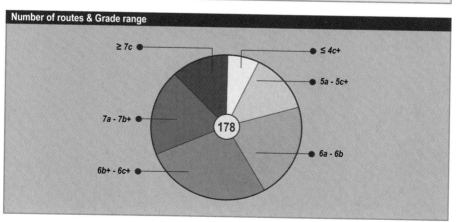

≥ 7c
7a - 7b+
6b+ - 6c+
178
≤ 4c+
5a - 5c+
6a - 6b

Napoleonica

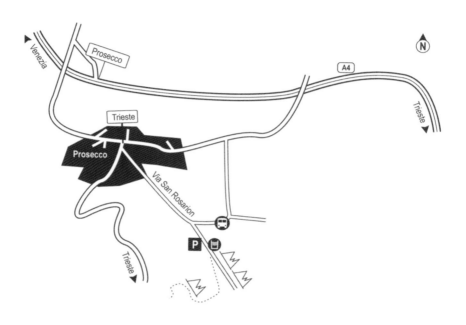

Directions

Leave Osp in the direction of Italy and pass through the village of Caresana after the border. Take the Trieste-Venezia highway (A4) and leave this at the junction for Prosecco, a small village just north west of Trieste. Follow the road to Prosecco and, in the village, turn right at the sign for Trieste. After only 10 metres turn left onto Via San Rosarion. Follow this street and, when it makes a curve to the left, go straight over into the car park. It is possible to drive on a bit further but it is best to park here.

There are also two buses, the numbers 39 and 42, from Trieste that stop just before the car park (see detailed drawing).

Climbing area Celje

Celje, in the north east of Slovenia, is the third largest city after Ljubljana and Maribor. Locals consider the crags of Kotečnik to be the best in Slovenia. People from Osp however will debate this. Have a look and judge for yourself! Besides the crags of Kotečnik there is also a smaller climbing venue called Kamnik. This place offers a good alternative to Kotečnik if you are looking for easier routes more in the 4th and 5th grade range. Both Kotečnik and Kamnik are perfect summer destinations as the crags lie in a forest.

This north eastern part of Slovenia is popular with bikers in particular - there are many small roads that take you through wonderful scenery and charming little villages.

Spring   Summer   Autumn   Winter

When to go

The climbing season in Kotečnik starts in April and lasts until October, although there could be some rainy days in spring and autumn.

Kotečnik in autumn

Crag		
Ⓐ Kotečnik		
Ⓑ Kamnik		

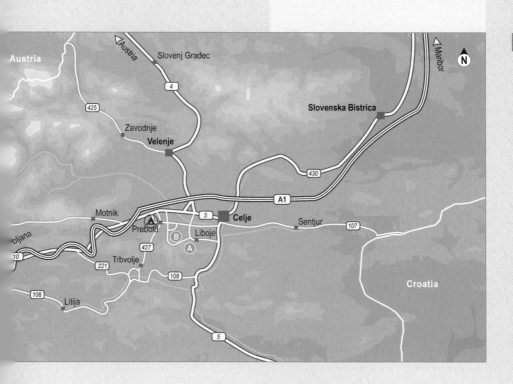

How to get to the area & how to move around

You definitely need a car to get to the crags of both Kotečnik and Kamnik as there are no buses going there. See the tips for car rental in the 'Moving around' section in the country introduction pages.

 By car

From Ljubljana it takes less than an hour to cover the 75km to Celje.

Camping Dolina

Where to stay

The closest campsites are in Prebold from where it is 15 minutes by car to both Kotečnik and Kamnik.

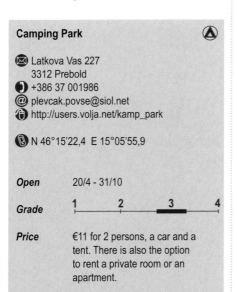
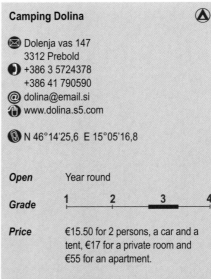

Where to buy groceries

From Camping Dolina it is a 5-minute stroll to a small supermarket. They open early in the morning and their freshly baked bread is delicious. Larger supermarkets are found in Celje.

Where to find the local climbing guidebook

The closest place in which to buy the "Slovenija, Športnoplezalni vodnik" climbing guide is in Ljubljana.

Annapurna
Krakovski nasip 4
1000 Ljubljana
+386 14 263428
info@annapurna.si
www.annapurna.si

Jernej Kruder bouldering at Kotečnik

What else is there to see & do

Celje
The city has numerous cultural and historical treasures offering an outstanding snapshot of history. Furthermore it offers a panoramic view over the Savinjske Alps and the ruins of the Old Castle, which preserve the memories of one of the most powerful medieval families.

Natural health resorts
There are numerous natural health resorts around Celje (Laško, Dobrna or Topolšica) where you can enjoy the beneficial effects of the spa waters complete with healing mud, mineral peloids and peat and brine. That's for sure something different to do on a rest day!

Celje

Kotečnik

The wall of Kotečnik is an impressive one kilometre in length and lies hidden in a forest above the village of Liboje. It is a great place to climb in midsummer since the trees provide good shelter from the sun. The climbing is very nice in varying styles and, from 6a onwards, in all grades. There are over 225 routes so there is little chance of getting bored here. Be aware that access to the sectors is across private land so please heed the warnings.

Kotečnik in summer

Sign at the car park at Kotečnik

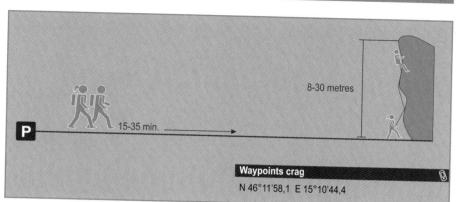

Waypoints crag

N 46°11'58,1 E 15°10'44,4

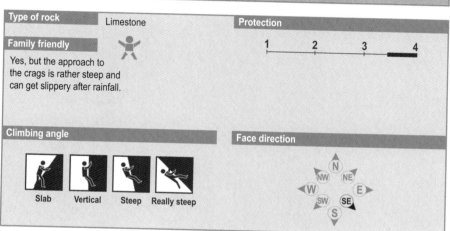

Type of rock

Limestone

Family friendly

Yes, but the approach to the crags is rather steep and can get slippery after rainfall.

Protection

1   2   3   4

Climbing angle

Slab   Vertical   Steep   Really steep

Face direction

N NE E SE S SW W NW

Number of routes & Grade range

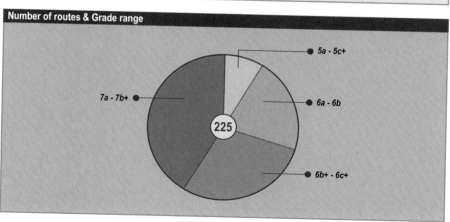

5a - 5c+

7a - 7b+

6a - 6b

225

6b+ - 6c+

Divji otrok (8a)

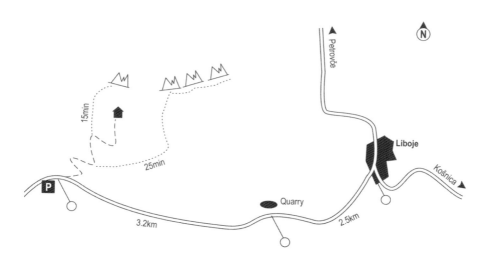

Boštjan Božič on Guernica (8a)

▶ Leave the Ljubljana – Maribor highway (A1) at Žalec, just before Celje. Follow the signs for Arja Vas / Petrovče. Continue to the village of Liboje. After you have driven through Liboje you will pass a quarry from where it is about 3km to the car park on the same road. The car park is clearly signposted.

Kamnik

In the forest near Kamnik lie some smaller crags that are perfect for the less advanced climber. The routes are easy, short, and have been recently re-equipped. It is also the perfect place to escape the heat in summer.

The small crags of Kamnik lie in a forest

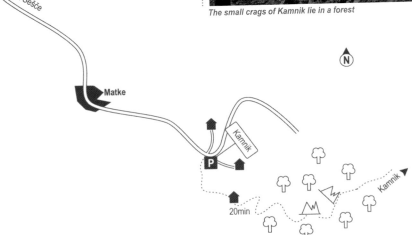

Directions

▶ Leave the Ljubljana – Maribor highway (A1) at Prebold, just before Celje. In the village of Dolenja Vas turn left towards Sesče. Drive through Sesče and continue to Matke. Still following the same road, you reach a junction of multiple roads and you can park there. There is a sign pointing to the path that leads up to Kamnik.

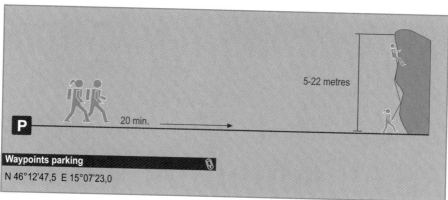

Waypoints parking

N 46°12'47,5 E 15°07'23,0

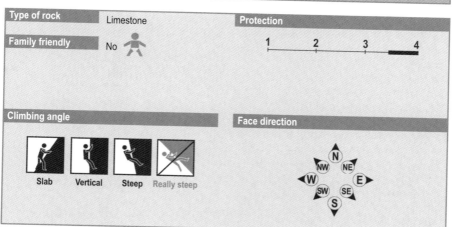

| Type of rock | Limestone |
| Family friendly | No |

Protection

1 2 3 4

Climbing angle

Slab Vertical Steep Really steep

Face direction

N NE E SE S SW W NW

Number of routes & Grade range

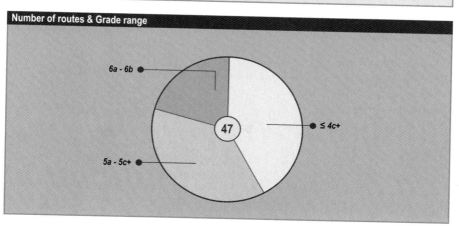

6a - 6b

5a - 5c+

≤ 4c+

47

List of photographers

Photo	Photographer
Alexander Huber	Michael Meisl
Vika Kollerova on Evanjelijum (5c), Cliffbase, Croatia	Miroslav Stec
Klemen Vodlan on the beautiful Dr. Ivan Merz (6b+)	Vicenco Bartulin
Ida Gandeva is at home on Nezen Kravopietc (7c), Sector Vrajite Dupki at Lakatnik	Iva Tsankova
Yavor Panov swings through on Koza Nostra (6c) at Kamen Briag	Iva Tsankova
Pure slab climbing at Sector Bezengi, The Slab (6b)	Peter Petrov
Relaxed climbing	Peter Petrov
Where next? - Paolina Miteva on Kolkoto-tolkova (6a), Sector Vrajite Dupki	Iva Tsankova
Yavor Panov in action on Trite Kelesha (7c), Sector Vrajite Dupki	Iva Tsankova
Ivajlo Radkov reaching for a tiny crimp on Thriller (8b+)	Ruslan Vakrilov
Split	Juraj Kopač
Dalmatian Coast	Josip Madračević
Marko Miscevic on one of the best difficult routes at Omis, Leon (7c)	Vicenco Bartulin
Beautiful climbing in Omiš - Ante Predovic on Dr. Ivan Merz (6b+)	Vicenco Bartulin
Gorana Jelic on Svemir (6a), Omiš	Vicenco Bartulin
Makarska with the crags of Brela	Milan Babić
Ana Kolovrat on HPD - Imotski (6b+), Omiš	Vicenco Bartulin
Filip Harna on Gentlemans' agreement direct (7c)	Miroslav Stec
Pakleni Islands	Milan Babić
The routes at Cliffbase are up to 60 metres in length	Miroslav Stec
Unknown climber on Domžalski (6a, 120m) at Anića Kuk	Boris Cujic
Danube-bend panorama	Hungarian National Tourist Office
Lorand Istvan on Régi ut, 5c	Andor Záhonyi
Lorand Istvan on Disszertáció, 6a	Andor Záhonyi
Vesna Talevski at Matka	Igor Talevski
Brasov view from above	Romanian Tourist Agency
Some smooth vertical walls at the Turda Gorge	Catalin Ionut
Mount Triglav	Bobo
Family hiking in the Julian Alps	Bobo
Triglav Lakes	B. Kladnik
Rafting on the Soča River,	B. Kladnik
Jorg Verhoeven sending Sanski par extension on his fourth attempt (9a)	Katharina Saurwein
Kotečnik in autumn	Rasto Jereb
Jernej Kruder bouldering at Kotečnik	Rasto Jereb
Celje	D. Mladenovič
Divji otrok (8a)	Rasto Jereb
Boštjan Božič on Guernica (8a)	Rasto Jereb
Website Hermann Erber: www.outdoor-fotos.at	

Most other photos are taken by the authors.

This Rock Climbing Atlas wouldn't have been here if it weren't for the many climbers that developed all the routes in the climbing areas. They all spend their free time and private money to do what they love most. Some of them we have met while we were on the road and their names follow below. Nonetheless, we would like to acknowledge all climbers that have contributed to the climbing possibilities in all countries. Keep on going!

First of all we are very grateful to have worked together with Irene Pieper and Daniel Jaeggi, both climbers and both excellent in their work. Your contribution to the Rock Climbing Atlases has been enormous!

Linda Rutten and Judith van de Geijn deserve a special word of gratitude as well. They not only accompanied us on our trips to Slovenia, Croatia and Macedonia, but also turned out to be first class Rock Climbing Atlas consultants. Thanks for your great contribution and support!

Boris Čujić is the man who knows all about the climbing in Croatia. Thanks Boris for helping us out in your beautiful country! Also a word of appreciation to Vicenco Bartulin and Goran Marusic for all the information they have given us about climbing in Omiš. Miroslav Stev is one of those few persons that really do what they love most. He bought a piece of land in Croatia that is filled with good rock and developed many great sport routes. Thanks Miro for your help and the good wine!

In Bulgaria we would like to thank the super friendly Iliyana Petrova and George Dimitrov, from the Trapezitca Tourist Office in Veliko Tărnovo, for their genuine interest and help. Of course, a very warm thanks goes to Kalin and Petya Gyrbov for their guidance and friendship. We will meet again!

In Hungary we definitely would like to thank the friendly Lorand Istvan Zahonyi, he was of great value to us. We also thank Gergő Gozony for all his help.

We would have been lost without Macedonian Vladimir Trpovski who literally helped us with just about everything that we needed during our stay in his wonderful country. Ile Ristovski joined us too on our adventure in Macedonia – thanks for the great time together guys!

We are very happy to have met Neatzu and his friends in Romania and we thank them for their help and night outs. In the Bicaz Gorge it was Issidoris with his friend who showed us around and shared their knowledge with us. We would also like to thank Roel Kalter and Neeltje Tops for the good moments we spend together in Romania.

In Slovenia we would like to say thanks to Maja Vidmar and Rasto Jereb.

Other people we would like to thank that one way or the other contributed to this edition of The Rock Climbing Atlas are:
Alex Vaklen, Alexander Huber, Alexander Klenov, Andrei Simu, Angelique Schreuders, Bas & Freya Westerbeek, Betty Roza, Catalin Ionut, Charles Bollen, Cristian Stoisor, Croatian National Tourist Office, Dana Floricioiu, Daniel Tulp, Elsje van Beek, George Stroie, Hermann Erber, Hugo & Agnes Verkuil, Jorg Verhoeven, Kilian Fischhuber, Maaike Kalse, Natko Bajic, Peter Petrov, René Geerlings, Richard Reese, Richard Simpson, Rinus van Denderen, Ruslan Vakrilov, Slovenian Tourist Board and of course our families.

Thank you all!

Wynand & Marloes

Grade conversion table

Climbing

UIAA	French (Sport Grade)	USA	British Tech	British Trad	Australia
1	1	5.1			9
2	2	5.2		M	10
3-					
3	3a/3c+	5.3		D	11
3+					
4-		5.4		VD	
4				HVD	
4+	4a/4c+	5.5			12
5-		5.6		S	13
5	5a/5b	5.7	4a	HS	14
5+			4b		15
		5.8			
6-	5b+/5c+		4c	VS	16
6		5.9		HVS	17
	6a				
6+		5.10a	5a		18
6+/7-	6a+	5.10b			19
7-		5.10c		E1	20
	6b				
7		5.10d	5b	E2	21
7+	6b+	5.11a			22
7+/8-	6c	5.11b	5c	E3	23
8-	6c+	5.11c			
8	7a	5.11d	6a	E4	24
8+	7a+	5.12a			25
8+/9-	7b	5.12b		E5	26
9-	7b+	5.12c	6b		
9	7c	5.12d			27
9+	7c+	5.13a	6c	E6	28
9+/10-	8a	5.13b			29
10-	8a+	5.13c		E7	30
10	8b	5.13d	7a		31
10+	8b+	5.14a		E8	32
11-	8c	5.14b			33
11-/11	8c+	5.14c	7b	E9	34
11	9a	5.14d			35
11+	9a+	5.15a			36
12-	9b	5.15b	7c	E10	37

Bouldering

V grade (Hueco)	B grade (Peak)	Fb (Fontainebleau)
		4-
V0	B0	4
V1	B1	4+
V1+		5-
V2	B2	5
V2+	B3	5+
V3	B3+	6A
V3+	B4	6A+
V4	B4+	6B
V4+	B5	6B+
V5	B5+	6C
V5+	B6-	6C+
V6	B6	7A
V7	B7	7A+
V8	B8	7B
V8+	B9	7B+
V9		7C
	B10	
V10		7C+
V11	B11	8A
V12	B12	8A+
V13	B13	8B
V14	B14	8B+
V15	B15	8C
V16	B16	8C+